MW00627332

"Communicating is the most important thing leaders do. Communicating *well* is the most important thing successful leaders do. Greg Stone's *Branding with Powerful Stories* ranges from Greek philosophy to Hollywood blockbusters to provide an invaluable guide on how to convey your message powerfully, memorably, and reliably. If you're a leader or you want to be one, *Branding with Powerful Stories* belongs on your bookshelf."

—Gautam Mukunda, Research Fellow, Center for
Public Leadership, Harvard Kennedy School, and author,
Indispensable: When Leaders Really Matter

"Greg Stone is the go-to resource for all who want to hone their presentation skills and public speaking acumen—whether you are giving a keynote talk for thousands or an update at your book club or leading a conversation at a dinner party. Stone is a master craftsman of storytelling with a successful track record of transforming novices into confident presenters. His book offers both a practical roadmap and an entertaining narrative that will enlighten, entertain, and change the way you talk. *Branding with Powerful Stories* is a standout, radiating sound advice and commonsense approaches that will make a difference in your life."

—Gina Vild, co-author, *The Two Most Important
Days: How to Find Your Purpose—and
Live a Happier, Healthier Life*

"Greg Stone understands that the most potent language is the language of story. In this trenchant work, he draws on a wealth of sources—from Bezos to Bogart to Lear to Degas—to construct a compelling guide to the storytelling arts. A must-read for anyone who seeks to engage, inspire, and persuade."

—Francis Flaherty, former columnist and editor,
New York Times, and author, *The Elements of Story:
Field Notes on Nonfiction Writing*

Branding with
Powerful Stories

Branding with Powerful Stories

The Villains, Victims, and Heroes Model

Greg Stone

PRAEGER™

An Imprint of ABC-CLIO, LLC

Santa Barbara, California • Denver, Colorado

Library of Congress Cataloging-in-Publication Data

Names: Stone, Greg J., author.
Title: Branding with powerful stories : the villains, victims, and heroes model / Greg Stone.
Description: Santa Barbara, California : Praeger, [2019] | Includes bibliographical references and index.
Identifiers: LCCN 2018034971 (print) | LCCN 2018037865 (ebook) | ISBN 9781440864780 (eBook) | ISBN 9781440864773 (hardcopy : alk. paper)
Subjects: LCSH: Branding (Marketing) | Storytelling.
Classification: LCC HF5415.1255 (ebook) | LCC HF5415.1255 .S76 2019 (print) | DDC 658.8/27—dc23
LC record available at https://lccn.loc.gov/2018034971

ISBN: 978-1-4408-6477-3 (print)
      978-1-4408-6478-0 (ebook)

23 22 21 20 19   1 2 3 4 5

This book is also available as an eBook.

Praeger
An Imprint of ABC-CLIO, LLC

ABC-CLIO, LLC
130 Cremona Drive, P.O. Box 1911
Santa Barbara, California 93116-1911
www.abc-clio.com

This book is printed on acid-free paper ∞

Manufactured in the United States of America

To my loving family—
my wife, Mary; my daughter, Lauren;
and my son, Jack—whose stories are an indelible part of mine

Contents

Preface

The great enemy of communication, we find, is the illusion of it.
—William H. Whyte[1]

As a "thinking manager," you undoubtedly want to become a better story-teller or presenter. I wrote this book with you in mind. Whether you are a newcomer to leadership, a seasoned speaker, a senior executive, or some-one who wants to rise in prominence or rank, I will help you improve your ability to tell your customers stories about the benefits that your products or services bring to their lives. The techniques are also applicable to many other audiences, including colleagues, suppliers, distributors, job inter-viewers, and the press.

For many decades I have devoted my full attention to storytelling. In every article or script I wrote as a print and broadcast journalist, every commercial video I produced, every consulting session I have ever con-ducted, I have dedicated myself to improving narrative skills—my own and, most important, my clients'. Many people envy those who seem "nat-ural" in front of an audience. They were just born with that innate talent, right? Wrong. Those who make it look easy work very, very hard behind the scenes. There is a myth, for instance, that Abraham Lincoln wrote the Gettysburg Address on the train from Washington to the cemetery in Pennsylvania. As Garry Wills tells us, however, in an entire book dedi-cated to the speech, the 16th president was generally a slow writer, honing sentences to smooth perfection.[2] (We'll revisit this later.) In the modern era, many regard Bill Clinton (in his prime) as a great orator. Yet we forget that his speech nominating Michael Dukakis at the Democratic National Convention in 1988 was so boring and so long-winded that the audi-ence applauded when he finally said, "And, in closing." Plus, we must remember that Clinton was elected attorney general of Arkansas at age 30 and that he proceeded to serve five terms as governor of the state. He has been a public speaker for virtually all of his adult life. The same could be said of Ronald Reagan, the so-called great communicator, who had a long apprenticeship as a radio announcer, actor, and president of the Screen Actors Guild before he entered politics.

Yes, storytelling is a craft, and there are formulas to be learned. You can and will improve with practice. Think of the process as a constant refinement of messages. As Rudyard Kipling once wrote:

> I keep six honest serving-men
> (They taught me all I knew)
> Their names are What and Why and When
> And How and Where and Who.[3]

I submit that the two most important characters in this poem are What and How, as in, "*What* does your business do?" (the substance of the story) and "*How* does it do it?" (the mode or style of operation). The answers will inevitably lead to your best stories. Accordingly, I have divided the book into two parts: the first (chapters 1–6) focuses on the essential *elements* of successful stories and the second (chapters 7–14) on the *techniques* of delivery, with a few details about my own experiences at the end.

If I may digress for a moment, I refer you to Tana French, a wonderful mystery writer who posted this memorable message to readers on her website: "It's not just your money that you're putting on the line; it's your time. . . . I'll do my absolute best not to waste [it]."[4] Like her, I have pushed myself to write a book that I hope will be worthy of your attention.

Note: The genesis of this book was my article "For Better Presentations, Start with a Villain," published in *Harvard Business Review* online on November 12, 2015.

Acknowledgments

I am grateful to these kind people who shared their insights and experiences: Professor Ethan Rouen of Harvard Business School; Professor Emerita Mary Jo Hatch of the McIntyre School of Commerce at the University of Virginia; Dr. Steve Schlozman, Assistant Professor of Psychiatry at Harvard Medical School, also a friend and neighbor; Dr. George Daley, Dean of Harvard Medical School; Jerry Shanahan from the Salute Military Golf Association; Jesse Laflamme, CEO of Pete and Gerry's Organic Eggs; Sree Sreenivasan, friend and social media expert extraordinaire; Marci Schorr Hirsch, friend and frequent advisor; Gale Pryor, writer; Ian Todreas, friend and neighbor; Lisa May, real estate agent from Sotheby's in Cambridge, Massachusetts; Attorney Dan Dwyer, wordsmith and orator; Debbie Burke, consultant and new friend; Christy McMann, Assistant Director of Digital Engagement at Harvard Business School; my fellow entrepreneurs, Suzanne Schalow and Kate Baker, from Craft Beer Cellar in Belmont, Massachusetts; and my brother-in-law Tony Castro, a skilled attorney and close friend.

I owe special gratitude to Ken Lizotte, my literary agent and pal, who has been a loyal coach and confidant. He believed in me from the start and has always been a man of his word and an all-around smart guy.

The team at Praeger has been outstanding. My editor, Hilary Claggett, gave me the benefit of the 600 books (!) that she has shepherded. She is kind, smart, and collaborative. I could not ask for a better partner in this venture. I echo the praise for Erin Ryan, who reviewed the copy once Hilary was done. She too is kind and supportive. I also salute the wonderful Michelle Scott and Suchitra Raghavalu, who did a great deal of heavy lifting in the copyediting process. All of these smart women caught many errors and lapses, though I take full responsibility for any that might remain.

Helen Zhai created the graphics inside the book. She was efficient, flexible, and massively talented.

I also want to acknowledge my best friends, who have supported me throughout my life in ways I could never repay. I list them in alphabetical order, along with the years we first met: Ken Bachman (1970), Greg Bauer (1982), Allen Cypher (1970), Frank Flaherty (1973), Russ Frye (1971), Phil Landa (2013), Jon Sarkin (1963), Jack Stilwell (1962), and John Strahinich (1980).

I thank those who wrote kind comments about this book: Frank Flaherty (see above); John Brodeur, a PR maven and long-standing confidant; the ever-witty Professor Jenny Knight from the University of Brighton Business School in the United Kingdom; Justin Drake, a wonderful client from Dunkin' Brands; Gina Vild, a friend, comrade in communications and co-author of the insightful book *The Two Most Important Days*; Francesca Gino, friend and Professor at Harvard Business School, and author of the outstanding book Rebel Talent: Why it Pays to Break the Rules at Work and in Life; and Gautam Mukunda, friend, research fellow at Harvard's Kennedy School, and author of the superb book *Indispensable: When Leaders Really Matter*.

And last, I salute my family, to whom this book is dedicated. Without my wife, Mary; my daughter, Lauren; and my son, Jack, my own story would have no consequence.

PART 1

The Elements of Your Story

ONE

Why Bother with Storytelling?

The Payoff Is Executive Presence

Is storytelling really *that* important?

Communication is a necessary component of the job description for virtually any business leader. It's not enough to simply do the work. You have to be able to *explain* yourself fluently in clear, crisp language. You need to deliver forceful, colorful, compelling messages, translated into narratives, with human actors, sensory details, and drama. As I always tell my children, now 21 and 26, presentation skills are not just for the podium. "One day," I'll say, "your boss or a colleague will suddenly appear at your office door and ask, 'So how's that project going?' If you can describe your work succinctly and, you hope, with nuanced logic, you'll make a good impression. If not . . ."

As this is a book about storytelling, let's begin with a story. A cabinet official at the Lincoln White House was startled to see the commander in chief engaged in a rather mundane task: "Mr. President," he asked, "are you shining your own shoes?" Without taking a beat, Lincoln replied, "Whose shoes would I shine?"[1] This anecdote reveals that our 16th president was at once unpretentious, humble, and quick witted. Those traits point toward executive presence—an elusive quality that is easy to recognize but hard to describe. One useful definition is the "ability to connect authentically with the thoughts and feelings of others . . . to motivate and inspire them toward a desired outcome."[2] To achieve this, you must first ask yourself a very tough question that will stun a room into silence: "Why would anyone want to be led by you?"[3] Would your colleagues use any of these words to describe you: inspiring, motivating, commanding, credible, confident, or compelling? If you're the boss, you are on stage all the time.

Employees will notice if your door is open or closed, whether you stay in your office all day or walk around, and even how you interact with fellow passengers in an elevator.[4] Above all, remember that a key element of leadership is the ability to tell forceful and persuasive stories that *resonate* with the audience. That is at the core of executive presence.

Before we go any further, however, let's debunk some myths about storytelling. First, you do not have to be Brad Pitt, Meryl Streep, or Cicero to hold an audience's attention. Rather, storytelling is "action oriented—a force for turning dreams into goals and then into results."[5] Second, you don't have to memorize a "script." In fact, a story "should sound different each time. Whether you tell it to 2,000 customers at a convention, 500 salespeople at a marketing meeting . . . or three CEOs over drinks, you should tailor it to the situation."[6] Feel free to improvise.[7]

Eloquence occupies a special position at the core of management. But do not be discouraged. Persuasive speaking may be essential, but it is only part of the equation. Napoleon reportedly believed that half his genius lay in his ability to inspire his soldiers to die for him and the other half in his aptitude for calculating "with great accuracy just how long it would take to transport a herd of elephants from Paris to Cairo."[8] (This book, however, deals with eloquence and not elephants.) Yet you don't have to be a creative writer. Bear in mind that your audience is already familiar with hundreds of stories or memes, "a culture's version of genes," and it is your challenge to supplant and augment them,[9] otherwise the most mundane tales will dominate. First, you need to choose the right elements. As you are about to learn, the villain is your best friend.

TWO

Find the Villain to Uncover the Story and Make Your Company the "Hero"

In my consulting practice, I have often watched senior executives start presentations with bland and platitudinous themes with as much pith as a puff of smoke, for instance, "We have a new focus on customer satisfaction," or "Our current strategic goals are execution and innovation."[1] Do these examples sound familiar? Sadly, leaders who utter such drivel might actually believe they can motivate their staff with vague abstractions. I call this the "stratosphere syndrome." It's not only lacking but lackluster. Did Shakespeare begin *Hamlet* by saying, "This is a play about indecision"? Of course not. Yet most executives like to reside in the stratosphere, where they can bask in the safety of generalities. A cynic might note that no one ever gets fired for uttering bromides. Yet by the same token few are promoted by clichés either. So please, come down to sea level and tell the audience about the daily experiences of your customers.

Focus on the three principal "players" in any good story: the villain, the victim, and the hero. There is an old Hollywood adage that great scoundrels make great movies. Alfred Hitchcock said it best, "The better the villain, the better the picture."[2] That's why so many of his crooks were attractive, distinguished, well bred, and, yes, evil too. That combination of conflicting traits is captivating. In the same vein, the hero should be flawed as well as noble, with both kindness and a hint of cruelty, otherwise the story will be comic-bookish.

"Fair enough," you may be saying to yourself. "But what does all this have to do with my business?" The answer: "Everything."

When you try to tell the *story* of your company, ask yourself who, or what, the heroes, villains, and victims may be. And start with the villains. Often they are not animate. In the mind of the consumer, mere frustration is a recognizable evil, as is a transaction that is incomplete or unsatisfying (anything from a faulty product to cold coffee to melted ice cream). It is important to note that the villain need not have a name, or even an identity (think of Voldemort in the Harry Potter tales—the one whose name cannot be spoken), but must be recognizable. The victim, as it were, is the customer whose problem you're trying to solve. The hero? Your company or team.

Table 2.1 provides a few examples.

When you're telling a story, start with a colorful explanation of your customers' difficulties, and be sure to display ample sympathy for their plight. Be as dramatic as decorum permits. Describe the "villains" in bold terms, but not from your perspective. It would be crude, if not insulting, to begin by saying "XYZ organic fertilizer will make your lawn greener and safer" because you would be speaking from your own point of view. Instead, cast the customer in the starring role: "You will be happy knowing that your children and your puppy will not be harmed when they roll around on the grass." Let the audience recognize themselves as the victim, with your product or service acting as the solution. It would be inappropriate to describe your company as the "hero," but that message will be conveyed implicitly. Again, notice that the "characters" are not necessarily people. Pollution has no name, but it surely is a villain, is it not?

Let's take a look at actual stories that illustrate these concepts in action. Muhammad Yunus is known as the architect of microcredit. The idea for this innovation came to him in Bangladesh in the 1970s when he was a young professor of economics. On a field trip to a poor hamlet, he and his students met a woman who made stools out of bamboo on a muddy patch of land outside her shabby hut. A local "banker" loaned her money to buy the raw materials, yet he retained the sole rights to the merchandise at prices *he* set. To compound matters, no pun intended, he was charging unconscionable interest rates, as high as 10 percent *per day*. Yunus came to the rescue with a loan of less than $27—enough to free that woman and 41 others from the cruel grip of the moneylender. "If I could make so

Table 2.1   Applying the Model

Industry	"Villain(s)"	"Victim(s)"	"Hero(es)"
Health care	Disease; suffering; bad outcomes; death	Patients and their families	Efficient, effective, and compassionate care
Software	Unreliable programs; slow processing; blue screens of death; porous security	Consumers who are frustrated or hacked	Technology that works, safely
Manufacturing	High cost; restricted markets; unfulfilled promises; dangerous products	Those who pay too much for inferior goods, or who are harmed by them	Efficiencies and fairness
Education	High tuition; degrees that don't lead to useful employment; irrelevance	Students who graduate with a mountain of debt and no job prospects	Affordable education providing marketable skills
Lawn care	Poisonous chemicals	Anyone who breathes the air or drinks the water	Organic products that help plants grow without polluting

many people so happy with such a tiny amount of money," Yunus said, "why not do more of it? That is what I have been trying to do ever since."[3]

This tale simply works, doesn't it? It has all the elements: a classic villain (the greedy moneylender), powerless victims (the people struggling to escape his clutches), and a hero in the form of humane microbanking (as evidenced by a tiny loan whose impact far exceeds its paltry dollar value). Note that the theme comes at the end, as a natural outgrowth of the facts.

The villain-victim-hero paradigm is effective in personal stories as well. Look at the way Amazon CEO Jeff Bezos described a "villain" he faced in college:

> I went to Princeton primarily because I wanted to study physics. . . .
> Things went fairly well until I got to quantum mechanics [and] I real-
> ized "I'm never going to be a great physicist." . . . At the same time I
> had been studying computer science and was . . . drawn to that more
> and more. . . . One of the great things Princeton taught me is that I'm
> not smart enough to be a physicist.[4]

We can recognize ourselves in this anecdote because Bezos casts himself
as the sweating victim of a villain called quantum mechanics, and the university becomes the "hero" for showing him a different way forward.
Again, the overarching theme comes at the end. There is no need to explic-
itly identify the roles the "characters" play. We understand the structure
intuitively.

Here is another example. Dateline about 2010, holiday season, Wayne,
Pennsylvania. An 89-year-old retired engineer, snowed in, worries that he
won't have enough food. His granddaughter calls several grocery stores,
but none will deliver—except Trader Joe's. Managers tell her they do not
ordinarily deliver, but they make an exception for the elderly man. Moreover, they suggest low-sodium items to help him follow his dietary restric-
tions. The groceries arrive in *30 minutes, free of charge*.[5] This anecdote is
more powerful than a thousand platitudes about customer service, isn't it?
The "characters" are the blizzard that shuts down the city (that is, the villain), the helpless old man (the victim), and the compassionate store that
rescues him (the hero).

In sum, try to emulate Bezos's personal touch, Yunus's eloquence, and
Trader Joe's compassion when you describe your brand's "heroism," especially the way your product or service vanquishes problems. If you depict the
consumer's predicament in gritty, sympathetic terms, then the "virtue" of
your company should resonate with customers, colleagues, and media alike.

If you haven't thought about the "villains" your company is fighting, or
if you are deaf to the cris de coeur of your customers (that is their passionate appeals, complaints, or protests), then you need to do some legwork to
add power to your messaging. Here are some suggestions:

- Interview your best customers and ask them what their key problems
  are. (In my case, for instance, many of my clients fear public speaking
  or have trouble telling their stories.)
- Interview both former and prospective customers. (If you think it's
  awkward to have this conversation yourself, then hire a researcher to
  do it for you.)

- Find out what clients need to resolve their predicaments and the solutions they currently lack.
- Try to discover what your competitors are saying about customer pain.

GRAPHICS PORTRAY HEROES AND VILLAINS TOO

Power corrupts, and PowerPoint corrupts absolutely. For me, the first rule is "Don't use PowerPoint." If you must, however (and I understand that in many large corporations the "deck" is a necessary element of any presentation—so fundamental that its absence could be perceived as a dereliction of duty), then by all means use graphics sparingly. Remember this: *you* are the presentation, not the slides. If you are simply reading the text on your PowerPoint, then do us all a favor and e-mail the copy to us and sit down. We can certainly read faster than you can speak.

In any case, bear in mind that graphics have heroes and villains just as stories do. For instance, take a look at this bar chart:

Without any information about the content of the X and Y axes, we can immediately see that the second bar from the left is prominent. If it represents revenues in EMEA (Europe, the Middle East, and Africa) and the other bars depict the results in other regions, then we instantly comprehend that the tallest item is the "hero." And if we label the vertical axis clearly as "Sales in Dollars" and tag the bars with the names of the regions, then we can turn a dull PowerPoint slide into a narrative whose basic story arc is abundantly clear.

Here's another example:

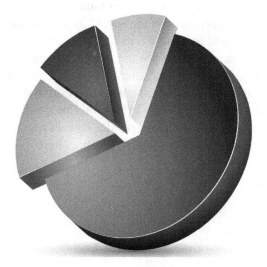

Let's assume that this pie chart represents Cost of Goods Sold. Clearly, then, the huge segment in the lower right-hand corner is the "villain." If we label it "Raw Materials," then we have already written the first chapter of our novel and introduced our "scoundrel." Any sixth grader could instantly grasp that the money we are paying for those components is inordinately and disproportionately large, and therein lies the tale. Whenever I see PowerPoint graphics, I wish that the presenter would just take the time to simplify the concepts so that I could intuitively grasp the message without having to work at all. Here are three simple rules to follow:

1. Always explain what the X and Y axes represent. There is nothing worse than puzzling over the meaning of the lines and missing the point. Once we are confused by even one slide, we generally tune out altogether.

2. Assume all graphics and concepts are unclear without careful explanation. Tell us why they matter and how they fit into the context of your presentation.

3. When in doubt, show a relevant picture. If you're discussing sales from the unit in France, for instance, a shot of the Arch of Triumph would orient us immediately. Plus, it would be a visual break from the monotony of financial results.

A DEEPER VIEW OF VILLAINY

Let's examine *why* picaresque tales of "bad guys" resonate so deeply with audiences. Evil has an ineffable appeal, which is why horror is such a popular genre at the movies. In essence, it "scares so good." A recent article in the *Journal of Consumer Research* cites "growing evidence suggesting that mixed feelings" (what psychiatrists call co-activation) are "not only possible but quite common."[6] That means we can experience both happiness and sadness, or fear and comfort, at the same time. In some ways, this is counterintuitive because our basic drives are hedonistic (a "tendency to pursue pleasure and avoid pain"[7]), but many horror movie aficionados willingly immerse themselves in "nearly 2 hours of fear, disgust, terror and depravity."[8] Even Edmund Burke, known as the father of modern conservatism, noted this dichotomy: "Whatever . . . [elicits] pain, and danger . . . is a source of the *sublime*."[9] As professor of media psychology Stuart Fischoff explains, "If we have a relatively calm, uneventful lifestyle, we seek out something that's going to be exciting for us because our nervous system requires periodic revving, just like a good muscular engine."[10] It has been said that fear is the backbone of great fiction: fear of loss, of failure, of success, of being unmasked, and so on. As Hitchcock noted, "I aim to provide the public with beneficial shocks. Civilization has become so protective that we're no longer able to get our goose bumps instinctively."[11]

Part of the appeal is metacognition, that is, thinking about thinking about fear. Dr. Steve Schlozman, a psychiatrist, author of the novel *The Zombie Autopsies: Secret Notebooks from the Apocalypse*, and an all-around horror expert, explained the appeal of terrifying villains:

People who engage in metacognition have increased respiratory rates, increased heart rates, increased skin conduction, which means they're sweating more. So they've got a fight-or-flight response. And we're assuming it's flight at this point. They're not ready to fight the movie screen, although they might be imagining it. But they get home, and then they think, "Oh yeah. That scene was scary, but why? I mean like why would he go into a tunnel with a match instead of a flashlight? Because it made me more scared." And then you have a good time thinking about it again.[12]

Dr. Schlozman explains that villains appeal to the rebel in all of us:

Darth Vader never has to make his bed, ever. Darth Vader never has to clean up his room. Darth Vader never has to do anything for himself. If Darth Vader is angry at you when you refuse to do what he wants, he can do that dark force thing with you and strangle you. . . . [Kids say that] Luke Skywalker's kind of boring. He's shallow. He's one-sided. . . . But Darth Vader could say no, and nobody could push back on that. So one of the reasons we like villains is they get away with stuff that we're not allowed to. . . . So it means that you get to sort of break the rules. You get to be a little bit of the villain yourself, but in a way that's pretty risk-free. You get to experiment. And you know, as a parent, I'd much rather have my kids break that kind of rule than, you know, get drunk on a Saturday night or something.[13]

Audiences for horror tend to be very sophisticated about the genre and enjoy remaining in a state of disorientation until some sort of resolution is reached. Sometimes the tension is so extreme because of the vibrating presence of opposing forces, as in the movie *Fallen* (spoiler alerts), where the hero Denzel Washington is actually a carrier of the evil spirit, or the film *Angel Heart* where the detective is the very person he is seeking. Yes, the hunter can also be the hunted. M. R. James, a noted medievalist at Oxford and master horror writer, said that a successful ghost story should force the reader to say to herself, "If I'm not very careful, something of this kind may happen to me!"[14] He wanted the pressure to build slowly, as we are "introduced to the actors in a placid way; let us see them going about their ordinary business . . . and into this calm environment let the ominous thing put out its head, unobtrusively at first, and then more insistently, until it holds the stage."[15] And hold the stage his evil spirits do: a room numbered 13 appears and disappears; a dead woman sits in a tree infested with spiders; a specter made of bed linens is summoned by a whistle. James believed that the ghost should be "malevolent or odious:

amiable and helpful apparitions are all very well in fairy tales or local legends, but I have no use for them in a fictitious [horror] story."[16]

You no doubt recall *Grimm's Fairy Tales* from your youth—stories like Snow White, Sleeping Beauty, or Hansel and Gretel. The plots often include decidedly non-child-appropriate subjects like murder, mutilation, cannibalism, infanticide, and incest. "Wilhelm Grimm had . . . no . . . scruples about violence. He rarely let slip the opportunity to have someone burned at the stake, drowned, forced to dance in red-hot shoes, torn to pieces, or stripped naked and put in a barrel studded with nails and harnessed to a horse."[17] This is all part of what Maria Tatar, the Chair of the Folklore and Mythology Department at Harvard, calls the intersection of beauty and horror. "How do you move from boredom to curiosity—how do you animate the child?" she asks. "[B]y using . . . shock value . . . administering jolts and shimmers that flip a switch in the mind."[18] At once we want to "look and look away."[19] There is some evidence that children are "rarely squeamish when they hear about decapitation or other forms of mutilation. Grisly episodes often strike them as amusing rather than horrifying. . . . Obviously [their] laughter is more a release for pent-up anxieties than an expression of delight."[20] And why focus on the pathological? "It seems so much more interesting than the good, the true and the beautiful."[21] Children's books offer "arsenals of beauty and horror" to construct "'peak experiences,'" combining "the exquisite, the terrifying and everything in between."[22] As Dr. Schlozman explains:

> [In fairy tales] the truth doesn't lie in the themes themselves. It's the rare parent who eats their kids. It's the rare stepmother who sends their kids out in the woods to starve to death. . . . There are a billion fairy tales written. But the ones that stick around have this universal appeal, the idea that someday your parents, as they transition towards conditional love from unconditional love, might throw you out. They might have had enough. No more tantrums. We're done. It's not a timeout, it's an out, period.[23]

Yet in the end, fairy tales have the "power to calm the 'cauldron of seething emotions'"[24] in children. Many adults also actually seek out disturbance or perturbation in horror stories, yet part of the joy of the experience is the relief that follows. Afterwards, we are reassured to find that our lives are unaltered and that we can return to the safety, comfort, and warmth of our homes. Similarly, successful products or services in many cases provide soothing antidotes for our frustrations. Had a tough day? Curl up with your Kindle.

THE PITH OF MYTH

Business professor Mary Jo Hatch says people think myth is false, but it's probably the truest thing there is.[25] It's timeless, located "beyond past, present and future."[26] It has occurred before and is reoccurring today. Myth has been called "a repository of allegoric instruction, to shape the individual to his group,"[27] a "conviction or credo" (rags to riches),[28] a communal experience, and a "special form of shared fantasy"[29] about something beyond our ken.[30] Often a hero's journey is involved ("When you take a trip, you return with something to talk about"[31]), and sometimes the protagonist "rides on the great rhythm of the historical process,"[32] for example, Napoleon at the beginning of the Russia campaign: "I feel myself driven towards an end that I do not know. As soon as I shall have reached it, as soon as I shall become unnecessary, an atom will suffice to shatter me. Till then, not all the forces of mankind can do anything against me."[33] The drive toward mythos is at the opposite pole from logos, that is, the need to master the practical details of life with logic: "From the very beginning, therefore, homo sapiens . . . used logos to develop new weaponry, and myth, with its accompanying rituals, to reconcile himself to the tragic facts of life that threatened to overwhelm him, and prevent him from acting effectively."[34] Yet myths don't just occur spontaneously. They seem to emanate from a deeper part of our unconscious.

> I don't think anybody sits down to write a myth . . . Myths form organically. So the myth of Steve Jobs wasn't the myth of Steve Jobs until Steve Jobs made Apple. Then this mythology emerged, some of which is true, some of which isn't true. I think it's very similar to fairy tales, in that it's less about the facts and more about the feeling that gets created by the story. So the truth comes out of the conclusions you draw, as opposed to the details.[35]

In business, the aura that mythical leaders cast often exceeds the footprint of their actual achievements as their stories grow in magnitude, particularly after their demise. This is redolent of the legend of the apotheosis of Caesar, whose soul was rescued from his bloody body and transformed into a comet following his assassination in the Senate (as the tale is told by Ovid). As the goddess Diana carried Caesar's spirit heavenward,

> . . . she felt it glowing and catching fire,
> So she let it escape from out of her bosom and fly right upwards.
> Higher than the moon it soared, displaying a sweeping

trail of flame in its wake, til it finally took the form
of a gleaming star.[36]

We see similar deification in the lore surrounding towering commercial
leaders, especially inventors. Take Thomas Edison, generally hailed as the
lone genius behind the light bulb, which is just one of 1,093 inventions he
patented in the United States. Yet his lab housed 14 engineers and scientists who worked in the background. When they tried to market themselves, they were unsuccessful because the public wanted to credit just one
man. Thus, the assistants "created Edison, the archetypal inventor. They
saw that [he] made for a more viable brand than their collective group, and
capitalized on that by mythologizing him."[37] Edison "did not 'invent' the
lightbulb in any meaningful sense"[38] because electric lighting had already
been in existence for a while. Instead, he pioneered filament made from a
type of bamboo that had greater resistance and therefore produced more
intense illumination. This sort of unjustified glorification is common.

> The canonical story of the lone genius inventor is largely a myth. . . .
> [S]urveys of hundreds of significant new technologies show that almost
> all of them are invented simultaneously or nearly simultaneously by
> two or more teams working independently of each other. Invention
> appears in significant part to be a social, not an individual phenome-
> non. Inventors build on the work of those who came before, and new
> ideas are often either 'in the air' or result from changes in the market
> demand or the availability of new or cheaper starting materials.[39]

Just as Edison benefits from unjustified, exclusive credit for the light bulb,
so too did Bell with the telephone, Morse with the telegraph, the Wright
brothers with the airplane, and so on. Bell had a competitor who filed a
patent for the telephone on the same day, but he won because he brought a
suit that went all the way to the Supreme Court. (In fact, the case was so
complicated that it filled an entire volume of the United States Reports.[40])
Although Morse did in fact invent the code named after him, he was not
the first to create a working telegraph. He merely used electromagnets that
carried the signals over great distances.[41] Similarly, the Wright brothers,
who were bicycle mechanics, were indeed the first to fly a powered plane
that was heavier than air, but the central concept dates as far back as Da
Vinci. Moreover, at the time the brothers were active, many other inventors were simultaneously struggling to master flight.[42] So much so that the
Wrights wrote to the Smithsonian Museum in 1899 and asked for all the

research data on planes. As Orville Wright noted, "We were much impressed with the great number of people who had given thought to [mechanical flight], among some of the greatest minds the world has produced."[43]

I offer these historical anecdotes not just because they are fascinating. They show that forging a myth surrounding your products can be very powerful. At worst, the lore might obliterate objective reality and aggrandize your achievements beyond a justifiable level. I am therefore not suggesting that you deliberately indulge in hyperbole. I do, however, advocate crafting strong messages, particularly about innovations, with an emphasis on the team behind them, the response to market demands or the timely capitalization of a new trend or unmet need. In the meantime, there is certainly enough sensationalism to go around, which brings us to the next section . . .

HARD TO AVOID TABLOIDS

What makes a tabloid story? Sex, celebrity, crime, or all of the above.

Unfortunately, the sensational style has infected mainstream publications, now often indistinguishable from their gory counterparts. At the same time, tabloids are imitating "legitimate" publications. For my part, the shift toward the lurid surged in the mid-1990s when conventional papers made significant space on their front pages for the OJ Simpson murder trial, day after day over 11 months. Not even *The New York Times* was immune. Covering a story of this nature seemed to make the sensational acceptable, even for the "intelligentsia."

Yet the tabloids actually do generate "real news," not just stories about Elvis appearing in a shopping mall or spaceships landing in backyards. In 2010, the Pulitzer Board actually allowed *The National Enquirer* to compete for a prize for investigative journalism. Moreover, mainstream publications have even gone as far as crediting the paper as a source. Columnist Michael Kinsley said this illustrates a "process whereby the daintier elements of the press can enjoy sex while claiming to have preserved their virginity: they simply wait for their less fastidious brethren to report something, then report—with distaste—that it has been reported."[44] Yes, sensationalism is now the norm. Yet the appeal of the lurid extends far back in history, to the ancient Greek playwrights, whose works featured suicides, homicides, and plenty of sex. Even Shakespeare, at the core a popular *entertainer,* fully exploited the Elizabethan audience's bloodlust. Many other classic writers have done likewise. If you doubt this, try to match the items in the two columns below.[45] (The answers are at the end.)

1.	To Kill or Not to Kill Dad's Murderer: Son Wavers	(a)	*The Story of Jesus*
2.	Judge Suggests Cutting Boy in Two in Custody Dispute	(b)	*Crime and Punishment*
3.	Angry Mob Votes to Kill Prophet Preaching Peace	(c)	*King Lear*
4.	Penniless Student Robs and Kills Elderly Landlord	(d)	*Casablanca*
5.	Ruler Banishes Daughter for Refusing to Flatter Him	(e)	*Hamlet*
6.	Manipulative Wife Pushes Husband to Murder His Way to Throne	(f)	*King Solomon*
7.	Wartime Bar Owner Pines for Mysterious, Disappearing Beauty	(g)	*Macbeth*

Answers: 1: e; 2: f; 3: a; 4: b; 5: c; 6: g; 7: d.

Please understand that I am not suggesting for a second that you should "go tabloid" when you tell the story of your business. I am, however, recommending that you exploit the impact of repugnant subjects, particularly when explaining the problems your customers face. If, for instance, there is a widespread belief that the typical veggie burger tastes like shredded, unsweetened, dried out hay, should you shy away from that in your messaging? Not if you are trying to make the point that *your* flavorful burgers move in the opposite direction. Another example: All you have to do is turn on any TV news show to see a constant stream of drug ads describing the abject suffering of patients who are struggling mightily with the debilitating symptoms of disease *X*—symptoms which the pills magically promise to alleviate.

Do not hesitate to play to the emotions. You may have heard the infamous expression "the banality of evil." In marketing, try to avoid the "evil of banality."

THREE

Travel to Your Islands

The Key Elements of Messages

When I help executives hone presentations, I let them run through the entire speech then ask what exactly they were trying to say. The answer is usually quite simple, such as "Most of our innovations have been unprofitable." Then I ask, "Why didn't you say that?" The response is often silence, followed by head-scratching. They begin to realize that their key message might have been left unsaid in a clutter of subsidiary facts, arrayed in a bewildering swirl of PowerPoint slides. Or, they sheepishly admit that their main point is on Slide 16. "Why didn't you start with that?" I'll ask. Why indeed? There is an old journalism adage: Good stuff up high. That means begin with your main point, your key fact, or your most interesting tidbit, to hook the reader. In television, start with your best video. Yes, good stuff up high. The rub is that this presupposes that you know what your main message is. If not, trouble will surely ensue. As the great sage Yogi Berra once said, "If you don't know where you're going, you'll end up someplace else."[1] Above all, don't start with a bromide like "I am honored to be here today to speak with the _____." Winston Churchill put it best: "Opening amenities are opening inanities."[2] When asked why he never began with the phrase "It's a great pleasure to _____," he said, "There are only a few things from which I derive great pleasure, and speaking is not one of them."[3] Sometimes you might begin with no words at all, just silence. Napoleon would often stand mute in front of his troops for 40 or 50 *seconds*,[4] no doubt as a way of collecting himself and at the same time ensuring that all eyes and ears were upon him.

LAND ON YOUR ISLANDS

Think of your messages as a group, or archipelago, of islands.

Each island should showcase three elements:

1. a general statement
2. proof points (preferably statistics) to substantiate the main message
3. anecdotes to bring the ideas to life.

The overall message, item number 1, is largely self-explanatory. It might be, "Our new goal is to introduce as many products as possible this year." Too often, however, as mentioned earlier, a given executive might simply utter a message and leave it at that. For instance, she might observe merely that the business is growing. That's why we need item number 2. She might add that market share has risen by 22 percent in Latin America alone. As the name implies, proof points prove or support the principle assertion, usually with numbers. I prefer to think of statistics as quantitative braggadocio that can supercharge the narrative.

Please bear with me as I digress for a moment. (We'll turn to anecdotes, item number 3, shortly.) I recently read Walter Isaacson's biography of Leonard Da Vinci. We all know that the great artist was a supreme innovator, in many fields. But what if we explain the range and power of this mind this way?:

> He filled the opening pages of one of his notebooks with 169 attempts to square a circle. In eight pages . . . he recorded 730 findings about the flow of water; in another notebook, he listed sixty-seven words that describe different types of moving water. He measured every segment of the human body, calculated their proportional relationships, and then did the same for a horse. He drilled down for the pure joy of geeking out.[5]

This numerical list of projects displays Leonardo's genius in a manner worth a thousand adjectives. (And speaking of adjectives, Mark Twain once said, "When you catch [one], kill it."[6] Adjectives can be vague beyond description, though they are hard to avoid. Notice that I just used one: vague.) Yet numbers speak with a precision that adjectives can never match.

For more insight on the power of statistics, I turned to Professor Ethan Rouen from the Accounting Department at Harvard Business School. An experienced communicator, he spent several years as a crime reporter at the *New York Daily News* earlier in his career. In these excerpts from our conversation, he recounts his fascination with the consummate authority of numbers:

> So I did an MBA and in my Intro to Accounting class, on the first day, the professor showed how you could use ratio analysis to actually predict Enron's [demise]. He demonstrated exactly how, with just four numbers, you can watch Enron's descent from greatness into fraud. It sparked something in me. All of a sudden I realized that accounting and finance are just storytelling in a different format.[7]

Be aware that numbers can cut in two ways. I often point out to clients that some audiences will be impressed by revenue of say $1.5 million, to pick an amount at random, whereas others might think it's paltry:

> A statistic can be incredibly powerful or incredibly confusing. And it's really all about context. Is a hundred people a lot or a little? A hundred people in this office would be a lot. A hundred people on a football field would not be that much. And so the numbers tell the

story just like words do, but you wouldn't just cut and paste a whole transcribed interview and say, "This is the story." Same thing with numbers. It's about selecting the numbers that actually really capture what you're trying to tell and then putting it into context. We think of ratios, earnings per share, because it's something you can pair across companies. Whereas if you have a billion dollars of revenue and one shareholder, that shareholder's much happier than if you have a billion dollars in revenue and a billion shareholders.[8]

I was taught in business school that an income statement (a.k.a. a "P&L") is like a video that depicts dynamic flows of money over time, whereas a balance sheet is like a stop-action photo that portrays just one moment. Yet Rouen points out that the balance sheet also tells a story of moving parts:

> [It's] the history of the business from day one. Every single transaction that this company has ever entered into is reflected in that balance sheet in compressed terms.[9]

I mentioned that in that sense it would be akin to a photo of Rouen himself, encompassing everything that had happened to him to that point, every mountain he climbed (he's an avid outdoorsman), every book he read, every news story he wrote and so on:

> That's a great analogy. Just like we are the sum of our experiences, the balance sheet is the sum of the company's experiences. So, from day one, every sale that's ever been made is reflected in the firm's cash, its accounts receivable, its inventory. . . . Whenever you go into a restaurant, you see their first dollar bill hanging up behind the cash register. . . . But that first dollar bill is really hanging up in the balance sheet.[10]

He agrees that numbers have a rare power for storytelling in many settings.

> If you are the manager or owner of a business, you know it better than anyone else. So anybody else talking about it is going to sound uninformed. Be concise and specific. Avoid vague terminology, use statistics and then provide examples to back them up. . . .
>
> There is a challenge in telling the story. Because you love the organization so much, you're so connected to it that you just expect everyone else to understand it. So try to sell your love of the business to the people that you're talking to.[11]

And that brings us smoothly to the next element on each island in the archipelago. In addition to the message itself and the supporting statistics, you need anecdotes, item number 3. (See: I'm keeping my promise to return to this.) Simply put, build your narrative around *people*, not abstractions. Politicians often use this technique in a corny way, as in "Ms. Jones, from X-town USA, raised five children in a two-room apartment and still managed to show up at work every day." Their anecdotes frequently sound hollow and canned, mainly because the candidates are merely mouthing words. As an executive, however, you should be intimately familiar with the customer and his or her feelings, aspirations, and desires. Too often clients tell me stories that are imprecise to the point of meaninglessness, as in "A customer in a focus group said she loves the product." I press for more details. Was it a young woman with hair dyed blue, a nose ring and tattoos, or a grandmother, with a different sort of blue hair, who sat silently the entire time until she finally opened her mouth and stunned everyone with her insight? These are two very different scenarios, giving context to the quote. Don't just relate the story, tell it. (We'll have more to say about sensory details later.) Above all, specifics *matter*.

And so does compression. If you communicate efficiently, your messages will take the form of a bouillon cube. The audience can simply add water, construct a bowl of soup, and feel the steam on its face. Take a lesson from Gabriel García Márquez, the Nobel Prize winner best known for the novel *One Hundred Years of Solitude*. The first sentence of that book could be a novel in itself: "Many years later, as he faced the firing squad, Colonel Aureliano Buendía was to remember that distant afternoon when his father took him to discover ice."[12] In those mere 26 words, we learn the character's name and rank, informing us that he spent some time in the armed forces; we also hear that he would one day face a firing squad—intriguing foreshadowing that is certain to spark interest given the extremity of the scenario; we also discover that his father once took him to discover ice. That last fact tells us that the Colonel no doubt came from a poor family in a rural area where refrigeration was an oddity rather than a commodity. Márquez specialized in a form of writing called magical realism, combining fact and fantasy to great effect. He once said that it's the details that make illusions credible:

> [I]f you say that there are elephants flying in the sky, people are not going to believe you. But if you say that there are four hundred and twenty-five elephants flying in the sky, people will probably believe

you. *One Hundred Years of Solitude* is full of that sort of thing. That's exactly the technique my grandmother used. I remember particularly the story about the character who is surrounded by yellow butterflies. When I was very small there was an electrician who came to the house. . . . My grandmother used to say that every time this man came around, he would leave the house full of butterflies. But when I was writing this, I discovered that if I didn't say the butterflies were yellow, people would not believe it.[13]

Let's take a detour into the sciences with a glimpse at Stephen Jay Gould's book about evolution and natural history called *The Panda's Thumb*. Here's how he introduces the main characters of his story:

Giant pandas are peculiar bears, members of the order Carnivora. Conventional bears are the most omnivorous representatives of their order, but pandas . . . [subsist] almost entirely on bamboo. They live in dense forests of bamboo at high elevations in the mountains of western China. There they sit, largely unthreatened by predators, munching bamboo ten to twelve hours each day.[14]

Wonderful, no? Notice the details. Pandas live in *dense* forests, at *high* altitudes, and they chew bamboo for *10 to 12 hours* a day. "What about the thumb in the title of the book?" you may be wondering. Gould goes on to explain that pandas actually have six fingers on each paw, and that their thumbs are not really fingers at all, in the classic sense. They're actually extensions of a bone called the radial sesamoid, normally part of the wrist. Between the elongated thumb and fingers they have a groove—and through that they slide bamboo stalks—stripping off foliage in the process.[15] Perhaps this is more than you ever wanted to know about pandas, but Gould uses this as a means of introducing concepts of natural selection, evolution and so on. This surely beats a dry recitation of scientific principles, doesn't it?

Specificity certainly enlivens stories, but so can personal touches, particularly when a spokesperson shows *vulnerability or candor*. Here is one of my favorite examples, from an address by a former CEO of John Hancock at a conference on work and family issues:

Well, my instructions were to be as provocative and visionary as I can. . . . I am, by training, an actuary. A common definition is that an actuary is someone who didn't have enough personality to be an accountant. . . . I might add, on a personal basis, that my own situation does give me a fairly broad range of experience in family matters. I have a ninety-year-old mother; three daughters whose ages are forty-one, twenty-six and eight; a nine-month-old grandson, and a baby-boomer wife whose mother is a World War II Icelandic war bride, and who lives in another city to which I commute on weekends. So I believe that I can relate closely to practically any demographic or family situation that anyone can bring up.[16]

This is a rather remarkable introduction encapsulating statistics, humor, and personal detail. We will have much more to say about intimate revelations in a later chapter on radio techniques, but suffice it to say that many of the best stories will come from your own life. In many senses, every tale is an autobiography, every poem a confession, and every painting a self-portrait.

It is important to remember that you should return to your islands, and their messages, stats, and anecdotes, when challenged. In media relations, we talk about bridging. When a reporter (or a harsh customer, for that matter) asks you about something unpleasant, irrelevant, or centrifugal to your main points, *answer the question first*, then "bridge" to your islands. This requires intense preparation. Again, you need to know where the islands are and how to get there. Sometimes you can bridge with two simple words: "but" or "however." Here are some examples:

- It is true we've had a rough quarter, BUT let me tell you about our new product line.

- Yes, our previous CEO had some legal troubles, HOWEVER current management has charted a new course.

- Yes, we did miss the deadline for the product revision, BUT initial reports are quite favorable.

Think of these bridges as one-way thoroughfares with the intimidating spikes we often see at the exits at rental car facilities in airports with the no-nonsense warning sign "Don't Back Up: Severe Tire Damage Will Occur." In other words, once you've transitioned away from swamps to your islands of paradise, don't go back. Advance, don't retreat, and be sure to bridge from island to island in the process. As a general rule, stay high-level on negatives and be specific on positives. A reporter may try to focus the conversation on unfavorable issues, but you should attempt to expand the discussion of the useful attributes of your product or service. Emphasize the advantages, not just the features. As Professor Theodore Levitt famously said, "People don't want to buy a quarter-inch drill. They want a quarter-inch hole,"[17] presumably to hang pictures on their walls. A photo gallery is not just the benefit, but the benefit of the benefit. Consider the phrase "which means that" to make the transition, as in "The new version of the software reduces RAM usage, which means that speed will increase by 10 percent." Don't just inform, persuade and answer questions implicit in the audience's mind. There is no more powerful way to engage listeners than to anticipate their objections and to alleviate confusion before it appears.

JOB-INTERVIEW STRATEGIES

Just about everything we have discussed to this point applies to job interviews. There is perhaps nothing worse than the dreaded prompt "So tell me about yourself." Most applicants immediately resort to a list of adjectives: "Well," they'll stammer, "I'm conscientious, hard-working, and creative"—a statement that tells us precisely nothing. Instead, fall back or, should I say, fall forward onto the archipelago of islands and villains-victims-heroes paradigm in the following way:

Island 1

Message: I'm hardworking.

Proof point: I generally arrive at the office before eight, stay until six and usually work at home after my kids go to bed. Plus I make a point of spending two to three hours working on Saturdays and Sundays.

Anecdote: One morning I noticed a gentleman in the foyer at five after eight. The receptionist wasn't in yet so I asked if I could help him. Though he was sloppily dressed (a key detail), I sensed he might have something to offer. We struck up a conversation and he told me that he had a new idea for product design. I sat down and we chatted for the next hour. It turns out that he was an inventor, and a very accomplished one at that. I invited him in and introduced him to our boss. The product he proposed was . . . etc.

Island 2

Message: I was successful in my previous job.

Proof point: We moved into 22 new cities during my tenure.

Anecdote: One in particular stands out in memory. We had never sold a single unit in Rochester, Minnesota before. When I first walked into the wholesaler's office the VP of Sales there looked at me like I was speaking another language. She brusquely told me, "I'll give you 10 minutes, talk fast." Taking that as a challenge, I proceeded to . . . etc.

A job interview is nothing else but story time. One more note: follow this formula in the "Objective" section of your resume, where you state your goals. Most job applicants write something like this: "Seeking senior position involving major responsibility for product development, marketing or sales in a growing company east of the Mississippi etc." Would you hire this person? Unlikely. I'd rather see something less abstract such as "Seeking senior marketing position where I can utilize my experience with three national campaigns with budgets ranging from $1M to $9M and my extensive network with major advertising agencies, etc." Now we're talking.

YOUR ABOUT FACE

There is another essential aspect about messaging that we should address, and I just mentioned the key word: about. Most executives use this term in a narrow way, as the old joke indicates. CEO to writer: "I need a speech." Writer: "What's it about?" CEO: "It's about 30 minutes." Bear in mind that audiences want to hear about their own lives. Choreographer George Balanchine once sharply ridiculed the type of theatergoer who wants to see his life on stage so he can grieve over it: "I'm married," Balanchine said in mocking imitation, "my wife and children have left me, and I'm unhappy and feel that I'm going to kill myself. And that's what I think Art [*sic*] is—people should pay me for my story."[18] Kidding aside, you should be familiar enough with your customers to be able to describe their predicaments in detail. This is not cynical marketing. Instead, it's real communication.

In that process be sure to orient your thinking with the correct preposition. Don't just talk *to* the audience, talk *about* them. FDR understood this intuitively. Let's take a look at his first inaugural speech from 1933, when the nation was mired in the Great Depression. This address is best known for the quote "The only thing we have to fear is fear itself," but I draw your attention to this section instead:

[W]e face our common difficulties. . . . Values have shrunk to fantastic levels; taxes have risen; our ability to pay has fallen; government of all kinds is faced by serious curtailment of income; . . . the withered leaves of industrial enterprise lie on every side; farmers find no markets for their produce; and the savings of many years in thousands of families are gone. More important, a host of unemployed citizens face the grim problem of existence, and an equally great number toil with little return.[19]

This speech resonated because most Americans at the time could recognize their own lives in the words. Roosevelt was drawing a portrait of the plight of the average citizen.

On a lighter note, National Public Radio's host Terry Gross, of *Fresh Air* fame, used a similar approach in a graduation speech at Bryn Mawr College:

So many of you know me as the lady you were forced to listen to in your parents' car, or in the carpool on your way to and from school every day. And here you are on one of the most important days of your lives, forced to listen to me again. And you're probably wondering, "So what's she gonna do today, ask questions?"[20]

As we can see, Terry Gross and FDR alike made it clear that they understood what their listeners were thinking or feeling. Try to do likewise, even on your website. Consider adding an "About You" section, perhaps as the landing page. When customers perceive that you grasp their needs, they're more likely to delve further into your site.

Think of storytelling as a form of *kindness* directed toward people who want to feel that you comprehend their lives. Once expressed, the story becomes a gift that belongs to them. It will no longer be yours because it will be theirs. Your message does not reside in what you say, but in what they retain, and *what they repeat to others*. As management professor Mary Jo Hatch says, "[I]t isn't just about what you [express], it's what they're hearing and what you're hearing them hearing. And when you get into really good storytelling, there is this give and take between the audience and the storyteller . . . with emotional and aesthetic messages going back and forth."[21] Hatch also notes that you should not just speak about the audience, but *for* them as well. That's why you need to cast them in the starring role so they can learn, internalize, and retell the story.

I have done a great deal of political consulting, and I always remind candidates that voters will seek answers to three questions before supporting them:

1. What will he or she do for me?
2. Does he or she care about my life?
3. Does he or she understand me?

Ideally, a great political leader will elicit affirmative responses to all three questions, but that is nigh impossible. Number 2 is essential, as we all like to feel that people sympathize with our plight, but number 3 is arguably the most important of all. We want our leaders to *understand* us.

The great Russian filmmaker Tarkovsky said nothing made him happier than this sort of reaction: "Thank you for [your film] 'Mirror.' My childhood was like that. . . . Only how did you know about it? There was that wind, and the thunderstorm. 'Galka, put the cat out,' cried my grandmother. . . . It was dark in the room. . . . And the paraffin lamp went out."[22] This viewer felt that Tarkovsky had filmed *her* life. This is what resonance all about.

WHAT "JOB" DOES THE PRODUCT PERFORM?

Professor Clay Christensen, who popularized the concept of "disruptive innovation," has written a useful book advancing the theory of "job marketing"—that is, posing the question "What job did you hire [the] product to do?"[23] He deduced, for instance, that customers bought milkshakes at an unnamed major food chain because "they had a long and boring ride to work" and they "needed something to keep the commute interesting."[24] Bananas were too quickly consumed, doughnuts were too messy, and bagels required too much acrobatic skill to eat in the car. Christensen said that jobs theory is focused on "why" rather than "who or what,"[25] and that it requires "writing a resume for every competing product."[26] This certainly dovetails with the villain-victim-hero paradigm because "customers may not be able to tell you what they want, but they can tell you about their struggles."[27] As observers of work or life, or as spectators at horror movies, we often ask the wrong questions. Dr. Steve Schlozman explains:

> [Horror movies] lead you down a certain road, and everybody thinks it's going in that direction. And then they throw this curveball at you, maybe a third to two-thirds into the movie. In *Nightmare on Elm Street,* for instance, Freddy appears to be a demon. He invades kids' brains

when they're dreaming. If he kills you in your dream you're going to die when you're awake. He's got to go. He's a bad actor. But then you find, two-thirds into the movie, that he was burned to death by the people in the town, without any due process. And then you feel a little bit conflicted. And you can even identify and understand his motivations.

The villain isn't Freddy. The villain was the lack of understanding and un willingness to remain civil by the elders of the town. So there's this kind of asking the wrong question. And that happens a lot in horror films. And they want the viewers to ask the wrong question too.[28]

We might make another query with regard to Christiansen's theory: Does it apply to the "job" that a story fulfills? Whose need is it satisfying, yours or the customer's? Christiansen notes that Levitt's famous insight about customers buying drill holes, not drills, coupled with Peter Drucker's observation that they rarely purchase what the company believes it is selling, "are the two most profound marketing insights of the last century."[29] Between firm and client lies a deep misunderstanding in many cases, and it is up to you to probe the buyer's mind to discover the exact nature of the villainy she is facing and to ascertain the substance of your "heroism." The answer is not often found in segmentation, with endless divisions by function, price, demographics, and so on.[30] Nor does it lie in cross-referencing data that may be correlated but not causative. As Nate Silver said, "ice cream sales and forest fires . . . both occur more often in the summer heat. But there is no causation; you don't light a patch of the Montana brush on fire when you buy a pint of Häagen-Dazs."[31]

Here are some examples of "job marketing" that may spark ideas: Harley Davidson is really selling freedom with its motorcycles. Aston Martin offers not just elite transportation but also a fantasy that you too can be James Bond. Brooks Brothers is not simply marketing clothes, but timeless tradition. Notice I stopped at three examples, which segues smoothly to the next section.

HARD TO DISAGREE WITH THE POWER OF THREE

You have certainly heard the expression "blood, sweat, and tears," allegedly from a speech Winston Churchill delivered in 1940 at the dawn of war. What he *actually* said, however, was "I have nothing to offer but blood, toil, tears and sweat."[32] Our collective memory has reduced those four words down to three, from what is called a tetracolon (in rhetoric) to a tricolon (three parallel words). The number three resonates deeply in the human mind in a visceral, fundamental, and pleasing way. There are three primary colors (red, yellow, and blue), three wise men, three acts in plays, and so on. There is even an old Latin proverb "Omne trium est perfectum," meaning every group of three is perfect.

When it comes to messaging, three items suffice and four are too many, according to Professor Suzanne Shu from UCLA's business school and Professor Kurt Carlson from Georgetown's. Their seminal article in the *Journal of Marketing*—called "When Three Charms but Four Alarms"[33]— shows that people either discount ads that contain four claims or disengage entirely. This phenomenon applies across the board to descriptions of shampoo, cereal, candidates, and restaurants. The same holds true with quotations. We tend to recall those with three items: "the government of the people, by the people, and for the people"; or "life, liberty, and the pursuit of happiness." Julius Caesar's brisk summary of a military campaign in 47 BCE comes to mind too: "I came, I saw, I conquered," which is even more terse in the original Latin: "Veni, vidi, vici." (Notice, I provided just three instances here.)

This principle even applies to "marketing" of potential mates. Shu and Carlson devised an experiment where they asked university students to imagine a scenario where an old friend from high school mentions that she's dating a guy named John. If she describes him as intelligent, kind, funny, and cute, then the listener probably won't be convinced that he's the best partner for her. If she merely says her new love interest is intelligent, kind, and funny, however, she'll be more persuasive. In this context, cute doesn't matter. Each successive message adds weight to the argument when the speaker moves from one point to two, or from two to three, but diminishing returns set in thereafter. That means you should not overwhelm your customers with a basketful of messages. Fewer are better.

It is important, however, to give examples. I often advise clients to employ the "colon" form of communication, that is, to make a statement followed by the phrase "such as," in turn followed by a colon, as an introduction to illustrations. But just a few! My children often bring me up short with the curt phrase, "Too many examples, Dad."

I can't resist a couple more instances of the power of three, though: "Eye it, try it, buy it" was a marketing slogan for Chevrolet in the 1940s. And then we have the infamous quote attributed to Dorothy Parker: "I require three things of a man. He must be handsome, ruthless, and stupid."[34]

It is worth remembering that there is an oddity in the English language that further underscores the force of three. When we indicate the position of items in a series, we use ordinal numbers. Although the words first, second, and third have unique endings, those from 4th to 10th, end in *th*. Once you go beyond three, everything sounds the same, literally, and has the same incrementally paltry persuasive punch.

FOUR

Brand with the Heart

Because Consumers Often Think Products Have One

There has been so much written about branding. Perhaps no field of business is rifer with cliché. A friend of mine was always amused when he overheard salespeople extolling their "value proposition" to potential customers at his high-tech firm. At least they didn't say brand promise or brand essence. The terminology may be shopworn, but the concept is about as essential as can be. Your "brand" incorporates your story, your myths, your history, your core, your collateral, your website, your videos, your wardrobe, your ethics, and just about any other tangible or intangible aspect of your business. It is important to keep in mind, however, that products or services are bundles of physical and psychological attributes. As Charles Revson once said, "In the factory we make cosmetics; in the drugstore we sell hope."[1] But before we enter the realm of the emotional aspect of branding, let's start with a list of rather tough questions that you should spend a great deal of time answering—questions that will take you on a trip to the skeleton and soul of your business:

- What is your *core* message?
- What are your *desired* messages versus the messages you actually convey?
- Why was your organization created?
- What do you do best and how do you do it?
- What business category are you in?
- Whom do you serve?
- How do you measure success?

- What do you *not* do?
- What benefits do you offer?
- If you could change the behavior of customers or stakeholders, what would you prefer that they do?
- What would the world miss if you did not exist?
- Who are the villains, victims, and heroes in your space?
    - What is the problem, and how do you contribute to the solution? (In other words, if your product/service is the answer, what is the question?)
    - What keeps your customers awake at night?
    - How do they feel about these issues?
    - How do you resolve their difficulties?
- How do you reduce the pain of those you serve?
- What is your competitive advantage?
- Who are your competitors?
    - What markets do they serve?
    - What are their key messages?
- What would surprise your audiences?
- What different messages do you want to convey to your customers, the public, the media, your competitors, your distributors, your shareholders, your stakeholders or your suppliers—both internally and through advertising, collateral, media or outreach?
- What is your overarching mission and does anyone care about it?
    - How many employees could articulate it?
    - How many have no inkling about it?
- Is your organization perceived as credible, intimate, or both?
- What are the trends and challenges in your space?

If you did this exercise correctly, you should have walked away from this book for a month or two. Kidding aside, this is an essential endeavor. At the risk of sounding like a taskmaster, I will add another assignment to the list: a positioning exercise. The goal is "to own **one word** in your customer's mind." Here are some examples: FedEx = overnight; Jaguar = style; Volvo = safety; McDonald's = hamburgers; Dunkin' Donuts = awake.

There is a fine distinction to be made, however: a *position statement* objectively explains the image you *actually* convey. On the other hand, a position*ing* statement details the impression you would *like* to convey. It may be aspirational, but it should delineate your core messages as follows:

To the (target audience) you are the [only?] _____

that provides _____

by _____.

If it's helpful, here are the so-called Top 10 positioning categories:

- Low Cost
- Value
- Innovation
- Domain Expertise
- Leadership
- Customer Intimacy
- Performance Excellence
- Service Excellence
- Depth or Breadth of Solution
- Low Risk

Begin by asking yourself what single word would define your business.

So much for the context. Let's turn now to the *emotional* aspect of branding.

BRANDS HAVE "FEELINGS" TOO

Consumers are quick to notice that brands have personalities just as humans do: they're either reliable or irresponsible, friendly or unfriendly, and so on. We *interact* with them and expect give-and-take and flexibility. (I was acutely aware of this phenomenon when I worked as a business reporter. The companies I covered readily exhibited their true nature in their relationships with the press. Some were open and accessible, in good times and bad, and others were hostile yet still expected reporters to write positive articles about them.) Yes, firms have temperaments, just like people. This is the phenomenon of anthropomorphism at work—the attribution of human characteristics to other beings. The concept dates back to Xenophanes in ancient Greece. He noted that images of the gods resembled those who worshipped them.[2] He observed that Greek deities were thought to be light-skinned and blue-eyed, like the citizens of Greece itself.[3] He even reportedly joked that if cows and horses had the capacity to draw, they would create gods that looked like them.[4] Indeed, Princeton professor Susan Fiske suggests that *people* were the first "brands," that human faces may have been the original "logos" and that our minds perceive brands as "stand-ins" for people.[5] She says we interact with companies just as "we have evolved" to interact with one another.[6] Even computers or websites elicit surprisingly emotional reactions, though we are fully aware that they're not real.[7] We curse at them when they fail to "behave,"[8] yet we regard them as warm and competent social agents[9] when they do our bidding and see them as accessible when phone numbers are posted on websites. We know that Amazon, for instance, is not alive, but we tend to regard her (or him) as a shopping partner bringing the world to our screens. When we can't find what we want right away, we react just as we would if a salesperson in a retail store were rude or uncooperative.

Marketers have long tried to link their products with real or fictional characters. The Marlboro Man, the World's Most Interesting Man, the Michelin Man, or the Twitter Bird come immediately to mind. (This is why environmentalists emphasize the phrase "Mother Earth"—an entity we dare not harm.[10]) Companies have even employed anthropomorphic cognates for everything from Kool-Aid to condoms[11] and have designed the front end of cars and motorcycles to look like faces.[12]

We find another example in the watch industry. Did you ever notice that the time is 10:10 in practically every picture in ads for watches? I thought the V formed by the hands in that position was designed to move our gaze toward the product name, which is invariably at the apex. I discovered, however, that the idea is to mimic a smile so that the product appears to be more lifelike and appealing.[13] There is even some evidence that personifying a product makes it harder to throw it away. Drivers, for instance, are said to be less likely to replace a car if they are called upon to judge its personality.[14] My own experience reflects this. My first car was a 1966, hand-me-down Chevy Impala, with a vinyl convertible top that lowered electrically. I nicknamed it "Charlie" for no reason other than the random thought patterns of a 17-year-old Jersey boy. I would pat "him" on the dashboard as my friends and I wreaked havoc on the local roads. I wasn't the only one who personified his car. My pal Mike Winett had a mid-1960s Mustang (that would be worth a fortune today) and he called it "Hubert," or "Hubie," for short. He described "him" as a "gleaming red bullet." When we were about to make the rounds with our band of brothers, we'd ask, "Are we taking Charlie or Hubie tonight?" Of course, we knew that the cars weren't really people, but we all treated them as though they were two more members of the gang. They were better than friends because they were loyal and consistent and they never complained. Charlie kept me company when I drove back and forth to college in Massachusetts. He was a faithful chariot when my dorm friends and I would head out to Walden Pond with the top down and the warm breezes caressing us on spring days. Eventually, I sold Charlie to a pal for $100. Sadly, my devoted Impala ended up in a junkyard because the electric windows started failing one by one as the vinyl top cracked and corroded. I hate to admit it, but I still miss him.

NAME IT AND IT'S YOURS

As with Charlie, naming is an essential part of branding and storytelling. You probably wouldn't order grilled Patagonian Toothfish at your favorite restaurant, for example. That's why a wholesaler named Lee Lantz renamed it "Chilean Sea Bass" nearly 30 years ago to give it more cachet. Ever heard of Minnesota Mining and Manufacturing? The engineers who founded it back in 1902 thought the name was so dull that they started using the moniker 3-M instead. Nike was originally called Blue Ribbon Sports, then renamed after the Greek goddess of victory. Good move. Somehow a "Blue Ribbon" swoosh wouldn't cut it. Then there's Sir Richard Branson. He was just 20 when he started a mail order records business. He was wondering what to call it and his associate came to the rescue: "What about Virgin? We're complete virgins at business." Verizon? A combination of the Latin word *veritas* (truth) and horizon. Cisco? An abbreviated version of San Francisco, where it was founded. Ikea represents the first letters of the late founder's name (**I**ngvar **K**amprad), the farm where he was raised (**E**lmtaryd) and his hometown in Sweden (**A**gunnaryd), which has a population of just 220.

If you're trying to figure out what to name a business or a product, here are some possibilities:

- Color it (literally): Red Hat or Green Giant
- Combine words: Laserjet or Dreamworks
- Add alliteration: Dunkin' Donuts
- Rhyme it: Reese's Pieces

- Evoke a concept: Amazon
- Describe the product: Whole Foods or Burger King
- Abbreviate: AOL, AT&T, FedEx
- Go sci-fi: Quark or Quasar
- Wax abstract: Akamai, Acura
- Add whimsy: Yahoo
- Invent words: Wii, Häagen-Dazs

Then again, sometimes the founders' name(s) work best: Dell, Hewlett-Packard, or Disney. I first called my business Greg Stone Productions, and I was doing, as you might have guessed, just video production as the time. (I had been a TV reporter so I was capitalizing on those who knew me in Boston.) As the company grew, however, I migrated into strategic consulting and changed the name to Stone Communications. Should I have chosen something trendier? Maybe. Yet Johnson & Johnson, Ford, and Steinway are still with us. I guess I'm in good company.

The name of your business is only part of what has come to be called brand journalism, a term coined by Larry Light, the former CMO of McDonald's:

> [It] is a chronicle of the varied things that happen in our brand world, throughout our day, throughout the years. Our brand means different things to different people. . . . It is positioned differently in the minds of kids, teens, young adults, parents and seniors . . . differently at breakfast, lunch, dinner, snack, weekday, weekend, with kids or on a business trip.[15]

When you contemplate your own form of brand journalism, try to think like a reporter. With social media, which we'll discuss in a later chapter, it's much easier to generate ongoing news. Ideally, it's possible to create a "lovemark"—a trademark on steroids, the ultimate emotional play—along the lines of Harley Davidson:

> Its logo is probably tattooed onto more human beings than any other. . . . It is a brand of mystery and legend, which inspires a quasi-religious devotion among its customers. The throaty growl of the engine, the low leather seats, the high handlebars. None of these things improve the quality of the bike, but they give it a character.[16]

Character indeed. Besides mystery, lovemarks of this sort exude sensuality and intimacy,[17] but we should maintain in close sight the overall dimensions of the brand experience: sensory, affective, behavioral, and intellectual. For a final lesson in this chapter, let's turn to one of the greatest communicators of the previous century.

DON'T PROVOKE, EVOKE

Tony Schwartz produced some 20,000 radio and TV commercials for illustrious clients like Jimmy Carter, Bill Clinton, and Ted Kennedy, but he is best known for the "daisy ad" for President Johnson's campaign in 1964. That spot showed an innocent little girl who was pulling petals one by one off a flower. (It is very easy to find this ad on YouTube.) The child counts to 10 and looks up with visible concern as a rocket countdown overwhelms us. Next we hear a loud explosion, accompanied by a mushroom cloud that permeates the screen.

Lyndon Johnson's distinctive voice, echoing W. H. Auden's famous anti-war poem *September 1, 1939*, warns us: "These are the stakes . . . we must either love each other or we must die." This searing ad was broadcast only one time, on NBC's *Monday Night at the Movies*, yet it had so much impact that it laid groundwork for LBJ's huge victory. The commercial suggested that his opponent, Senator Barry Goldwater, might have been a dangerous hawk.

Schwartz sought to create ads that would evoke, rather than provoke. He wanted to *elicit* emotional responses, instead of merely propounding facts. He explained his approach in his seminal book, *The Responsive Chord*: "The listener's or viewer's brain is an indispensable component of the total communication system."[18] In fact, the audience is called upon to put the final touches on the feedback loop: "The best political commercials are similar to Rorschach patterns. They don't tell the viewer anything. They surface his feelings and provide a context for him to express those feelings.[19] Surprisingly, Schwartz thought the "daisy" ad was "the most positive commercial ever made,"[20] perhaps because of its anti-war impact.

Schwartz's work was so memorable that all of it resides in the Library of Congress. I was fortunate enough to meet him in 1980 when my political writing class at Columbia Journalism School journeyed to his home studio in the West 50s in Manhattan. Striding alongside lab benches that were cluttered with microphones, tapes, and production paraphernalia, Schwartz captivated us. Despite his palpable energy, though, there was something melancholy about him. I later discovered that he was a recluse, driven indoors by the agoraphobia that afflicted him since his teens. Although he rarely left his brownstone, he was quite worldly and displayed deep familiarity with current events, fads, and fashions.

At base, he was a sonic *artist*. His fascination with all things audible began when he went blind for six months at age 16—perhaps due to psychosomatic causes. As he said, people are born without ear lids. "They listen to anything that concerns them."[21]

FIVE

Why Stories Resonate

Neuroscience Meets Homer

The human brain weighs just three pounds yet it consumes 20 percent of the body's energy. This productive organ houses some 100 billion neurons, each one connected through a dazzling array of networks with 10,000 of its mates. When you look out at an audience, try to imagine that your goal is to transmit ideas from your brain into theirs, without distortion or noise. The best conduits are stories, which are up to 22 times more memorable than facts alone.[1] Fortunately, there are biological phenomena that can facilitate this process: for instance, speaker-listener neural coupling, a wondrous effect that links brains when the audience is actively engaged. Princeton University cognitive neuroscientist Uri Hasson has been in the forefront of research in this area. In one experiment, he placed a grad student inside in an fMRI and recorded her as she told a story about a wild and complicated high-school prom night. He asked her to speak as if she were telling the tale to someone she knew well. Here's the setup: her prom day happened to coincide with the final leg of a scuba diving course she was taking with her family. Unfortunately, the boat broke down, they were late going home and disaster ensued:

> Pretty much the worst you'll ever look is after you go scuba diving. . . . You've been under 60 feet of water, which is two atmospheres of pressure, for an hour and a half. You have a goggle mark permanently sketched into your face, which takes like 5 hours to get rid of that. And um, just your hair, it's just a mess, you're just a mess. And now I have approximately 5 minutes to get ready for the prom. So I'm like trying to put on make-up while my sister is shaving my legs,

while my mom is brushing my hair. . . . [later in the evening] So we're walking to the car, and _____ had drove but he obviously couldn't drive 'cause he was drunk, so I drive. And _____ is going through his pockets to find his keys . . . and he trips in the parking lot [and] falls flat on his face . . . and he's just a bloody mess. . . . And so I'm driving on US1. . . . And I'm driving slowly, there's lights and traffic and stuff so I'm not going quickly at all. And there was this fender bender and _____ . . . sort of grabs my arm and I sort of turn, and I end up crashing into this accident that's already there. . . . So the policeman comes over, and I don't have my license, by the way. I have a permit so I can be driving with _____ cause he's 18, but he's wasted, I mean, he's still playing air guitar when the policeman comes over and his face is bloody. . . . And I'm thinking I'm done for. I'm thinking I'm going to jail . . . [After 20 minutes the policeman returns.] He hands me back my license and he says to me, "I'm sorry Miss _____, but somehow your registration has blown away and I cannot find it." And he was so embarrassed about losing my registration that he tells me to drive on my way. For real. So I drive away as quickly as I can and I finally get to the after party house and I get out of the car and _____ passes out on the beach and I call my mom and have her pick me up. And that's it.[2]

Whew! Professor Hasson and his colleagues played the tape of this remarkable tale for 11 volunteers, also stationed inside fMRIs. The results were startling. The speaker's and listener's brains mirrored one another with coupled response patterns (with a slight delay to allow for comprehension to occur).[3] Moreover, Hasson and his co-authors found that the stronger the coupling, the more successful the communication. The researchers further discovered that the listener's responses actually *anticipated* the speaker's on occasion, and that effective comprehension "requires the active engagement of the listener."[4] Think of the process as a *pas de deux*, with two performers in synch with one another. This research shows that interaction is "really a single act performed by two brains."[5]

Neural coupling was observed in many different parts of the brain: Broca's area (where speech is produced), Wernicke's area (where language comprehension occurs) and in "extra-linguistic areas . . . [where processes affect] the capacity to discern the beliefs, desires and goals of others."[6] This is not exactly like the Vulcan mind meld we know from *Star Trek*,[7] but it takes a step in that direction. (These wonderful benefits of communication, by the way, can be severely compromised by mental impairments. Dementia caused by Korsakov's syndrome or Alzheimer's, for instance, can diminish the ability to process narratives. The effect is quite dreadful and has the sinister name dysnarrativa. Korsakov's is particularly debilitating because "selfhood virtually vanishes" to the extent that neuroscientist Oliver Saks said one of the patients was "scooped out, de-souled."[8] Indeed, it would perhaps not be an exaggeration to say that the ability to follow, enjoy and appreciate stories makes us "souled" beings in the first place.)

Savoring a narrative is a multimedia phenomenon. In another experiment, Professor Hasson asked volunteers (inside fMRI machines again) to watch part of episodes of TV shows like *Sherlock*, which are full of complicated plot twists. They would then recount the stories to other volunteers (whose brains were also analyzed by fMRIs during the process.) The result: similar areas in the storyteller's and listener's brains were activated, whether they were watching, recalling, or imagining scenes from the shows.

> The more similar the patterns in the brain of the person who originally viewed the episode and the person who mentally constructed it when listening to the description, the better the transfer of memories
> . . . "Perhaps the key function of memory is not to represent the past, but to be used a tool to share our knowledge with others and predict the future," Hasson says. He expects the results would be even more pronounced in real-time or face-to-face conversations.[9]

The implications of this for business storytelling are immense. Try to imagine your listener's brains lighting up just as yours does when you convey a dramatic tale. This is not ESP or magic, it's simply neural electricity at work, and it might change your customers' actions given the link between cognition and behavior.

There is another biological phenomenon that supercharges the impact of stories. You have probably heard of oxytocin, the so-called hug hormone or cuddle chemical that facilitates social bonding. It turns out that captivating stories stimulate the release of this substance. Professor Paul Zak, who directs the Center for Neuroeconomics Studies at Claremont Graduate University, has studied this extensively. In one of his experiments, he infused synthetic oxytocin into a group of volunteers who watched emotional ads called Public Service Announcements, dealing with smoking, drinking, speeding, or global warming. They were incentivized to pay attention with the promise of a $5 payment if they could successfully answer a factual question about the stories (for example,

"Was there a car in the video?"). Then they were asked if they'd like to donate some of the money to the cause featured in the spot. Those who received the oxytocin donated 56 percent more than the control group. The hormone's effect was

> associated with concern for the character in the story. . . . If you pay attention . . . and become emotionally engaged with the story's characters, then it is as if you have been transported into the story's world. This is why your palms sweat when James Bond dodges bullets. And why you stifle a sniffle when Bambi's mother dies.[10]

Moreover, "character-driven stories with emotional content" enhance both understanding and recall even after weeks have passed.[11] Moreover, this persistent effect may galvanize the audience into a change in behavior. Zak's work underscores the impact of the villain-victim-hero paradigm I have outlined, starting with employees who will be

> substantially more motivated by their organization's transcendent purpose (how it improves lives) than by its transactional purpose (how it sells goods and services). Transcendent purpose is effectively communicated through stories—for example, by describing the pitiable situations of actual, named customers and how their problems were solved by your efforts. Make your people empathize with the pain the customer experienced and they will also feel the pleasure of its resolution—all the more if some heroics went in to reducing suffering or struggle, or producing joy.[12]

The same effect will occur with customers, the most important audience for your business, and they will either choose to buy or not. In general, most decisions are made through what Dr. Steve Schlozman calls a "wonderfully subtle dialogue"[13] in our brains between the visceral limbic systems and the higher, more rational regions in the frontal lobes. Here's a brief anatomy lesson:

> [T]he primitive region of the brain . . . [is] governed by a wordless and excitable despot called the amygdala [whose] job is to perceive all of existence through the binary scope of fight versus flight. . . . [But] we have more advanced compartments to "talk" to the amygdalae. These compartments rest in our frontal lobes. The frontal lobes tell the amygdalae what do with all of its excitement.[14]

Since our primary motivation is to avoid threat, pain, and fear, a story about a product or service that will blunt the power of the "villains" will have innate appeal. Moreover, effective narratives tend to cause a cascade of dopamine, which can enhance the accuracy of memory. My own view is that memory is akin to a script that we are constantly revising and combining, conflating or perhaps confusing with prior or subsequent recollections, further complicated by distortions or biases. If there is a way to penetrate this morass with a telling narrative that obscures all extraneous material, then we can increase the chances that the customer's "script" will match our own.

Scholars have long noted that stories function in an intertextual manner, meaning that all collections of words or ideas, be they oral, written, visual, or social, are interrelated in an intersection of

> several speech acts and discourses (the writer's, the speaker's, the addressee, earlier writers' and speakers'), whereby meanings emerge in the process of how something is told and valued, where, to whom, and in relation to which other utterances. "Stories echo with other stories, with those echoes adding force to the present story. Stories are also told to be echoed in future stories. Stories summon up whole cultures."[15]

Russian theorist Mikhail Bakhtin said that language is dialogic because the words we are using now are linked with past and future statements,[16] in the same way that memes circulating within the confines of a company reflect the future views of external stakeholders. "Corporate" messages like IBM's old motto "Think" or Apple's "Think different" or Nike's "Just do it" express more than the simple connotations of the words because they connect with every other statement uttered before, during, or after. Reading and listening are constant processes of reinterpretation and participation, just like watching films. The late Italian semiologist Umberto Eco felt that *Casablanca*, for instance, was an intertextual collage encompassing past and future works.[17] It "became a cult movie," he said, "because it is not one movie. It is 'movies.'"[18] Borges envisioned a similar amalgamation in his short story "The Library of Babel," where he wrote that "there must exist a book that is the cipher and perfect compendium *of all other books*, and some librarian must have examined [it]; this librarian is analogous to a god."[19] In a world where the Internet and mobile technology supplement television, radio, and print, this convergence effect is multiplied. We know from McLuhan that the media extend our senses (allowing us to see and hear things far beyond our physical capacities), yet we might add that the media also expand our ability to combine narratives in ever more creative ways. Just as Freud said that each person is "like an entire cast of characters in a novel or play,"[20] so too are businesses made up of a whole collection of personalities and tales. We learn stories to retell them, and in adding our own words we make them our own and transcend time to "reinvent yesterday and tomorrow":[21]

> Just as each age reinvents Shakespeare, constructing new meanings out of the very words read by other generations, each age creates its own folklore through rereadings as well as retellings. The prominence of certain stories is in itself symptomatic of cultural production—of the way in which culture constitutes itself by constituting us.[22]

Even if the result is a palimpsest where the underlying themes or memes are invisible, their impact is still palpable, especially if iterated in narrative form. Seminal thinker Claude Shannon of Bell Labs fame believed that "information can be treated very much like a physical quantity, such as mass or energy,"[23] and he saw the process of communication as a resolution of uncertainty rather than a transmission of meaning—sending the recipient new data—ideally with "error-correcting codes."[24] I submit that one of the most airtight and foolproof of those corrections would be narrative itself.

THE STORY OF STORIES: WHERE THEY COME FROM

Daily life tends toward the mundane. Routine and repetition dominate. Maybe that's why stories are so powerful because they help us climb to the balcony and get a wider-angle view. Their appeal is indelibly seared into our DNA:

> Folklorists have recognized their tales in Herodotus and Homer, on ancient Egyptian papyruses and Chaldean stone tablets; and they have recorded them all over the world, in Scandinavia and Africa, among Indians on the banks of the Bengal and Indians along the Missouri. The dispersion is so striking that some have come to believe in Ur-stories and a basic Indo-European repertory of myths, legends, and tales.[25]

When scholars mention "Ur-stories," they mean basic elements, from which all other compound tales are composed. Underlying the urge to share anecdotes is the desire to create a *new world* in a way "that makes some particular future not only plausible but also compelling."[26] Fairy tales, in particular, are said to work in an "optative" manner, that is, by expressing a wish that invites us to "dwell in astonishment and explore new possibilities" in "announcing what might be" and taking us "off course, or off socially sanctioned paths."[27] Likewise, stories also function in the subjunctive mood because they can express a desire for something that has not yet occurred, keeping "the familiar and the possible cheek by jowl"[28] but "without diminishing the seeming reality of the actual."[29] They can also exploit what philosophers call an "illocutionary force" (meaning they advise, command, or warn.)

This reminds me of a telling anecdote I heard. An executive I know took one of his young associates on his first trip to Europe. After a few days had passed, during a conversation over dinner, the boss asked the younger man what his initial impressions were. "Well," he said, "in America everything is permitted unless it is forbidden, but here in Germany everything is forbidden unless it is permitted." An Italian gentleman at the next table apologized for intruding on the conversation, then added this comment: "In Italy, everything is permitted *because* it is forbidden." Somehow this exchange sheds light on the nature of business stories. We constantly bump up against the limitations of what is permitted and forbidden in life, but in chronicling our endeavors we can let the imagination flow in a way that turns us all into sightseers. Truly transformative products or services call for transformational stories that take us into a new realm of expectation, be it optative, subjunctive, or illocutionary.

This ongoing rewriting of our narratives will change business archetypes over time. The age of the "organization man" has given way to the hero, the magician, the intrapreneur, the ruler, the convener, or some other category we haven't begun to even consider yet. Perhaps this is the era of the storyteller. We don't mean shaman or entertainer, but rather she or he who can lead by weaving a narrative. Anecdotes can effect change in three ways: as "light," that is, highlighting the fault lines, illuminating outliers, and revealing the future; as glue, building empathy and coherence; or as a "web" that changes cultural narratives and helps the vulnerable reframe.[30] We can attempt to close the "myth gap," which seems to occur when evidence and arguments alone don't suffice.[31] Perhaps that's why "Chief Storyteller" is a hot new job title. Microsoft has one, and so does the city of Detroit.

Let's turn to Microsoft first. Go and visit their Story Labs at news .microsoft.com. It is far from what you'd expect. You'll see a gumbo of sumptuous photos and lively graphics, with the feel of a clever magazine.

Here's a sampling of some of the copy, which is decidedly not like your uncle's Microsoft:

Headline: Block Party

Earlier this spring, 45 schoolgirls in matching uniforms crowded into the computer room at the custard-colored North Thanglong Economic & Technical college on the outskirts of Hanoi, Vietnam. Beyond intermittent ripples of laughter and excitement, the 15- and 16-year-olds stayed focused throughout the day on the hard work at hand: playing Minecraft.

Together they built 3D models that reimagined the darker corners of their neighborhood as a safer, more functional and more beautiful place for them and their families to inhabit. But this wasn't just an exercise in imagination. The girls were taking part in the newest project from Block by Block, a program from the United Nations and Mojang, the makers of Minecraft, that uses the power of Minecraft and designs sourced from local residents to improve public spaces around the world.

Headline: The Fusionist, Asta Rosway

FoodFutures, an exhibition addressing food production needs in the year 2050, melds the seemingly strange bedfellows of urban farming, machine learning, research engineering and design.

Its self-sustaining hydroponic and aquaponic farm modules use computer vision analysis to maximize efficient yield and crop health. The retro-futurist aesthetics nod to 2050 while remaining approachable and inspiring discussion about the challenges of feeding a world facing increasing climate change and urbanization.

. . . In her Redmond, Washington, office stuffed with research white papers, mannequins in high-tech haute couture and a vintage Ms. Pac-Man mini-arcade, [Asta] Roseway [principal research designer at Microsoft Research and co-founder of FoodFutures] said, "We are entering an era of design-driven collaboration where the designer's role will be to act as the 'fusion' between art, research, science and engineering."[32]

Note the oblique, featurish approach, instead of a normal bland press release. This sort of storytelling is transforming Microsoft's image from stodgy to state of the art.

Likewise, the city of Detroit, subject of many "ruin porn" stories showing urban blight and abandoned factories, has as of March 2017 a new voice belonging to Chief Storyteller Aaron Foley. His mission is to give Detroiters a stronger platform by describing the variety in the city's 200 neighborhoods. He brings deep pride to the task:

> I can't stand the term "gritty" when it's used to describe my hometown and my residence of Detroit. It's empty. It's lost all meaning. It's an overused term that, far too often, simplifies this city to an easily digestible narrative when there are several storylines here. . . .
>
> Detroit is a large city, yes, but it's one of few that has a majority black population. And because of that, writers and other observers never take the time—the real time—to dig deep enough into our population here. It's far easier to apply a simple label instead of understanding nuance.
>
> Not only that, but there's an expectation that black people—through the viewpoints of onlookers, mind you—must forever endure a level of hardship.[33]

Foley wants to publicize stories about the African American community to counteract the media's emphasis on nonblacks. In a column called "Can Detroit Save White People?" he asked some provocative questions:

> What is it like being born into the most spoiled classes on the planet and wanting to move to a city full of black folks who have been ruined by centuries of your tyrannical rule? . . . Why don't we just make a deal that when you move to Detroit, you just move here and shut up about it? Buy your abandoned building, build your lovely studio space and make art to your heart's content, but at the same time, keep that maudlin B.S. to a minimum. Get off this endless spiel of trying to "save yourself" and just pay some property taxes. Welcome to Detroit.[34]

Foley is believed to be the first Chief Storyteller hired by a city in the United States, and he probably won't be the last. Ads for positions like his in businesses are cropping up more frequently on personnel sites, with job descriptions like these:

- "Define customer engagement plans.
- Create consistent, compelling storytelling content.
- Create and support overarching messaging framework.

- We are looking for someone who can breathe life into the stories about _____'s unique brand and mission on a global scale.
- [You should be] a brilliant writer, able to inhabit other people's voices."[35]

It won't be long before novelists, short story writers, and screenwriters will be common sights in the Fortune 1,000. Who says literature majors don't have a place in corporations?

SIX

Examples of Great Business Stories

The Formulas in Action

Let's take a break from analysis and enjoy a few more business anecdotes. We'll start in the 1500s and move forward to the present day.

First: Michelangelo. From the age of 26, the legendary artist was consistently employed. He was constantly doing what today we call networking, principally with the nobility, especially the Medicis, and the leaders of the church. In fact, he worked for *nine* popes over the course of his 88 years. Falsely claiming noble blood, Michelangelo disdained the label of artisan: "I was never a painter or sculptor like those who run workshops."[1] Style mattered to him. He wore fine clothes in public—following the rule of the three Ns: "nero, nuovo, netto" (black, new, and neat). Here is a story told by Giorgio Vasari that encapsulates Michelangelo's business acumen: A wealthy merchant named Agnolo Doni commissioned the famed *Tondo*, a round portrait of Jesus, Mary, and Joseph that is the artist's only surviving free-standing, or easel, painting. Doni and Michelangelo had agreed on a price of 70 ducats, more money than a skilled worker would make in a *year*. When Michelangelo delivered the finished product, however, the merchant balked and paid only 40. The artist gave him a choice: Pay 100 ducats or send the painting back. Doni eventually caved and agreed to pay the original fee of 70. Game not yet over, though. As a matter of principle, so the story goes, Michelangelo doubled the price and the miserly merchant ended up paying 140 ducats. "The era of the superstar artist was dawning." This was in the 1500s![2]

Moving ahead a few centuries, let's sip Courvoisier, the so-called brandy of Napoleon. Before leaving for exile on the remote island of St. Helena in the South Atlantic, where he spent the last six years of his life, the emperor reportedly sampled several drinks before choosing Courvoisier. He liked it so much that he brought several barrels with him.[3] That was in 1815, and we're still telling this story today. Cachet in a bottle.

The combination of outsized personalities and great companies certainly can produce robust stories. For instance, the late Helen Gurley Brown, of *Cosmopolitan* magazine fame. She infused the publication with her personality and ethos and made it sizzle with salacious copy. "We were inspiring. We tried to help you solve problems, realize dreams,"[4] she explained. Unabashedly ambitious and frank, she "taught unmarried women how to look their best, have delicious affairs and ultimately bag a man for keeps, all in breathless aphoristic prose."[5] Her messages may seem quaint today, but she ruled the magazine from 1965 until 1997 and represented, for many young women, not just the brand but a lifestyle too. I had occasion to interview her on camera for a corporate video and can attest to her iconic presence. Her office was decorated like a living room, with floral wallpaper and sumptuous furniture. She preferred to use a typewriter rather than a computer and hammered at the keys at an astounding rate—100 words per minute as I recall—a skill no doubt developed at the 17 secretarial jobs she held at the beginning of her career. She showed up for the pre-light in a bathrobe—with curlers in her hair—without the least bit of self-consciousness. She exuded unapologetic sensuality despite her advanced years, not to mention the artificially taught skin on her cheeks. Brown was very slight and short of stature, but commanding nonetheless—a true "walking brand."

WATER WORKS

The problem/villain: Some 660 million people on earth "have no reliable access to clean, safe water year-round."[6] Every day, water-related diseases kill 4,100 children under the age of five.[7]

The "hero": WATERisLIFE. The organization has developed, among other products, the CleanSip straw. As a child drinks through it, the straw purifies water from any source as it removes chlorine, lead, mercury, aluminum, arsenic, and cadmium and protects against giardia, E coli, fungus, cholera, typhoid, and dysentery.

Proof point: The straw can purify hundreds of liters of water and it costs just $10.[8]

Anecdote: The tale of any child the device has helped.

SHOES AND SOLACE

Zappos prides itself on customer service. Its "loyalty team" is on call 24/7 in the hope of delivering "the wow experience."[9] Example: "I received a call from Lisa," said Team member Shaea Labus. "We talked for 9 hours, 37 min. I took one bathroom break about two hours in. [Another person] took care of me by bringing me food and drinks. We talked about life, movies and favorite foods."[10] The previous record, by the way, was 8 hours and 47 minutes. "Sometimes people just need to call and talk," customer service representative Mary Tennant said. "We don't judge, we just want to help."[11]

Zappos seems to be a never-ending source of colorful anecdotes. CEO Tony Hsieh has lived in a trailer park in a 240-square-foot Airstream. Why? "I just love it because there's so many random, amazing things that happen around the campfire at night. I think of it as the world's largest living room."[12]

The Villain: Loneliness
Victims: Customers who need a friend
Heroes: Salespeople who care

THE ROOM IS ONLY THE BEGINNING OF THE EXPERIENCE

Ritz-Carlton believes it sets the "gold standard" in hospitality. Every day employees meet for a brief lineup where "wow stories" are read and circulated to all workers around the world. For example,

[O]ne family staying at the Ritz-Carlton Bali needed a particular type of egg and milk for their son who suffered from food allergies. Employees could not find the appropriate items in town, but the executive chef at the hotel remembered a store in Singapore that sold them. He contacted his mother-in-law, who purchased the items and personally flew them over 1,000 miles to Bali for the family. This example showcased Service Value Six: "I own and immediately resolve guests' problems."[13]

Apparently, encounters like this are commonplace at the Ritz. Here's another:

> [A] waiter overheard a man telling his wife, who used a wheelchair, that it was too bad he couldn't get her down to the beach. The waiter told the maintenance crew, and by the next day they constructed a wooden walkway down to the beach and pitched a tent at the far end where the couple had dinner. . . . As part of company policy, each employee is entitled to spend up to $2,000 on a guest to help deliver an anticipated need or desire.[14]

I can add a personal story: About 20 years ago, my wife and I won a weekend at the Ritz in Boston in a raffle at our daughter's nursery school. When we checked in, the person at the front desk greeted us by name: "Welcome, Mr. and Mrs. Stone." I'm not sure how he knew who we were. When we stepped into the elevator, the operator, who had been out of earshot of the front desk, said, you guessed it, "How are you, Mr. and Mrs. Stone?" The tiny, discreet earpiece was a giveaway: No doubt management quickly gave him our names before the doors closed. When we walked into our room, the phone rang. You know where this is going: The voice on the other end asked, "Is everything up to your satisfaction, Mr. Stone?" My wife later joked that if we went for a walk in nearby Boston Common, an employee disguised as a random stranger on a park bench would probably say, "Have a nice stroll, Mr. and Mrs. Stone."

Villain: Anything that frustrates a hotel guest

Victims: Customers who need attention, of any sort

Heroes: Hotel employees who go way, way beyond the norm

A NIGHT TO REMEMBER

George Daley is the new Dean of Harvard Medical School. He would prefer to be called simply George, but quickly realized that his name now carries the honorific "Dean" and with it a responsibility to lead through public speaking. This is how he recounted a formative night in his training:

> I was halfway through my internship. It was Christmas Eve. I was assigned to take call on the Cardiac Step Down Unit at Mass General Hospital. I was in the first crop of interns entrusted with that responsibility. I took 14 hits that night, 14 admissions. I think that was the

record that year. Alarms were beeping all around me and there were three codes. I was frazzled. I was terrified. But I survived that night—without sleep. On rounds the next morning, I came to a profound realization. I realized that there were only a small number of ways a patient could die while on my watch—lack of oxygen, lack of blood pressure, or lack of a heartbeat—and I had proven to myself I was capable of managing each one of those life-threatening clinical scenarios.

It was a transformative moment for me. As long as I could handle the acute challenges of critical care medicine . . . I could relax and be thoughtful about systematically securing a diagnosis and formulating a therapeutic plan. From that day forward, I became a better doctor.

I also learned that even when on call by myself, I was never alone. In the hospital I was supported by a host of remarkable colleagues—other residents, nurses, technicians, even occasionally attending physicians. I didn't have to shoulder all the responsibility because I was part of a team. I learned that others would have my back, as I had theirs.[15]

Villain: Potential death of patients, via three pathways

Victims: Patients in acute distress

Heroes: Dean Daley's training and skill and the support of the team

"CLOTHESING" THE DEAL

Ian Todreas, a senior environmental consultant who pays careful attention to his wardrobe, shared this story about his personal stylist Maria Rowley, whom he calls the most service-oriented person he has ever met:

She comes to my office or home for appointments to walk me through the new products and evaluate gaps in my wardrobe (there are zillions).

She brings her husband's jackets and pants so I can see what the swatches can look like as a finished piece of clothing.

She scouts out affordable accessories that she *doesn't* sell upon my request (such as shoes, overcoats, pocket squares) or even affordable pieces that she *does* sell but that I don't need to spend such big money on (e.g., belts). She has offered to purchase them for me and return them if I don't like them.

When my pieces arrive she comes to see how they fit, if necessary. She takes them to her tailor to be altered and also offers to have other stuff she has sold me cleaned, pressed, and altered.

All of that is great, but the best part is she comes to my home or office for our appointments.

I don't know about you, but I have never seen such detailed, nuanced service. She really makes me feel like a king.[16]

Villain: The complexity and difficulty of maintaining a stylish wardrobe

Victim: A married, middle-aged father of two with no time and little inclination to shop

Hero: The stylist extraordinaire who solves every minute problem, anticipated or unanticipated

WELL BREAD SERVICE

Ian Todreas is a font of stories. Here's a shorter one he told me:

At Trader Joe's yesterday, I was hemming and hawing at the gluten-free bread selections. One of the employees offered to help me, opened a package and let me try a piece. Tasted like cardboard. Then the guy picked up a loaf from a second brand, scratched out a note for the cashier and said, "Take this one home and try it—on the house."

That was pretty extraordinary.[17]

Villain: Feeling overwhelmed by multiple options and lacking specific knowledge about the products

Victim: The customer who has to guess about the product

Hero: A salesperson who helps you make up your mind and also gives you free merchandise

TOLLS FOR THEE

Deborah Burke is a PhD consultant specializing in corporate culture and employee engagement. This story defies the notion that bureaucracies are impersonal:

My Massachusetts E-ZPass didn't appear to work when I drove on to the New York Thruway. I got no message at the toll booth sign, it just didn't register. I was stuck. Couldn't back up, couldn't stop. I had to proceed to my appointment in Albany.

Afterwards I called E-ZPass, using the phone number conveniently listed on the transponder, right next to the unit's registration number. After just a couple of moments clicking through a clear, sensible, automated menu, I was quickly connected with a live human, Eileen. She swiftly located my records. No mysteries, no confusion, no lag time. I explained what had happened, and she told me there were no apparent problems with my account, but that it was too early to see today's transactions. She suggested that the transponder, which I got in 2003, might be failing, so I should probably replace it. I could either stop by an E-ZPass service center or wrap it in aluminum foil and mail it in for a swap.

I thanked her and said I'd stop by the service center some distance away on the Turnpike but I then sort of muttered a question of whether there was a closer one. She heard me, and quickly read me the list of locations, which included a center right near where I live. With some enthusiasm and relief, I said I'd stop there on my way home. I thanked her and told her that I appreciated how helpful she had been. We bid each other happy holidays, and hung up.

Within a minute, my phone rang, showing the E-ZPass caller ID. I first assumed it was a faulty call back of some technical sort, but I answered anyway. It was Eileen calling back to tell me that the center in Lee would only be open until 3:00.

I couldn't believe it. Not only had automated, standard parts of the call gone perfectly, but Eileen cared enough about me to add to the information I might need to fully resolve my issue. AND THIS IS A PUBLIC AGENCY! Not Amazon or LLBean, or Nordstrom's, where I spend money voluntarily, where I choose to be a customer. But an agency that is intended to serve the public. And serve it well, it does![18]

Villain: A failing transponder

Victim: A worried driver who thought she'd get a ticket

Hero: A governmental employee who cares and follows up

THE PERSONAL IMPACT OF AN ASSASSINATION

What you are about to read is not a business story. It is instead a column that the late Jimmy Breslin wrote for the *New York Herald Tribune* following the assassination of President Kennedy in November 1963. Breslin focused not on the impressive collection of world leaders who came to pay their respects, not on the formal ceremony, but on the experience of a humble man who dug the grave in Arlington National Cemetery where the president was laid to rest:

> Clifton Pollard was pretty sure he was going to be working on Sunday, so when he woke up at 9 a.m., in his three-room apartment on Corcoran Street, he put on khaki overalls before going into the kitchen for breakfast. His wife, Hettie, made bacon and eggs for him. Pollard was in the middle of eating them when he received the phone call he had been expecting. It was from Mazo Kawalchik, who is the foreman of the gravediggers at Arlington National Cemetery . . . "[C]ould you please be here by eleven o'clock this morning?" Kawalchik asked. "I guess you know what it's for." . . .
>
> When Pollard [arrived at the cemetery], Kawalchik and John Metzler, the superintendent, were waiting for him. "Sorry to pull you out like this on a Sunday," Metzler said.
>
> "Oh, don't say that," Pollard said. "Why, it's an honor for me to be here."
>
> Pollard got behind the wheel of a machine called a reverse hoe. Gravedigging is not done with men and shovels at Arlington. . . . At the bottom of the hill in front of the Tomb of the Unknown Soldier, Pollard started the digging. . . .
>
> Pollard is 42. He is a slim man with a mustache who was born in Pittsburgh and served as a private in the 352nd Engineers battalion in Burma in World War II. He is an equipment operator, grade 10, which means he gets $3.01 an hour. . . .
>
> Clifton Pollard wasn't at the funeral [the next day]. He was over behind the hill, digging [other] graves for $3.01 an hour in another section of the cemetery. "I tried to go over to see the [president's] grave," he said. "But it was so crowded a soldier told me I couldn't get through. So I just stayed here and worked, sir. But I'll get over there later a little bit. Just sort of look around and see how it is, you know. Like I told you, it's an honor."[19]

Villain: Assassination of a president

Victim: A low-paid gravedigger who is shut out of the funeral

Hero: Also the gravedigger, displaying exemplary valor, humility, and
    dignity

This is a masterpiece of what one might call microstorytelling—describing
an event from the eyes of a humble gravedigger who is also serving his
country. It also shows one aspect of the craft that we have not described so
far: the admirable application of old-fashioned shoe leather. Walking the
streets to find out what is happening. Interviewing people. Paying attention
to details. And taking the trouble to get quotes that reveal character. Jimmy
Breslin's brand of reporting is rare in this era. But we can all learn from
his style. This column has been called a "mentor text" for generations of
journalists: "Rather than follow the pack toward conventional sources,
reporters have been trying to find their own 'gravediggers' ever since."[20]

THE STORY OF THESE STORIES

Michelangelo knew how extensive his talents were and made sure that
those who paid him did too. Courvoisier had a taste imperious enough for
a deposed but still haughty emperor. Helen Gurley Brown *personified* her
magazine. WATERisLIFE is saving kids one purifying straw at a time.
Zappos sells shoes for many and companionship for a needy few. The
Ritz-Carlton offers employees up to $2,000 to satisfy a customer. Dean
Daley saved 14 lives in one night. Ian Todreas's personal stylist sets a new
style for personal service. An E-ZPass worker made it all so easy for worried driver Deborah Burke. And a humble gravedigger made a huge contri-
bution to his country and took home just $3.01 an hour. All of these tales
are told with specificity, clear heroes and villains, and innate drama that
takes us beyond the particulars of the situation.

This carries us smoothly to the next section of the book where we'll
delve into the techniques of storytelling. We've covered the "what," and
now it's time to pursue the "how."

PART 2

How to Tell Your Story

SEVEN

The Pictures Are Better on Radio or Podcasts

Especially with Sound Bites, Rhythm, and Brevity

Why in the world should we even bother talking about radio? Isn't it antiquated? Not at all. At a time when the Internet so dominates the landscape, 91 percent of Americans 12 and older still listen to terrestrial AM/FM radio.[1] The pictures are simply better on radio. And they're in color. Although it directly affects only one sense (that is, your hearing), radio engrosses the entire mind. It's not a "lazy medium" like TV, film, or print, which make the process easier because the images are right there for ready assimilation. Radio, on the other hand, requires active participation because you have to call up pictures to supplement the narration. Due to this effort, the images will be more real, colorful, and poignant for you.

And the same is true for podcasts, which are soaring in popularity. More than one-third of Americans have tuned in, and 15 percent listen weekly.[2] Podcasts have spawned TV shows (*Missing Maura Murray*), books (*Untold: The Daniel Morgan Murder*), and extensions of newspaper brands like the *New York Times' Daily*. Samantha Henig, the paper's editorial director of audio, said "[It's] an inherently intimate medium, and 'The Daily' allows listeners to form a much deeper connection with our journalists than they tend to get from print."[3]

There is a lesson here. For best results imitate the style of radio sports announcers who make you feel as if you are at the stadium with them. You can play a similar role as the "narrator" of your business. Imagine that you are explaining a movie to a blind person. Bear in mind that the audience might as well be blind because they were not present to witness the events you're recounting. Describe what you have seen in detail, and then you will disappear when the captivating force of the story dominates the field. Dialogue and sound are so powerful that some who lack both hearing and sight say that deafness is the greater obstacle. Helen Keller, for one, said, "For me [being deaf] means the loss of the most vital stimulus—the sound of the voice that brings language, sets thoughts astir and keeps us in the intellectual company of man."[4] Even in movies, unadorned audio is most effective. Austrian Director Michael Haneke, whose films include *Caché* and *The Piano Teacher*, says that sound incites the imagination while pictures curtail it. As he explains, "You see what you see and it's 'reality.' . . . That's why for me [sound] is more useful . . . if I want to touch someone emotionally."[5] The great French director Robert Bresson agreed: "When a sound can replace an image, cut the image or neutralize it. The ear goes more towards the within, the eye towards the outer."[6]

In any case, try to include as much detail as possible in your stories. Take a lesson from the peerless CBS correspondent Edward R. Murrow, subject of the recent movie *Good Night and Good Luck*. Here's one of his radio reports from London in the aftermath of a bombing in World War II:

> Children were already organizing a hunt for bits of shrapnel. Under some bushes beside the road there was a baker's cart. Two boys, still sobbing, were trying to get a quivering bay mare back between the shafts. The lady who ran the pub told us that these raids were bad for the chickens, the dogs and the horses. A toothless old man of nearly seventy came in and asked for a pint of milk and bitters, confided that he had always, all his life, gone to bed at eight o'clock and found now that three pints of beer made him drowsy-like so he could sleep through any air raid.[7]

You can see it all, can't you? Murrow puts us *right there*. There are no clichés like the "horrors of war" or the "indomitable spirit of the Britons" that lesser writers might employ. That would be superfluous, *because we get the point from the details.* Who among us cannot identify with children who turn the aftermath of an air raid into a treasure hunt? What about the unexpected reference to the fear of the animals? This informs us, without saying so, that war is tough for beast and man alike.

Then comes Supreme Court Justice Sonia Sotomayor, who became a star on the book circuit with her memoir. "In examining witnesses," she explained, "I learned to ask general questions so as to elicit details with powerful sensory associations: the colors, the sounds, the smells that lodge an image in the mind and put the listener in the burning house."[8] This effect can be demonstrated biologically, as Dr. Steve Schlozman makes clear:

> If you look at somebody in a functional MRI scan as they're hearing a story, they actually recruit the regions of the brain that allow them to create a scene, a setting. So they're using somatic sensory data. They're smelling the area. They're seeing it. I mean they're literally experiencing another place. And then they're constantly kind of reloading that space as the setting changes.[9]

My brother-in-law Tony Castro, an attorney in Westchester County in New York, has a unique way of conveying sensory data. When he handled homicide cases during his time as an assistant District Attorney in the Bronx, he was often hamstrung by an apparent lack of witnesses. This presented a challenge, but a surmountable one. He would tell the jury that there was in fact one key eyewitness: the victim himself. Then he would proceed to describe what the dead person could "say," such as the direction of the bullet, the height of the assailant, and so on. Besides, "While a corpse can speak volumes, it can't be cross-examined," Tony says. "No attorney is ever going to try to impeach its credibility."[10]

So, we ask, did video kill the radio star, as The Buggles famously sang in the first rock video that MTV aired back in 1981? Nope. Radio not only survived the attempted murder, but it's flourishing. There's a reason why the famous concert hall in New York is still called Radio City.

SOUNDBITING WITH TEETH IN BRIEF

"Intellectual property has the shelf life of a banana."[11]

Bill Gates

"In the business world, the rearview mirror is always clearer than the windshield."[12]

Warren Buffett

"[A] brilliant diversity spreads like stars, like a thousand points of light in a broad and peaceful sky."[13]

George H. W. Bush

These are examples of memorable sound bites, aka quotable quotes. President Bush's metaphor, for instance, compared America's community organizations to a "thousand points of light." This statement is indelible because it paints a picture in our minds, in the manner of radio announcers. It is quite possible to engage all of the audience's senses with spoken words. Here are some tips for delivering quotable sound bites.

Sprinkle in "wow statistics": "Only one in three adults participate in the recommended amount of physical activity each week."[14] (And, you might add, "That's why our collective health is deficient in this country.") Or, "About half of employees find love at work, with slightly more women than men coupling with significant others."[15] Sharing your feelings is another way to enhance a sound bite. For instance, don't simply say "This product is selling well." Instead, tell your team, "Our success is so exciting that I don't mind postponing my vacation." You can also add impact through humor, especially when it's self-effacing. Steve Jobs was the duke of droll. He once said, "I'm the only person I know that's lost a quarter of a billion dollars in one year . . . It's very character-building."[16] And then there's Warren Buffett, who wryly described his terrible diet this way: "I'm one-quarter Coca-Cola. . . . I checked the actuarial tables, and the lowest death rate is among six-year-olds. So I decided to eat like [one]."[17]

One last tip: If you have a clever sound bite in mind, deliver it at the beginning of a media interview so the reporter can relax, knowing she has bagged a useful quote. Then tell the rest of the story.

A SHORT NOTE ABOUT BREVITY

Perhaps needless to say, brevity is essential not only in soundbiting but in effective speaking in general. "Be sincere, be brief, be seated,"[18] FDR aptly said. In the Bible, we learn that Moses came down from Mt. Sinai with 10 commandments, not 27. And, of course, we have Pascal's famous quote: "I made this [letter] longer, only because I did not have the time to make it shorter."[19] Then, we can point again to Lincoln's Gettysburg address, which we have mentioned elsewhere. The big draw that day at the cemetery was Edward Everett, a famous orator, blessed with a bold voice and the expressive body language of an actor. Everett had graduated from Harvard (as valedictorian, no less) at 17. Subsequently, he was a professor there, a congressman, governor of Massachusetts, president of Harvard,

US Secretary of State, then a Senator. This gifted man spoke for two hours—from memory—yet his remarks are forgotten while Lincoln's 272 words are indelibly etched in our minds. The president's speech followed Everett's and lasted just three minutes. Some claim that the audience was left wondering, "Was that all?"[20] Yet when we look at what Everett said that day, November 19, 1863, it is no wonder that his bombastic words are forgotten. Here's how he began:

> Standing beneath this serene sky, overlooking these broad fields now reposing from the labors of the waning year, the mighty Alleghenies dimly towering before us, the graves of our brethren beneath our feet, it is with hesitation that I raise my poor voice to break the eloquent silence of God and nature. But the duty to which you have called me must be performed; grant me, I pray you, your indulgence and your sympathy.[21]

I would say that it was the audience that needed sympathy, not the speaker!

Indeed, Lincoln had great consideration for his listeners and that is why he edited his copy so ruthlessly. Compare, for instance, William Seward's first draft of the conclusion of Lincoln's first Inaugural Address with his own. The president's changes not only shortened the copy but vastly improved the flow and clarity:

Seward's Draft	Lincoln's Final Draft
We are not, we must not be, aliens or enemies, but fellow-countrymen and brethren.	We are not enemies, but friends. We must not be enemies.
Although passion has strained our bonds of affection too hardly, they must not, I am sure they will not, be broken	Though passion may have strained, it must not break our bonds of affection.
The mystic chords which, proceeding from so many battle-fields [sic] and so many patriot graves . . . will yet harmonize in their ancient music when breathed upon by the guardian angels of the nation.	The mystic chords of memory . . . will yet swell the chorus of the Union, when again touched . . . by the better angels of our nature.[22]

In modern times, regard Twitter as your friend. Your central idea should fit neatly into a 280-character tweet. As Cato once said, find your message and the words will follow.[23] And don't be afraid to repeat it, in symphonic fashion. Think of the famous four-note motif "da-da-da-DUM" at the beginning of Beethoven's *Fifth Symphony*. We never tire of hearing it.

For amusement (and edification), let's take a look at some examples of very short stories taken from the book *Not Quite What I Was Planning: Six-Word Memoirs by Writers Famous and Obscure*:

- I fell far from the tree.[24]
- I still make coffee for two.[25]
- Married for money, divorced for love.[26]

Then there's the saddest of all, attributed to Hemingway when he was challenged to compose a six-word tale: "For sale: baby shoes, never worn."[27] On a more cheerful note, let's go back to 1975, when the inimitable Muhammad Ali spoke at Harvard. A student shouted out, "Give us a poem." Without hesitating a millisecond, the champ shot back, "Me . . . we," said to be the shortest poem on record.[28] Every businessperson should study those two words as an exemplar of a marketing message that is worth a thousand volumes.

GREAT SPOKESPERSONS "GOT RHYTHM"

I have what famed Cream drummer Ginger Baker calls the "gift of time." I'm not bragging, by any means. It's just that I have always had an instinctive ability to keep a beat—at least at the level of an amateur drummer. That skill crosses over to my business where I have found that rhythm is an integral part of any speech, story, or presentation. Stay with me. Sometimes you can speak at the speed of a gushing river, but if you keep that up you'll lose the audience. Eventually, rapids fade and the water slows and pools. Think of this image when you communicate. Vary your pace.

Let's look at Robert Frost's rhythmic genius in his two-line poem called *The Span of Life*. Read it out loud:

The old dog barks backward without getting up
I can remember when he was a pup.

This masterpiece of brevity scans as follows, with the stressed syllables in bold:

The **old**| **dog barks back**-| ward with-**out**| get-ting **up**
I| can re-**mem**-| ber when **he**| was a **pup**|

The rhythm in the first line is quite strange, with four accented syllables in a row at one point. This forces us to slow down, awkwardly, like the old dog himself. The next line accelerates, however, with a regular drumbeat mimicking a frolicking pup.[29] Here we have the aging process in reverse, in just 16 words, with language that is rather prosaic on its face. Frost would have been a great drummer. Ditto Winston Churchill. Here's part of his "Finest Hour" speech from 1940. Again, read it out loud:

> We shall go on to the end, we shall fight in France, we shall fight on the seas and oceans. . . . We shall fight on the beaches, we shall fight on the landing grounds, we shall fight in the fields and in the streets, we shall fight in the hills; we shall never surrender.[30]

Churchill captivates us with mostly monosyllabic old English words that arrive with the insistence of a bass drum. Does this seem simple? Try it and you will see how difficult it is. So much of the meaning depends on the tempo. Even as a child T. S. Eliot understood this too, as his sister Ada recalled:

> When you were a tiny boy, learning to talk, you used to sound the rhythm of the sentences without shaping words—the ups and downs of the thing you were trying to say. I used to answer you in kind, saying nothing yet conversing with you as we sat side by side on the stairs . . . And now you think of the rhythm before the words in a new poem![31]

When writing, Eliot would even bang out the beat with the help of a small drum, and he advised a young poet to do likewise.[32]

Although I have been a percussionist ever since I was a young lad, I never learned to read drum music until recently. I had no choice when I started performing with a parent-student-teacher band in the town where I live in Massachusetts. I was hoping to be able to follow along with the melody (since I do know how to read notes), but was horrified to see that the sheet music just showed the percussion parts, with no other references. Needless to say, there are gaps, sometimes long ones, where I had to stand by and wait—counting each measure in my head. Coming in at the wrong time, especially with something as noticeable as crash cymbals, could be very embarrassing. Then I thought about the significance of this. There is a time to speak, and a time to remain silent. A time to pound and a time to pause. This has vast implications for communication.

If you want to learn more about rhythm, by the way, listen to Babatunde Olatunji, Buddy Rich, or the virtuoso Conga Kings—Patato Valdes, Giovanni Hidalgo, and Candido. Another suggestion: imitate the metrics of poetry when you write or speak. There are several common patterns in the "feet" in poetry (that is, the components of a line). There's an iamb, which sounds like this: dee-DEE; or a trochee, DEE-dee; or an anapest, dee-dee-DEE; or a dactyl, DEE-dee-dee. Iambic pentameter consists of five feet per line, in this manner: But, **soft!**| what **light**| through **yon**|der **win**|dow **breaks**? (from *Romeo and Juliet*).[33] This is regarded as the most natural and conversational of all meters. Are you wondering what this has to do with business? Iambic pentameter (or an approximation) is often used in slogans or taglines. Here are some examples:

- Be all that you can be in the Army. (The US Army)
- Wouldn't you like to be a pepper, too? (Dr. Pepper)
- It takes a lickin' and keeps on tickin'. (Timex)
- When you care enough to send the very best. (Hallmark)

And here's another I just made up: To **speak**| with **force**| do **not**| ignore| the **beat**.

EIGHT

How to Compose a Compelling Story, in Person or on Video

A Dose of Dickens and a Splash of *Casablanca*

If you have a good story, report it; if not, *write* it. That's an old saying in journalism. Unfortunately, much of life is so straightforward that you have to reach for the poetry in the mundane, the best way to hold the audience's attention. If you are telling a story, you are at once narrator, director, and sometimes star. That means you can switch roles at will. In any case, try to convey the vitality of the events in the retelling. As Hemingway once said, "good writing is good conversation, only more so."[1] I think we can turn that epigram on its head: "Good conversation is good writing, only more so."

Remember: captivating the listener is the cardinal virtue. Mystery writer Elmore Leonard said the secret to pacing was to leave out the boring parts.[2] Alfred Hitchcock noted that some films were like slices of life, but his were like slices of cake: "What is drama after all, but life with the dull bits cut out?"[3] In fiction, we speak of a willing suspension of disbelief, but involvement in a real-life story requires affirmative trust. The audience needs to believe that the speaker is truthful and that the plot occurred as described.

In composing a story (and I repeat that I mean a *verifiable* story in this context), emulate the style of what used to be called "new journalism"—as practiced by the late Tom Wolfe and others—that is, the incorporation of these fictional techniques into nonfiction: scene-by-scene reconstruction, extensive direct quotation, a third-person omniscient point of view and the use of minute detail to describe manners and style.[4] Let's take these one by one:

1. Scenic reconstruction frees you from the constrictions of chronology. You can develop a story thematically rather than sequentially.[5] (When asked if his movies had any structure, even a beginning, middle and end, director Jean-Luc Godard said, "Yes, but not necessarily in that order."[6])

2. Direct quotation allows you to reconstruct dialogues to reveal the essence of the characters.

3. The third-person omniscient point of view gives you an opportunity to explore the inner thoughts of the participants. Contrary to popular belief, it is actually more liberating than the first person because the story can be told from several vantage points, instead of just your own. You can move your spotlight freely from person to person and even penetrate minds to reveal an "interior monologue." This is also called the "authorial-omniscient" point of view:

   > [T]he writer speaks as, in effect, God. He sees into all his characters' hearts and minds, presents all positions with justice and detachment, occasionally dips into the third person subjective to give the reader an immediate sense of why the character feels as he does, but reserves to himself the right to judge (a right he uses sparingly).[7]

4. Details of customs, manners, décor, and dress firmly place us on the scene.[8]

To utilize this approach, first learn to use your eyes. I recently read *Revenge*, consisting of 11 interlocking tales from the outstanding Japanese writer Yoko Ogawa, whose style is redolent of Hemingway, Raymond Carver, and Edgar Allan Poe. Here's the opening paragraph of a story called "Afternoon at the Bakery":

> It was a beautiful Sunday. The sky was a cloudless dome of sunlight. Out on the square, leaves fluttered in a gentle breeze along the pavement. Everything seemed to glimmer with a faint luminescence: the roof of the ice-cream stand, the faucet on the drinking fountain, the eyes of a stray cat, even the base of the clock tower covered with pigeon droppings.[9]

Who notices the way sunlight caresses the roof of an ice-cream stand, the faucet of a drinking fountain, or the eyes of a stray cat? A professional writer? Yes. But you too can be this observant, if you learn *how to look*. Use your eyes to collect precise images, then explain them as colorfully as you can for the benefit of those who were not there. As they might say in New Orleans, put some salsa in the gumbo. Stephen King is a master at that, even when telling the story of his own life. In his wonderful book *On Writing*, he openly discusses his former addictions and describes in excruciating detail his wife Tabby's intervention:

> [She] began by dumping a trash bag full of stuff from my office out on the rug: beercans, cigarette butts, cocaine in gram bottles and cocaine in plastic Baggies, coke spoons . . . Valium, Xanax, bottles of Robitussin cough syrup and NyQuil cold medicine, even bottles of mouthwash. A year or so before, observing the rapidity with which huge bottles of Listerine were disappearing from the bathroom, Tabby asked me if I drank the stuff. I responded with self-righteous hauteur that I most certainly did not. Nor did I. I drank the Scope instead. It was tastier, had that hint of mint.[10]

Needless to say, you can't do this without a precise *vocabulary*. A useful story: Degas, the famous painter, tried his hand at verse. He pleaded his case with poet Stéphane Mallarmé: "It isn't ideas I'm short of . . . I've got too many," cried the painter. "Degas," Mallarmé said, "You can't make a poem with ideas—you make it with words."[11] The same is true of stories. As Mark Twain said, the difference between the right word and the almost right word is the difference between lightning and lightning bug.[12] English may have 170,000 words, but the average person uses only 10,000 to 40,000 of them. Some can turn them into poetry, others into nonsense. It's even more humbling to contemplate the process of composing music. A piano has just 88 keys, and you can combine them in a myriad of ways that can yield either Mozart or a simple three-chord rock tune. There's a similar process at work in drawing. Artists will tell you that there are four principle shapes in the world, cylinders, cubes, cones and spheres, and that skillful hands can combine variations of these building blocks into virtually any object that the eye can see.[13]

Talent is not necessarily a prerequisite for sketching, at least at a rudimentary level. Instead, you need to learn to draw what you see and to train your eyes to notice what is around you in the first place. As you gaze

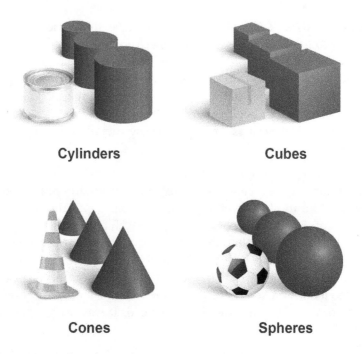

Cylinders   Cubes

Cones   Spheres

at the contours of your world, try to separate the novel from the quotidian, the startling from the rote. This will help with storytelling too.

BRAND NEW BRAND NEWS

Let's take a step back for a moment and consider how much of what you do is *newsworthy* in the first place—newsworthy in the sense of captivating press, public, and customers alike. It comes down to two categories: the wonderful or the shameful. Those words sum up the content of almost all news stories. Most fall into the shameful bin, unfortunately. The wonderful articles tend to end up on the sports or feature screens, but that is the category you should seek. But how do we define news in the first place? I think of it as information of the greatest interest, to the largest number of people, in a particular place, at a particular time—in other words, stories the public either *needs* or *wants* to know. Examples: we probably *need* to know about the state of the economy, but many *want* to know about silly celebrity gossip. (Cynical reporters, by the way, say that news is simply what their editor says it is, on any given day.)

Let's examine what motivates readers or listeners. Arthur Asa Berger tells us that "the media enable us to have powerful experiences without paying for them, so to speak, and to take risks without having to worry about being devastated."[14] Here are some of the benefits he lists:

- seeing authority figures exalted or deflated
- satisfying curiosity
- being informed
- finding models to imitate
- seeing others make mistakes
- participating in history (vicariously)
- exploring taboo subjects with impunity
- seeing villains in action[15]

French writer Guy de Maupassant understood this quite well. No wonder: he worked as a journalist for many leading newspapers during a hectic life that lasted just 42 years. As prolific as they come, with some 300 short stories to his credit, he wrote in a naturalistic manner, showing the world in all its ugliness, without embellishment. At the same time he believed that readers were seeking emotional stimulation. He believed they were crying out:

- Console me
- Amuse me
- Sadden me
- Move me
- Make me dream
- Make me laugh
- Make me tremble
- Make me cry
- Make me think[16]

Too often, unfortunately, corporate executives move in the opposite direction. They favor dry, vague adjectives like unique, revolutionary, innovative, useful, and the like.

If possible, connect your story with larger social or economic issues. Will your product or service help conserve energy, raise better children, or improve health care? Or are you merely seeking publicity for its own sake? Going back to the two categories of "wonderful" and "shameful," are you doing something that is utterly delightful, on the one hand, or solving an appalling problem, on the other? In any case, focus on the *audience's* needs and desires, not yours. Pleasing yourself merely makes you vain, not newsworthy. These standards apply to business interactions, too. A recent survey shows that the three biggest turnoffs for B2B buyers with regard to vendors are: "They talk too much about themselves and don't get to know our company" (27.5% feel this way); "they act more like vendors than partners" (19.6%); and "they don't provide me with objective information to help me frame my decision" (18.5%).[17] Overall, buyers want vendors to forge relationships, not just execute transactions.[18]

FACTS, FEELINGS, AND NOVELS

When I worked as a reporter I often met garrulous business executives who would "describe" the birth of a product this way: "In grad school 15 years ago, Sally and I were working on a new design for a carburetor. The fuel efficiency was off the charts but it was too expensive so we used more cost-effective materials, calculated the precise ratio of air to gas, first working on a motorbike engine over about 15 months. We logged more than 6,200 miles on the test track. Then we redesigned the contours of the device etc." What's wrong with this brief story? For one thing it's boring, but why? Too many facts and no emotion.

I learned valuable lessons from *The Basic Patterns of Plot*, written by journalism professor William Foster-Harris. Although the book is out of print, the messages still resonate:

> The "music" of fiction is the . . . feeling-fact rhythm. . . . [T]he emotional parts are upbeats, the . . . fact portions downbeats. . . . You can score a piece of competent fictional writing. You will come up with something that reads like this: feeling-fact, feeling-fact, feeling, feeling, fact, fact, feeling-fact, feeling-fact, feeling-fact, fact, fact. And so on.[19]

How does this apply to business stories, which presumably are nonfiction? Again, don't be afraid to intersperse your *feelings* about your product or service, or more important, the emotional reactions of your *customers, among the particulars.* For instance: "When we first introduced Product X in June (fact), we hadn't slept for weeks and we were at once exhausted and exhilarated (feeling). The customers told us that for the first time in their lives, they could relax (feeling) knowing that their information was secure (fact) because of our impenetrable firewall (fact)." You get the idea: upbeat, downbeat, fact, feeling. Be sure to tell the audience what gets *you* out of bed in the morning. It's probably more than the paycheck (at least I hope so, for your sake). Tap into the passion that you experience when you solve customers' problems or improve their lives.

We can turn to novelists for further lessons on storytelling techniques. If I may, and I'm attempting to read your mind here, you may be saying to yourself, "Why is Stone talking about fiction, it has so little to do with *business*." Please bear with me. The basic thrust of any fictional story, and, more to the point, a compelling business tale, is to ask the question "What if?" This works in science fiction ("What if we could travel through time?"—H. G. Wells), in traditional literature ("What if a shady, rich man keeps throwing fancy parties in his mansion in the hope that his long lost lover will show up?"—*The Great Gatsby*), and in business ("What if we could invent a computer that can think more creatively than humans?"). Beyond this, think in terms of conflict, which is the lifeblood of any story worth its name. Ask yourself, "What is the worst thing that could happen to my client at this time?" and keep raising the stakes. That sort of inquiry will lead to dramatic tension. The writer John Le Carré has a great quote about this: "The cat sat on the mat is not a story; the cat sat on the other cat's mat is."[20] Besides competition, fear is at the base of many plots, or perhaps we should say at the base of tension. Fear of loss, of exposure, of disappointment, and so on.

The novelist John Gardner offered many useful tips in his book *The Art of Fiction: Notes on Craft for Young Writers*, and his guidelines apply directly to business too:

- "Write the kind of story you know and like best."[21] Discuss topics that are at the center of your circle of responsibility and expertise. You will be much more effective describing the work you do and how it affects your key customers.

- "Drama [equals] character in action."[22] By the same token, the audience needs to *care* about the characters. Describe a situation with people we might know: a teenager, a homeowner, a traveler, and so on. Stories about arctic explorers or extreme skiers may be inspiring, but they are easy to ignore if they are outside the realm of common experience.

- "Fiction does its work by creating a dream in the reader's mind."[23] This may seem farfetched but it's directly applicable to business because the speaker needs to make us see and feel the movie he's describing, as if we are sharing a waking dream or a hallucination.

- Use shifts in psychic distance,[24] in the sense that we need to watch the action in a wide shot, as if from a balcony, and in close-up as the emotional content changes. A manager might first provide an overview of the market, for instance, and then "zoom in" on a particular customer or product.

- "When a novel's dénouement has been properly set up, it falls like an avalanche, and the writer's chief job is to describe stone by stone how it falls."[25] Dénouement is a French word that literally means untying, as in untying the knots of the plots. If you establish a conflict faced by a customer, make sure that you reveal the specific details of the outcome.

Norman Mailer, who was a journalist and a novelist, also offered many useful tips about his craft in a very entertaining book called *The Spooky Art*. "Write as if your life depended on saying what you felt as clearly as you could,"[26] he advises. That level of exigency may seem extreme, but it's nonetheless good advice. If you don't have that slight edge of intensity in your content and demeanor, you may not fully capture the audience. Mailer also notes that we love plots because they obey the rules of cause and effect,[27] unlike life which seems, I suppose, more haphazard. Our experience generally makes sense only when we play it back afterwards, but stories usually obey chronology in that they generally move forward in time (but not always, as we have seen before). Finally, from Mailer: "one of the better tests of the acumen of the writer [is] how subtle, how full of nuance, how original, is his or her sense of the sinister?"[28] I bet he would endorse our notion that the villains make the tale.

Stories, after all, are made of characters. Real or imagined people with hopes, fears, dreams, foibles, and strengths. E. M. Forster, who wrote *A Passage to India* and *Howard's End*, notably distinguished between round and flat characters. Round people can "surprise in a convincing way"; those who lack the capacity to astonish are "flat."[29] This is all part of an effort to "bounce the reader into accepting" what the writer says.[30] How do we apply this in business? Do you tell stories about a "customer who?" That is, "a" customer, preceded by an indefinite article? Why not "the" customer, with a definite article, pointing to the *particular* person, the teenager who swaggered into a room. Imagine that same teen (again with the demonstrative "that" referring to him and him alone), whose name was Carlo, by the way, fidgeting in his seat. Despite his youth, he explained the ergonomics of the design better than our engineers can and we realized that he had done a science project about it and . . . You get the idea. Carlo would be a round character, not a flat one. Another lesson from E. M. Forster: try to expand the scope of the story:

> When the symphony is over we feel that the notes and tunes composing it have been liberated, they have found in the rhythm of the whole their individual freedom. Cannot the novel be like that? Is not there something of it in *War and Peace*? . . . Such an untidy book. Yet, as we read it, do not great chords begin to sound behind us, and when we have finished does not every item . . . lead a larger existence than was possible at the time?[31]

A larger existence—those three words encapsulate the essence of the benefit of a successful product or service that augments our lives. I traveled similar terrain in my book *Artful Business: 50 Lessons from Creative Geniuses*, where I spoke about the breathtaking power of art that

> leaves you wanting more. It is an urgent and compelling experience, producing concentrated satisfaction. It creates a kind of superreality that is more stubbornly real than the everyday world, in a way that surpasses our normal perceptions. The process continues after, perhaps long after, you walk away from the museum, leave the theater, or put down the book. Art is news that stays new. Like a tyrant, it proclaims: "I insist that you look at me. Try to turn away if you dare."[32]

The same can be said of any transformative product, service, or platform. Think of the PC, the iPhone, the internal combustion engine, and so on.[33] The point here is that the *stories* of those products need to be equally compelling in a way that insists that we pay attention. We need to envision the merchandise as a character with a personality of its own: with likes and dislikes, strengths and insecurities, passions and frustrations. Think of *Casablanca*, whose characters are generally regarded as old friends. In fact, we know Humphrey Bogart and Ingrid Bergman in that film in many ways better than our friends because the celluloid heroes are "eternal and unchanging," unlike the rest of us who alter our circumstances all the time.[34] Fictional entities "let us in on their secrets, becoming our intimates as we are drawn into their lives."[35] When Harvard students discovered *Casablanca* at the Brattle Theater in Cambridge back in the 1950s and 1960s, it became such a cult favorite that it was like "a theater in ancient Greece . . . some people came twenty-five and thirty times."[36] On one fateful night, the sound failed at the last moment. No problem. As if in a church, the audience came to the rescue, and all together said, "Louis, this could be the beginning of a beautiful friendship."[37] Granted, it is very difficult to elevate a product, service, or company to such exalted status and to sear it so indelibly into the memory of the public, but we should at least try to treat it like an acquaintance or friend in the hope that the customers will too.

The story of *Casablanca* moves us smoothly into a broader examination of film. We should look no further than the mind of Alfred Hitchcock, who gave voice to many of his secrets about technique in an extended series of interviews with François Truffaut, the French director. Here we have the benefit of a conversation between two unmistakable geniuses. Hitchcock believed that suspense was paramount, making the audience wonder what is coming next. "They want to be one jump ahead of the action. . . . So, I have to take up the challenge. 'Oh, you know what's going to happen. Well, we'll just see about that.!'"[38] One way to hold attention is to hook one scene into another. In writing, use the last sentence of a paragraph as the basis for the first sentence of the next one. In a dramatic situation, one character might point toward another, for instance: "I don't know what will become of us," says Matilda, as she turns toward Sam.[39] How might this work in a business context? If you are telling the story of a particularly difficult interaction with a customer, you might say, "He was exasperated and impatient and said he didn't like sales people, period. Then he looked at me as if to say 'So why am I wasting my time speaking to you?' I quietly met his unspoken question with another: 'Do you feel they don't understand you?'" The links between the characters pull us into the scene.

And now let's turn to turning points, aka plot points (that is, events or circumstances that propel the story into a new direction). For instance, in *Casablanca*, Ilsa (played by Ingrid Bergman) suddenly shows up after a long interim. This is shocking to all, especially to Rick (played by Bogart). He thought he'd never see her again when she disappeared after their brief affair in Paris. In *Darkest Hour,* we are surprised when the seemingly bellicose Winston Churchill contemplates appeasement with Mussolini on the eve of World War II. Similarly, in *Three Billboards Outside Ebbing, Missouri,* we are astounded to learn that the gruff sheriff played by Woody Harrelson is dying of pancreatic cancer. Although current screenwriters speak of plot points as if they were a modern invention, that is hardly the case. We find this concept in Aristotle's *Poetics*—dating from 335

BCE—the first and probably most influential treatment of literary theory in the West. Aristotle called the plot twist *peripeteia*, a reversal of the situation, with the action swerving around to its opposite, in a manner that advances the story.[40] (Indeed, he believed that complex tragedy, by definition, required turnarounds of this sort.) We can also think of these about-faces as decision points, "dark moments" in the story that the hero must push through, by dint of reason or effort, sometimes against daunting odds:

> And at the climax . . . we cannot see our way at all, because we have arrived . . . the focal point of reversal, the place where objective reason fails, the instant of death and rebirth, the place of transition.[41]

Sometimes the plot point can create vertigo:

> You'll be going along, say, "Okay, I made it through the loop-de-loop. I made it through the big downfall, where I felt negative Gs." And then suddenly the roller coaster is twisting. And you didn't expect the corkscrew. Nobody saw that coming. Even though you watched it, you didn't expect it. That's the sort of unexpected jolt that then makes you feel like alive again.[42]

A plot point can also be a simple shift in perspective if the tale is suddenly told from the villain's point of view[43] (though it is important to keep in mind that many villains do not see themselves as evil, and therein lies their strange attraction).

In any case, in the most captivating stories life goes off track, and surprisingly the resolution for "*any possible problem or question you could pose*" can be "*in some fantastic manner the diametric reversal of the question.*"[44] Henry Ford's assembly line is a classic example of innovation through turnabout. His employee William "Pa" Klann reportedly brought the idea to the boss's attention after a visit to the Swift slaughterhouse in Chicago. As the carcasses moved along an overhead trolley, each worker performed the same task over and over. In 1913 Ford essentially reversed that process and created an *assembly* line for cars instead of a *disassembly* line. (If Aristotle were a business consultant, he'd applaud this insight.) The results were astounding: manufacturing time was slashed from 12 hours down to two and a half![45] Another example of the application of "about-face" thinking can be found in the creation of Google. Founders Sergey Brin and Larry Page were grad students at Stanford where their advisor Rajeev Motwani was studying algorithms to analyze purchase patterns in stores. Brin worked with Motwani on a project called MIDAS (Mining Data at Stanford) and Page on a Digital Libraries Project. After the Internet exploded with Netscape's $3 billion IPO in 1995, AltaVista came into being as the premier search engine in the new medium. While surfing, Page stumbled across something called links, a new concept at the time[46]:

> AltaVista let you "find pages that link to your site." These reverse links reminded Page of academic citations . . . [He said] "Citations are important. It turns out, people who win the Nobel Prize have citations from 10,000 different papers [which] means your work was important, because other people thought it was worth mentioning."[47]

Page's flash of insight was that web pages, like academic articles, could be ranked by the number of citations they receive.[48] In a sense, he was reversing the process, following the trail from the linking entities back to the source, to determine the value of the information. He proceeded to download the entire Internet onto computers at the university (a feat that would require acres and acres of server farms today!). Brin added a data mining algorithm to the mix. Thus was born a new business. At first they called it PageRank, then Google (a misspelling of the word "googol," a very large number representing 10 to the 100th power). The two young men weren't even aware that they had invented a search engine. Instead they considered the project a great PhD thesis![49] They tried to sell the patent to AltaVista for $1 million in 1998 but were rejected. Part of the problem was that Google wasn't a "portal"—a sticky destination site designed to keep users in place. The idea was to execute the search and send you on your way. Brin and Page persisted, however, and took a leave of absence from Stanford. They raised $1 million from angels, then another $25 million from VCs. Yet it was still unclear (in 1999) how the company could make money! The answer was advertising, of course, but not with annoying banners and pop-ups. Instead, they incorporated the listing format pioneered by a company called Overture. By 2000, when the dot.com bubble was leaving a residue of suds on the ground, Google was in effect a monopoly.[50]

What do we learn from these two reversal stories, Ford's disassembly-assembly and Google's citation-page rank? First, as we mentioned, the answer is often the opposite of the question. But going back to our villains-victims-heroes paradigm for a moment, the three categories emerge clearly. For Ford, the villain was an expensive, complicated manufacturing process; for Google, it was the slow pace of searches on a new medium.

The victims were Ford itself, saddled with onerous costs, and possibly consumers who would have paid much higher prices absent the innovation. For Google, the victims were every user of the web who would be unable to find what he or she needed quickly. And the heroes are threefold: the companies themselves, their products, and the innovative processes they were smart enough to implement.

In these examples, we see the concept of dialectics at work. As originally conceived by the philosopher Fichte, and attributed to Hegel perhaps falsely, the idea rests on the thesis-antithesis-synthesis triad. One force or concept (the thesis) opposes another (the antithesis), and they join together in the synthesis. We see this at play in stories involving a conflict between the established and the possible, or "familiar ground" and the "might-be, could have been [or] perhaps will be"), between expectation and reality, or norms and transgressions.[51] Fairy tales are very much in this mode:

> Like Hans [from "Hans in Luck"] who is both foolish and wise, poor and rich, lucky and unfortunate, the heroes of numerous fairy tales possess attributes that imperceptibly shade into their opposites. All the same, it is clear that certain oppositions (humble/noble, naïve/cunning, timid/courageous, compassionate/ruthless) are encoded on virtually every fairy tale with a male hero.[52]

Moreover, fairy tales often feature radical transformations:

> A fox [becomes] a beautiful shop; a dragon turns into a boar, the boar into a hare, and the hare into a pigeon; a witch changes into a bed or a fountain; a princess turns into a lemon or a fish, then into a lump of silver, and finally into a beautiful linden tree. A reed turns into a silver dress or into a . . . horse. A large castle can be changed into an egg and back again at will.[53]

Film is also inherently dialectic. Its principle editing technique is montage. As explained by Eisenstein, the collision of two shots in opposition produces a new concept. His fellow Soviet Kuleshov had pioneered this method in a short film that alternated between close-ups of the face of a famous Tsarist actor and images of a bowl of soup, a woman, and a coffin—apparently conveying either hunger, desire, or grief—when all the while the pictures of the actor were identical. The impact produced not a sum, but a product; it was not $A + B = C$, but $A \times B = C$, with C possessing a completely different meaning than either of the multipliers. The potential elements that could be juxtaposed span the catalog of cinematic grammar: line, scale, volume, mass, depth, close-ups, long shots, screen direction, darkness, light, dimension, and duration.[54] Eisenstein found evidence of montage everywhere: in Flaubert's cross dialogues, in Gogol's "cubism" (with the four legs of two bankers seeming to support the façade of the stock exchange),[55] and in the clashing details in Leonardo's paintings.[56]

Myths also exhibit dialectics, in conflict between equality and inequality, security and chaos, or control and turmoil. These ancient stories often feature metamorphoses, the very title of Ovid's book, the font of much of our knowledge of Greek and Roman mythology. There we learn, for instance, that Pygmalion made a statue of his ideal woman, fell in love with it, and beseeched the gods to give it life. Venus, the Roman goddess of desire, was happy to oblige.[57] Ovid also tells the story of Minerva, the jealous goddess of wisdom and magic. A young woman named Arachne was so skilled at weaving that she challenged her to an embroidery contest. Arachne created portraits in thread that were even more beautiful than the goddess's work, whereupon Minerva ripped up the tapestry and turned the challenger into a spider so she could "spin her thread and practice her art in the web" forever (hence, the term "arachnid").[58] Then we have the sad story of lusty Apollo and chaste Daphne. He pursued her so vigorously that she prayed to her father, a river god, to save her. He rescued her by transforming her into a laurel tree:

> . . . her hair was turned into foliage, her arms into
> branches.
> The feet that had run so nimbly were sunk into sluggish
> roots;
> Her head was confined in a treetop; and all that remained was her
>   beauty.[59]

The still-smitten Apollo decreed that her branches would be used to decorate the heads of generals in times of triumph—spawning the expression "rest on your laurels" and the word "laureate" for winner.

As we can see, the concept of transformation or metamorphosis is probably as old as our species. In keeping with this style, explain how your product or service *changes* the lives of your customers. Sometimes the dialectic in business stories takes the form of confounding expectation, setting up a clash between assumption and reality. A prime example is a *Harvard Business Review* article called "Stop Trying to Delight Your Customers,"[60] based on a survey of 75,000 B2C and B2B customers and their experiences with phone calls, chat, and e-mail interactions. The study showed that service above and beyond meeting the clients' basic needs does not build loyalty to any significant degree. Moreover, refunds, free products, or expedited shipping are only slightly more effective than the essentials. Surprisingly, "companies create loyal customers simply by helping them solve their problems quickly and easily."[61] They can do this by removing obstacles, instead of forcing people to contact the company over and over, to repeat their complaints, or to make an annoying switch from the website to phone support.[62] Merely reducing the effort they have to expend to resolve issues goes a long way.[63]

LESSONS FROM OTHER MEDIA

We've already seen how literature and mythology can contribute to your storytelling toolkit. Let's take a look at other media, starting with songwriting, in particular composers who start their lyrics in the middle of the story, with little introduction. For instance, here is the beginning of "Me and Bobby McGee," written by Chris Christopherson and made famous by Janis Joplin: "Busted flat in Baton Rouge, waitin' for a train." We *leap* into the story, you might say without warning. The details (paraphrased here) create indelible images of the "narrator's" predicament: Feeling as washed-out as her clothes, wearing a filthy kerchief, she plays an instrument she calls a harpoon (a strange term for a harmonica, perhaps signifying an aggressive attempt to escape life through art). All the while the windshield wipers keep the beat like a metronome. Hers is an authentic southern voice, befitting a story that could occur only in Louisiana. And speaking of that state, here's the beginning of Chuck Berry's "Johnny B. Goode": "Deep down in Louisiana close to New Orleans." Quickly we learn that Johnny is illiterate, that he lives in an evergreen forest in a log cabin, but he plays the guitar like a champion. We have no choice: we are thrust into Johnny's life. Then there's the opening of Joni Mitchell's "No Regrets Coyote," addressing her lover: "We just come from such different sets of circumstances." This is an abstract observation worthy of Tolstoy (redolent of the first sentence of *Anna Karenina*, "Happy families are all alike; every unhappy family is unhappy in its own way"). Thereafter, Mitchell parachutes down to sea level where we learn that she is a night owl, apt to be coming home from her recording studio at sunrise just when her man is likely to be found grooming a horse's tail on his ranch. This is a collection of very specific details that plunge us into the setting. At the end she rises to a great height and reminds us that the disparities in their habits are hard to understand.

Video techniques are also instructive. I have a great deal of experience with moving pictures, both in a prior life as a TV journalist and as an independent producer. Nowadays video, like still photography, has become a DIY (Do It Yourself) medium in a world where everyone is a cameraman and a director. After all, you can shoot virtually anything with an iPhone, right? That is certainly the prevailing view. I spoke at a marketing conference last fall and I attended two seminars on video there. One man started his workshop this way: "So, you want to produce videos at your company, but you don't think you can afford them. I'm going to show you how you can do it at three budget levels—$200, $2,000 or $10,000." I said to myself, "This I have to hear." He proceeded to explain that if you have just $200, you can beef up your iPhone with a special lens attachment and a portable microphone. (The latter would be a huge improvement over 99 percent of the homespun corporate videos. They are saddled with bad audio from the built-in mike, which captures not only the voice of the interview subject but all the distracting ambient sound as well—traffic, stray conversation, the hum of ventilators, etc.) "And . . . for $2,000," the seminar leader continued, "you can buy a decent camcorder, tripod and a few lights . . . and for $10,000 a more elaborate setup, etc." But what about experience behind the lens? And interviewing skills? How much does they cost?

Yes, if we lend credence to the infamous 10,000-hour rule, that it takes that long to learn how to do something, then we should not trust beginners to create a film to showcase our wares to the world. If you must be your own producer, however, please follow these guidelines:

- Remember that great directors use cameras to create, not merely to record. That means that you should treat them like paintbrushes or violin bows. Don't just shoot what's right in front of you. Try to view the world the way humans do, from many angles and points of view.

- At the same time, do not overdo the zooms. There is a lot to be said for a static shot that allows the action to unfold without fanfare. The human eye, after all, does not zoom. We merely cut from wide to medium to tight without transition. Hitchcock once showed the victim of an attack in *The Birds* with just that sort of movement in rapid succession. The effect was searingly abrupt and indelible.

- Don't pan (move the camera from side to side) or tilt it (up and down) unnecessarily.

- On the other hand, manipulation is an essential part of film and video. With editing, we can compress or expand time and heighten or reduce emotional impact. The infamous shower scene in *Psycho*, for instance, took 7 days to shoot, with 70 camera setups, yielding just 45 seconds of film.[64]

Let's pause, for a humorous interlude, to describe Hitchcock's concept of the MacGuffin—his term for an element in the plot that just does not matter. As he told the story, imagine that there are two Scotsmen on a train.

> One asks, "What's that package up there in the baggage rack?"
>
> The other explains, "Oh, that's a MacGuffin."
>
> "What's a MacGuffin?" the first asks.
>
> "An apparatus for trapping lions in the Scottish highlands," is the answer.
>
> "But there are no lions in the Scottish highlands," says the first.
>
> "Well, then, that's no MacGuffin," the second one answers. That's exactly the point.[65]
>
> The MacGuffin does not exist, and Hitch would often use similar "straw men" in his movies. Critics noted some of these lapses, for instance, the vague and unexplained reference to "government secrets" in *North by Northwest* or the formula for the airplane engine in *The Thirty-Nine Steps*, but he was unfazed. He agreed with Truffaut's observation that the filmmaker's job was to *show*, not to explain.[66]

Back to the business at hand: Here are a few more suggestions about storytelling on video:

- Compress stories down to the absolute essentials. "Leave them wanting more" when editing. Do not belabor an explanation, a sound bite, or an effect. For instance, you might shoot a time-lapse sequence showing pedestrians walking in traffic, then speed it up so much that you can depict 20 minutes in 30 seconds. Don't fall in love with the result and leave it on the screen for too long. The audience will get the idea quickly. Cut away to the next sequence before their pleasure is sated.

- Try not to use too much dialogue. Action is more essential.

- Employ narration sparingly. Directors resort to voiceover to fill gaps that they should have covered with interaction. I much prefer minimal narration, allowing the "stars of your movie" (that is, the customers) to speak for themselves.

- When interviewing, REMAIN SILENT AFTER YOU ASK A QUESTION. Rookies insert themselves with interjections like "Ooooh" or "Uh-huh." The audience will wonder who the unseen person in the background may be. Likewise, try not to laugh, even when the subject is hysterically funny. If you are not in the shot, then you should not be heard.

- Do not use digital effects such as wipes, page turns, or squeezes unless you have a good reason. Simple cuts and dissolves will work just as well. In fact, most films are edited with cuts only. You can usually count the dissolves on one hand.

- Use lighting to create a circle of interest, not simply for illumination. If the product in your VP's hand is the "star" of the movie, then light it accordingly.

- Do not use plants in the background, unless you are shooting in a greenhouse or a florist's shop. There is nothing worse than superfluous foliage. It is the ultimate corporate video cliché.

- Try to find the poetry in the ordinary. If you are shooting an exterior of a building, for instance, do it when the sun is most dramatic, with a chiaroscuro blend of light and shadow.

- If you are shooting b-roll (generic footage that shows relevant action) be sure to add audio. Without it the footage will be sterile. There is nothing worse than watching an assembly line without hearing the clanging of machinery.

- Use music tastefully, and set the audio levels so that voices, ambient sound and score can all be heard clearly. That process is called mixing, and it is best done slowly and carefully. Speakers' voices tend to rise and fall, just as music crescendos and diminishes. You need to "ride the levels" and adjust them scene by scene, sometimes second by second.

- Editing requires three faculties: eyes that can see, ears that can hear, and a brain that analyzes. Many editors are wizards with pictures, but have tin ears for music and mixing. Few can think conceptually to help you determine whether a particular shot works, or if a given sound bite adds or subtracts from the efficacy of the piece. If you find a competent video editor, stay with her forever.

Years ago I wrote the following guide for cameramen. The best ones are truly DPs—Directors of Photography—who bring an artist's eye and a producer's mind to the table. These "10 Commandments" are for the rest of us:

1. ***Do not change iris settings in the middle of a shot.*** If you do, you will satisfy yourself, and ***ruin*** the footage. Make a choice, and stick to it. Adjust on the next take. A shot that goes from light to dark for no apparent reason is not usable.

2. Do not talk over the b-roll. Cameramen often say, "Don't worry, you can 'fix it in post,'" meaning that audio can be redone in post-production, in the editing room, to remove the stray commentary. Those who say this are not considering, however, the additional time and absurd expense needed to find stock audio to match a basketball bouncing or fingers clacking on a keyboard.

3. *Always* capture wide, medium, and tight shots of a b-roll sequence. Context is key. The audience needs to know *where* the action is taking place. Counting to 10 for a wide shot, then zooming in and counting to 10 on the tight shot, then zooming out and counting to 10 again for a medium shot gives you three sequences at once. (Zooming does, after all, have a purpose.)

4. Shoot ***extensively, not intensively.*** That means that one decent take of six different shots is ***infinitely*** superior to six takes of the same shot. Go for ***variety.*** (Isn't that the name of a show-biz publication, come to think of it?)

5. Do not roll focus—a clichéd technique—unless you're in the jungle and you want to shock us as you move from the serenity of a blurry orchid in the foreground to a frightening close-up of a tiger snarling. This works best for nature documentaries. (Similarly, don't pan from drab inanimate objects like doorframes or blank walls to the main action. They add nothing. If you must pan, move from one point of *deep interest* to another. Ditto tilts. Starting from the rug adds nothing, unless you're shooting for a carpet company.)

6. Do not stage b-roll. Go for fake spontaneity instead.

7. Do not overshoot. If *you're* starting to get bored with something, how do you think the audience will feel?

8. Imagine people watching the footage. Will they be delighted? If not, see number 10 below.

9. ***Do not fall in love*** with your own technique. It's not about you, it's all ***about the project.***

10. When in doubt, see number 8 above.

NINE

Making Rhetoric Stick

Tips, Signs, and Lies

Rhetoric is the art of persuasive speaking or writing. It's a downright shame that it isn't routinely taught in schools today, as it was in Shakespeare's time, because it is one of the fundamental ingredients in stories. Without knowledge of oratorical technique, we might be as uninformed as the "would-be gentleman" in Molière's play, who has trouble understanding the distinction between prose and poetry:

> **Monsieur Jourdain:** . . . I'm in love with a person of high quality, and I'd like you to help me write her something in a little note . . .
>
> **Philosophy Master:** Is it verse that you want to write her?
>
> **Monsieur Jourdain:** No, no, no verse.
>
> **Philosophy Master:** You want only prose?
>
> **Monsieur Jourdain:** No I don't want either prose or verse.
>
> **Philosophy Master:** It has to be one or the other.
>
> **Monsieur Jourdain:** Why?
>
> **Philosophy Master:** . . . there is nothing to express ourselves in but prose or verse.
>
> **Monsieur Jourdain:** There's nothing but prose and verse? . . . And the way we talk, what's that then?
>
> **Philosophy Master:** Prose. . . .
>
> **Monsieur Jourdain:** Bless my soul! I've been talking prose for over forty years without knowing it, and I'm ever so grateful to you for teaching me that.[1]

Yes, we cannot apply the rules of rhetoric without knowing them. Let's start with the most basic concept in storytelling: write for the *ear*, not the eye. Write as you speak. Avoid long sentences or big, florid words. If you want to find the weak parts of your presentation, read it out loud. (I confess that I spoke the words in this book several times in an effort to find rough spots.) Try arranging the copy in the form of a poem. This will enhance your delivery and ensure that you add pauses at strategic points. Take a look at the difference between the two versions below. Read them both out loud and you'll immediately see which array is superior:

Prose	Poetry
Why are we here? Is it to celebrate success or learn from failure? It's true that our sales surged by 22 percent last quarter, and that's a plus. A big plus. But then we have to look at our turnover rate, which almost matches the growth in sales. It's 20 percent. That means one in five people here in January won't attend our Christmas party in December. And that's unacceptable.	Why are we here? Is it to celebrate success or learn from failure? It's true that our sales surged by 22 percent last quarter . . . and that's a plus. A big plus. But then we have to look at our turnover rate . . . which almost matches the growth in sales. It's 20 percent. That means one in five people here in January . . . Won't attend our Christmas party in December. And that's unacceptable.

Perhaps the most literate president the United States ever produced was Abraham Lincoln. As we mentioned earlier, there's a myth that he wrote the Gettysburg Address on the back of an envelope on the train, but that is no doubt far from the truth.[2] He reportedly worked on it in Washington, on the six-hour trip to Gettysburg, then that evening and again the next morning.[3] Yet in many ways he had been composing it all his life. He had always been a student of oratory, rhythm, and inflection. Moreover, he saw writing as a way to organize his thoughts (not surprising for a man who studied Euclid for fun!)[4] Like Mark Twain, he used words precisely, savagely chastising his rival Stephen Douglas for confusing "a similarity of words with a similarity of things—as one might equate a horse chestnut with a chestnut horse."[5] In fact, Lincoln often struggled to find the exact word to fit his ideas out of the vast array of English vocabulary.[6]

Like the 16th president, try to exploit the power of the language. Employ simple, direct words: serve instead of accommodate; guess instead of conjecture; clarify instead of elucidate. Try to use parallel constructions, with similar grammatical structure: "If a free society cannot help the many who are poor, it cannot save the few who are rich" (President Kennedy).[7] This is all-important in bullet points. If you mix nouns and verbs, for instance, the meaning is muddled, as in this list of priorities:

- Customer service
- Researching their needs
- More dialogue

It would be better to use all nouns, or all verbs, as in:

- Service
- Research
- Dialogue

Or:

- Serving
- Researching
- Speaking

Simplify the grammar: say many, instead of a large number of; did not know, instead of was unaware of. Never say "the fact that" because it adds nothing: say "I'm here because I care" rather than "The fact that I'm here means I care." Also, try to avoid the word "whom." (William Safire once said, "When whom is correct, recast the sentence."[8]) Use verbs, not adjectives or adverbs. It is much more effective to say, "He screamed," rather than "He spoke very loudly, or that he seemed angry." Speaking of verbs, use the active voice, not the passive: "The governor cut the budget, not the budget was reduced by the governor." Winston Churchill wryly noted that the passive voice is "exculpatory,"[9] meaning that it sounds as if you are shifting the blame away from yourself toward the fates. And speaking of Churchill, don't forget the value of repetition. I can't resist another look at his "Finest Hour" speech on Dunkirk to the House of Commons in 1940 at the dawn of World War II:

> [W]e shall fight on the seas and oceans ... we shall fight on the beaches, we shall fight on the landing grounds, we shall fight in the fields and in the streets, we shall fight in the hills; we shall never surrender.[10]

No wonder that JFK said that Winston Churchill mobilized the English language and sent it into battle.[11] The repetitions create an echo, just as the 272 words in the Gettysburg Address ring with reiterations. (Please note that we have designated the reappearing words and phrases in bold and italic):

> Four score and seven years ago, our fathers brought forth on *this* continent, a new *nation, conceived* in Liberty and *dedicated* to the proposition *that* all men are created equal.
>
> Now we are engaged in a *great civil war*, testing whether *that nation*, or *any nation* so *conceived and* so *dedicated*, can long endure.
>
> We are met on a great *battle-field* [*sic*] of *that war*.
>
> We have come to *dedicate* a portion of *that field*, as a final resting place for those who *here* gave their lies *that that nation* might live. It is altogether fitting and proper *that* we should do *this*.
>
> But in a large sense, we can not *dedicate*—we can not *consecrate*—we cannot hallow—*this* ground.
>
> The brave men, living and dead, who struggled *here*, have *consecrated* it, far above our poor power to add or detract.
>
> The world will little note, nor long remember, what we say *here*, but it can never forget what they did *here*.
>
> It is for us, the living, rather to be *dedicated here* to the unfinished work which they who fought *here* have thus far so nobly advanced.
>
> It is rather for us to be *here dedicated* to the great task remaining before us—*that* from *these honored dead* we take increased *devotion* to *that* cause for which they gave the last full measure of *devotion*—*that* we *here* highly resolve *that these dead* shall not have died in vain—*that this nation*, under God, shall have a new birth of freedom—and *that* the government *of the people, by the people, for the people* shall not perish from the earth.[12]

Note the linkages from sentence to sentence, and the repetitions that push us forward, yet firmly within guardrails. The word "here" appears 8 times, "that" 13 times, and "this" 4 times. In the hands of a less skillful writer, this copy could have been monotonous, but Lincoln's facility with the language was musical.

We are about to engage on a further tour of rhetorical techniques, many with complicated Greek names. Please do not be intimidated by the terminology. The concepts are simple and quite useful.[13]

Pronyche: this is a fancy word for a setup line. If you say, "This is the most important point I'm making today," chances are that people will listen to the words that immediately follow. Here's my pronyche: I will demonstrate each of the techniques in this section for a hypothetical company I will call The Mythical Software Emporium, a.k.a. TMSE. It was a challenge to do this. I hope I have succeeded!

Anadiplosis: repetition that bridges the gap between sentences. For example, Malcolm X once said: "Once you change your philosophy, you change your thought pattern. Once you change your thought pattern, you change your attitude," and so on.[14] Example for TMSE: "We serve our clients, our clients become our friends, and our friends recommend us to others."

Epistrophe: a related technique, where the same word or phrase appears at the end of sentences, clauses, or paragraphs. The best examples are, once again from the Gettysburg address, "of the people, by the people, for the people"; or Barack Obama's speech following a primary loss in New Hampshire, in January 2008: "It was a creed written into the founding documents that declared the destiny of a nation: *Yes, we can. . . . Yes, we can* heal this nation. Yes, we can repair this world. *Yes, we can.*"[15] Example for TMSE: "What are we all about? Development. What do our clients need? Development. What is our competitive advantage? Development."

Epizeuxis: repetition of a word for emphasis: "I am shocked, shocked to find that gambling is going on here" (from *Casablanca*);[16] or Demosthenes's observation that the three most important items in rhetoric were action, action, action.[17] Example for TMSE: "Our software is reliable—as reliable as the North Star."

Polyptoton: another form of repetition of words with the same root but different endings, as in "*Choosy* Mothers *Choose* Jif," a slogan for the peanut butter. Example for TMSE: "We are driven to make your hard drives work."

Antanaclasis: repeating a word or phrase, but with a different meaning each time. For example, the Beatle's song "Please Please Me"; or Vince

Lombardi's statement "If you aren't fired with enthusiasm, you will be fired, with enthusiasm." Example for TMSE: "Our ones and zeroes will ensure that the ones in your revenues are followed by many zeroes."

Diacope: repeating a word or phrase with intervening words, in a sandwich formation, as in "Bond, James Bond"; "All happy families are alike, but an *unhappy* family is *unhappy* after its own fashion" (Tolstoy); "You're not *fully clean* until you're Zest*fully clean*" (advertising slogan). Example for TMSE: "Software, scalable software."

Extended diacope: "A horse, a horse, my kingdom for a horse" (Shakespeare); or "Free at last, free at last, thank God almighty we're free at last" (Martin Luther King). Example for TMSE: "Our product line runs from customer to customer to customer." (There's yet another form of diacope called elaboration, by the way, which adds emphasis in this way: "from sea to shining sea." TMSE sample: "From triumph to greater triumph.")

Epanalepsis: one more form of repetition, beginning and ending with same word, at regular intervals, in a way that suggests circularity. For instance, "The King is dead, long live the King"; or Walmart's slogan "*Always* Low Prices. *Always.*" Example for TMSE: "The core of our business is our people and the people are the core."

Rhetorical questions (for which no answer is apparent): Example for TMSE: "Why do you spend so much on our competitors' products?"

Hypophora: a related technique, whereby the speaker poses a question then answers it immediately, as in this commercial: "Ask any mermaid you happen to see, 'What's the best tuna?' Chicken of the Sea"; or Bob Dylan's song "A Hard Rain's A-Gonna Fall": "Oh, what did you see, my blue-eyed son?" Example for TMSE: "Why do you need such complicated solutions? You don't."

Antithesis: the juxtaposition of two opposing elements to evoke a powerful message. A great example is the motto for the state of New Hampshire: "Live free or die"; or Dickens's "It was the best of times, it was the worse of times"; or Sara Lee's advertising slogan "Everybody doesn't like something, but nobody doesn't like Sara Lee." Example for TMSE: "Software as durable as hardware."

Chiasmus: a particularly useful form of antithesis, where the second element reverses the first in the form of verbal judo, with comparison and contrast.[18] The classic examples come from President Kennedy: "Ask not what your country can do for you—ask what you can do for your country"; or "Let us never negotiate out of fear. But let us never fear to negotiate."[19] In advertising, we have "Starkist doesn't want tuna with good taste,

Starkist wants tuna that tastes good." Example for TMSE: "We care about user interface and we interface with care with our customers."

Merism: another variety of antithesis, where the opposing elements create a unified whole. For example, "night and day" means constant. Example for TMSE: "We'll protect your data, be it near or far."

Alliteration: generally entails the repetition of an initial consonant sound. This is one of the most potent weapons in your rhetorical arsenal, as in Krispy Kreme, Gold's Gym, Burt's Bees, and so on. Example for TMSE: "Perfect programming produces profits."

Assonance: closely related to alliteration, but involving the repetition of similar or identical vowel instead of consonant sounds, as in "It beats . . . as it sweeps . . . as it cleans!" (advertising slogan for Hoover vacuum cleaners, 1950s). Both assonance and alliteration make phrases more memorable: linguists Frank Boers and Seth Lindstromberg discovered that it was easier for adults to learn English through word combinations such as green grass or home phone.[20] (One oddity of English, by the way, is that it has fewer vowels than any other language. The most common one, by the way, is the schwa, like the *a* in the phrase "a book."[21]) Example of assonance from TMSE: "Open source, of course, yields great force."

Synesthesia: A blending of the senses. Most artists know there is little separation between them in the first place. The composer Franz Liszt, for instance, once told his musicians, "Please, gentlemen, a little bluer, if you please."[22] Those with synesthesia might associate letters or sounds with colors. (In fact, I have a variant called spatial sequence synesthesia. That means I envision numbers as a line with hash marks extending forwards and backwards in space. I am happy to report that people with synesthesia are often creative.) Even if you do not see the world in a skewed way, it is worthwhile to *try* to do so. Energy flows back and forth between our senses. If you can see music, hear colors, or envision numbers in a different manner, you'll gain greater insight.[23] In telling a story, then, you might tell us how an idea or image might feel or taste, as in a silky voice or a sweet thought. Example from TMSE: "We think of software as a mellifluous flute, with bright red passion."

Hyperbaton: words in inverted order, such as "Uneasy lies the head that wears a crown."[24] Yoda, of *Star Wars* fame, spoke this way: "Truly wonderful, the mind of a child is."[25] Lincoln used this technique with "verbal athleticism," particularly in his Second Inaugural Address: "Fondly do we hope, fervently do we pray."[26] Example from TMSE: "Clever are our engineers, worry they do, so you don't have to."

Parataxis: words and phrases arranged independently, like a series of quick cuts in a movie, perhaps without cause and effect or logic. Here's an example from Raymond Chandler's Novel *Farewell my Lovely*: "I needed a drink, I needed a lot of life insurance, I needed a vacation, I needed a home in the country. What I had was a coat, a hat and a gun."[27] Example from TMSI: "When we started we dreamed all day. We ate a lot of pizza. We made no money."

Syllepsis: using a word in two divergent or unusual ways. "International Business Machines makes business machines, and Ford Motors makes Fords, and Sara Lee makes us fat."[28] Here's another example, from a bumper sticker: "PEACE. Live in it or rest in it." From TMSI: "We don't believe in feature creep but we are proud to say that our security measures keep the creeps out."

Enallage: a deliberate grammatical error, as in Got milk?; Be more dog (O2); or Think Different (Apple). "[They] stick in our minds because they're just wrong—wrong enough to be right."[29] Example from TMSI: "Software ain't simple and neither is your problems."

Catachresis: related to enallage—either a "sentence that makes you stop, scratch your head and say 'that's wrong'" (for example, "I will speak daggers")[30] or "the inappropriate use of one word for another, or an extreme, strained, or mixed metaphor, often used deliberately."[31] Another instance: "Changing birds of a feather in mid-stream." From TMSI: "Your software should protect your soft underbelly"; "A compass for your softwhereabouts."

Snowclone: a phrase with key elements alternating in a way that changes the meaning[32]—a relatively new addition to the rhetorical playbook. For instance, "Orange is the new black" or "60 is the new 40." Apple used this technique in marketing the iPod Shuffle with the claim "Random is the new order."[33] There is even a site called "The Snowclones Database."[34] offering many examples: "Yes, Virginia, there is an X; I'm not an X, but I play one on TV"; or, "X is hard, let's go shopping." From TMSI: "We software, therefore we 'knowwhere' the innovation lies." (By the way, the term "snowclone" was derived from the inaccurate story that Inuit people have many words for "snow." It's a pun on the snow cone, presumably referring to its artificial resemblance to real snow.[35])

Whatever rhetorical technique you use, try to fashion a new world in your story. Poet Marianne Moore wrote about creating "imaginary gardens with real toads in them."[36] Do whatever it takes to make your customers share your gardens.

SEALED, DELIVERED, AND SIGNED

We are now going to take an excursion into an area that may seem complicated but that is nonetheless quite relevant: semiotics, the theory of signs, involves three elements: the signifier (the pointer—a word or a picture, for instance); the signified (the concept); and the referent (the real-world object).[37] For example, the word "book" (the signifier) consists of four letters on this page, calling to mind an image of an object with a collection of printed pages (the signified idea), not to be confused with the actual book you are holding in your hand (the referent). Signs come in three varieties, iconic, indexical, and symbolic, as this chart shows:[38]

	Iconic	Indexical	Symbolic
Signifies by (that is, functions through)	Resemblance	Cause and effect	Convention/habit
Examples	Pictures, statues	Smoke and fire; Antibiotics and health	Words, numbers, flags
Processed or understood through	Seeing	Analysis	Learning

As soon as we see a picture of an animal with spotted, orange fur and an elongated neck, we immediately recognize it as a giraffe (an iconic sign). Similarly, smoke coming out of the window of a building leads to the conclusion that a fire may be raging inside because we have an indelible concept of the causal link (an indexical sign). Last, when we see these symbols on the page—$1,000,000—we immediately perceive them as a representation of one million dollars, because we have learned what those numbers mean (a symbolic sign).

By now you may be wondering what this has to do with storytelling. The answer centers on the concept of rules and codes, which are often hard to articulate. "Sometimes there is confusion and the code of the [speaker doesn't match] the audience's."[39] If you believe, for instance, that your product's image will enhance prestige, and your customers view it more literally as a simple car that transports them from place to place, then the communication is flawed. Or, suppose you are selling software that can facilitate collaboration in product design by allowing multiple users to manipulate 3D images in real time. You might regard it as a genius-level innovation that will spark creativity, but the customers may see it as a source of inefficiency with too many parties involved in the process. Imagine a designer saying to herself, "We used to choose the colors and the shapes ourselves. Now we have the VP of engineering and his entire staff providing input. What do they know about design anyway?" Also, bear in mind that codes are affected by class, ethnicity, and geography.[40] It is therefore important to consider all possible interpretations (signifieds) of your message and to understand that "aberrant decoding"[41] can be the norm when people hear your story through the lens of their own experience and assumptions—a lens that may significantly diverge from yours. One aspirational goal for new companies is becoming a "cognitive referent," which Professor Rory McDonald at Harvard Business School defines as a firm that customers, partners, analysts, and employees "automatically recognize as epitomizing the nascent [product]" in the manner of Google or Starbucks.[42] Companies with this exalted status "enjoy a privileged position that conflates [them] with the market in the minds of relevant audiences."[43] Achieving that is certainly a bold ambition. Under ideal circumstances, firms achieve secondary meaning in the sense that customers see their products as a verb that is synonymous with the function performed, as in "Fedex it" or "Xerox it." In any case, try to align the signs and codes in a way that conveys intended messages, not distortions. Ask your customers what they see when they experience your wares. The results may surprise you.

METAPHOR: CARRYING YOUR MESSAGES ACROSS

A clever metaphor is one way to ensure that your messages will be delivered with authority and impact. In many respects, metaphor is the progenitor of all figures of speech—the stem cell, if you will, from which all other parts can be generated. It consists of a comparison between dissimilars and is actually quite a potent form of semiology, since once element directs our attention to another.[44] The derivation of the word is instructive, coming from the Greek *phor*, meaning to carry, and *meta*, meaning across. It literally transports us from one concept to another, so much so that Aristotle described it as a sign of genius.[45] The philosopher also said that metaphors work best in two cases: when they convey information quickly (but not in an obvious way), or when they confuse us at first.[46]

Straightforward metaphors are called rhetorical, as in "our software opens doors for you," and the more baffling ones are cognitive, as in "our developers are gazelles in the lab." Rhetorical metaphors compress "an idea for the sake of convenience" but offer few insights,[47] whereas cognitive ones require analysis because the "relevance and meaning are not immediately clear."[48] We quickly understand that a company that sells software that opens doors expands the purview of your business, but the gazelle reference makes us pause and ponder because we have to imagine the nimbleness and grace of a gazelle and deduce how that might apply to developers. Please note that we are still in semiology territory, with one element (programmers) pointing to another (gazelles), with the first as a signifier, the second as the signified concept, and the referent (the real-world object) being the actual animals. The greater the theoretical distance between sign and referent, the more powerful the image. In other words, the harder we have to work to understand the comparison, the more satisfaction we derive.[49] (Linguists speak of the two elements as the source domain, the gazelle, an abstract concept, and the target domain, the workers, a concrete entity that we are trying to describe.) Cognitive metaphors bring about "an oscillation between two domains within a single mind."[50] This can be endlessly captivating to an audience. Perhaps F. Scott Fitzgerald was mistaken in saying that "the test of a first-rate intelligence is the ability to hold two opposed ideas in the mind at the same time, and still retain the ability to function,"[51] because geniuses and ordinary people alike can do so given that metaphors are a part of everyday speech. We use expressions like "It's raining in buckets" or "the grass is a soft carpet" so often that the linkage between the unrelated concepts seems to be second nature. Robert Frost said, "We like to talk in parables and in hints and in indirections—whether from diffidence or some other instinct"; he even suggests that "metaphor [is] the whole of thinking."[52] A word of caution: make sure that your metaphors (or analogies) don't go too far, otherwise they'll resemble "feathers on the scales of a serpent."[53] On the other hand, if the comparisons are too simple or obvious, they might seem condescending, as in "we're putting our arms around our clients."[54] Also bear in mind that the strength of metaphors is not just intellectual. They can also engage our emotions, even unconsciously, according to new research by Professor Adele Goldberg of Princeton University. When participants in an experiment heard expressions like "She gave him a sweet compliment" as opposed to the more literal statement "She gave him a kind compliment," the part of their brains controlling emotions lit up during fMRIs.[55]

Reaching for sensory references of this sort can add untold dimensions to your stories.

And while you're at it, you might consider an extended metaphor. Professor Mary Jo Hatch provides an excellent example in her effort to redefine organizational structure with jazz terms. She came by this naturally, since she was married to a jazz musician at the time.[56] She cites philosopher Richard Rorty who advocated "redescription, a constant recycling of old concepts, using new (even contradictory) language for the sake of replacing a worn out vocabulary with a new one."[57] Hatch gets us started by defining jazz terminology: while the soloist improvises, other musicians "comp," that is, accompany him or her with rhythmic or harmonic support and with ideas that he or she may (or may not) incorporate. This back and forth process is called swapping fours or simply fours.[58] Then there's groove and feel, meaning that the musicians (and the audience) are locked into one another in a way that creates an emotional and aesthetic communion.[59] She draws parallels with corporate structure as follows:

Jazz Activity	Emerging corporate vocabulary/concept
Soloing, comping, trading fours	Teamwork/Collaboration
Listening/responding	Strategic development
Groove and feel	Culture and identity[60]

Following Rorty, she advises us to embrace new vocabulary, not argue with the old one. Do we see how powerful this cognitive metaphor is? We need to ponder the complexity of the concepts to find connections with corporate structure, but once we get there the insights can be astounding. Too often managers try to stick to the same old melody (and there is no stronger insult for a jazz musician than accusing him or her of going "by the book" and failing to improvise.) Moreover, Hatch told me that these ideas are directly applicable to storytelling:

Learn to ride the emotions of story along with the audience. Be sure to notice the impact. . . . When you achieve a true groove, you should find yourself saying things you did not expect to say, or saying them in a way that you had not planned. . . . [During her marriage to the musician] I hung out with some very talented people and they really taught me what jazz is beyond theory and technical chops. It's very much about listening and responding in the moment and leaving everything else out of your consciousness. And when you can do that, a song will just take off. And I came to the conclusion the same thing was true of good storytelling.[61]

Hatch's work is related to the theory of framing, as put forth by cognitive linguist George Lakoff in his book *Don't Think of an Elephant*. He defines frames as "mental structures that shape the way we see the world,"[62] so much so that they are an invisible part of our unconscious—configurations "in our brains that we cannot . . . access [but that affect] the way we reason and [our notion of] common sense."[63] Frames and the metaphors that accompany them overwhelm objective evidence because they are indelibly etched into our neural circuitry: "When the facts don't fit the frames, the frames are kept and the facts ignored."[64] That means we tend to discount contrary evidence as misguided or downright stupid. Lakoff demonstrates that this phenomenon often leads citizens to vote against their self-interest when candidates project a worldview that accords with theirs. He shows, for example, how the phrase "tax relief" has informed political policy by portraying taxes as a disease for which we need an antidote, rather than a source of revenue supporting needed social projects.[65] In my own work, I have repeatedly seen that readers tend to classify articles as "objective journalism" when the slant is in line with their preconceptions. I am not suggesting for a moment that we try to manipulate audiences by pandering to their baser instincts in business messaging. I do recommend, however, that it is all-important to place messages in a larger context. Here's a simple example: I happen to have a pile of index cards on my desk at the moment. On the one hand, a card, is just, well, a paper rectangle measuring 5" × 8." So why would anyone buy them, at a time when everything is digital? Are they just paper qua paper or do they have greater significance? I find that it's very useful to print out ideas on cards that can be rearranged on a horizontal surface—literally allowing us to "touch" the concepts and facts as we sort and analyze them. In fact, I composed this section on framing that way. This "technology" might just be retro chic. For me the "frame," or should I say, reframing for the "index card market" might be something like this: "It's all in the cards: organize your thoughts." Corny? OK, how about this? "The index card is avant-garde." Or, perhaps better yet: "Get in touch with your ideas with index cards."

Here is another quick example of reframing: Recently I did a consulting project with a group of pharmacists from a leading supermarket chain.

One of them referred to the customers as "patients." This simple substitution could redefine their entire marketing approach. Those who use pharmacy services, in his view, are not just people filling prescriptions, but patients seeking health care. It is important to use a lexicon that fits the context. (For instance, in the novel *The Door*, Magda Szabó shows that two characters failed to communicate because their vocabularies clashed: "[One's] dictionary featured . . . scandal . . . and shame. [The other's] contained law, order, solutions, solidarity, effective measures. Both . . . were accurate, it was just they were in different languages."[66]) Try to ensure, then, that you and your customers are working from the same phrasebook. The first step in framing is defining the terms.

LIES THAT REVEAL THE TRUTH

There is a fundamental point to be made about signs and metaphors. They simply are not true. If we say that we are employing guerilla marketing, do we literally mean that we're using impromptu bands of small groups against a larger, more powerful foe? Of course not. When we speak of viral messages, do they actually spread with the, well, virulence of a disease? No, again. Metaphors may be a supercharged form of signage, but the comparisons, though insightful, are downright false. Here's Umberto Eco on the subject:

> Semiotics is concerned with every thing that can be *taken* as a sign. A sign is everything which can be taken as significantly substituting for something else. This something else does not necessarily have to exist or to actually be somewhere at the moment in which a sign stands in for it. Thus *semiotics is in principle the discipline studying everything which can be used in order to lie.* If something cannot be used to tell a lie, conversely it cannot be used to tell the truth: it cannot in fact be used "to tell" at all. I think that the definition of a "theory of the lie" should be taken as a pretty comprehensive program for a general semiotics.[67]

Eco is saying that a sign posits a complicated comparison (a "significant substitution") such as "business is a dance between the possible and the achievable." As we have discovered, that is a lie, since we generally don't dance at the office. The leap of imagination is nonetheless fanciful and perhaps helpful in plotting strategy.

I am certainly not advocating lying. When a narrator weaves a story that captivates and transports the audience, he or she is leading them on a pathway toward a world of his own creation. There is, however, a distinction between "trying to convince" and "seeking to mislead."[68] It is impossible to achieve complete objectivity, however, no matter how strenuously one might try, as any competent journalist knows. Village Voice writer Jack Newfield once said "objectivity is not shouting 'liar' in a crowded country" and that "truth is not the square root of two balanced quotes."[69] He believed that part of his job was to call out lies and to prevent sources from turning him into a stenographer. Yet is it permissible for a business spokesperson to combine several characters into a composite, or to compress long chains of events into a shorter time, or to invent quotes that support the desired conclusion? (These maneuvers would be forbidden in a responsible newsroom.) Some marketing people seem to feel that the disparate facts that compose an event are somehow separate and distinct from the ultimate truth, and that it's permissible for a writer to impose his own voice. Yet if "you pick up a book expecting a report and you find instead a man" that can "harm the unwary reader."[70] I believe that each of us knows when we are approaching the line between fact and fiction, between accuracy and deception. We don't need to resort to epistemologists (i.e., those who study the theory of knowledge) in philosophy departments to tell us when our language is doing the customer a disservice because we literally may not know what we are talking about.

CONVEY EMOTION FROM TEXT AND CONTEXT

In my consulting practice, I find that many executives share a common malady when it comes to expressing emotion: they try to convey enthusiasm by saying "I'm really excited about our new initiative." That is about as effective as claiming that your restaurant serves delicious, well-cooked food. It is important, make that *all important,* to project enthusiasm, and in turn to elicit desired reactions from the audience, but this effort requires a *nuanced* approach.

Let's take a look at T. S. Eliot's theory of the objective correlative. He said that the only way to invoke a particular emotional response in art is to establish a foundation in facts or circumstances. "[I]n other words, a set of objects, a situation, a chain of events" will be the "formula" for that feeling, so that "when the external facts, which must terminate in sensory experience, are given, the emotion is immediately evoked."[71] This is a fancy way of saying that you cannot produce a sentiment without the proper stimuli.[72] Eliot goes so far as to say that *Hamlet* is a failed play because the prince's frustration with his mother exceeds the factual justification. Hamlet, then, is a shallow character because there is no "objective equivalent" to his feelings. In short, "Shakespeare tackled a problem which proved too much for him."[73] Now I'll leave it to you to decide if *Hamlet* is a triumph or a failure as a work of art, but in the meantime let's take a closer look at this theory and its relevance to business.

First, let me digress for just a moment. Eliot famously said, "Immature poets imitate; mature poets steal; bad poets deface what they take, and good poets make it into something better, or at least something different."[74] The same is true of his theory, which can be traced back to 1840 when American poet and painter Washington Allston noted that just as air, earth, heat, and water are essential elements in the development of a common vegetable like a cabbage, "so too is the external world to the mind . . . which needs [as a precondition] its objective correlative," an object that yields the emotion sought.[75] Santayana was a professor at Harvard when Eliot studied there and he may have introduced this concept to the young poet. In any case, Santayana also borrowed the term, albeit in inverted form, when he argued that "the glorious emotions with which he [the poet] bubbles over must at all hazards find or feign their correlative objects."[76] Edgar Allan Poe is also a possible source. He believed that the writer should not extract an idea from the plot of a tale, but rather should reverse the process and conceive the desired effect first, then invent the "incidents" that evoke it.[77] We can find the seeds of this line of reasoning in the 1500s, when the so-called father of the modern essay, Montaigne, was suffering from what were probably kidney stones that were so excruciating that they made him wish he were dead. As he contemplated the end of his days, however, he reasoned that he would not miss life in the abstract but only in the particular. He thought of "a dog, a horse, a book, a glass" and the "tears of a footman, the disposing of my clothes, the touch of a friendly hand"[78]—"objective correlatives" for his sadness.

If you amass this sort of detail in your marketing, then the product may exude the coveted aura by its mere mention and may come to *represent* an emotion automatically. This is sort of an objective correlative in reverse—one that already contains the stimuli. For instance, the word "Bacardi" conjures up thoughts of outdoor bars, sunny days, palm trees, sandy beaches, tropical vacations, and so on. More specifically, we might immediately think of the sweet, thick elixir of rum, pineapple, and coconut, aka a Piña Colada, or a combination of crushed ice, lime juice, and rum known as a Daiquiri, and so on and so on. This is all contained in that *one word because we carry around those associations* that invoke a feeling of relaxation. As Judith Williamson noted in her book *Decoding Advertisements*, "the product not only represents an emotional experience, but *becomes* that experience and *produces* it: its roles as sign and referent are collapsed together."[79] Bacardi at once points to a beach scene in our mind and *is* that image.

This dovetails with the theory of predicates. In grammar, a predicate is a descriptor linked with the subject of a sentence that provides additional information. It can be a verb, as in Nutella *satisfies*; a noun, as in Nutella is a guilty *pleasure* (at least for me!); or, an adjective, as in Nutella is *delicious*. Just as the media are an extension of our senses, so too can transformative products that are bundles of physical and psychological attributes expand and intensify our lives as predicates. It's no longer verb-direct object, as in "I want a Porsche"; it's now subject-predicate, as in "I am the style I am purchasing." Products can thus reflect and even embody our desires and our very identities by imposing new concepts on the norms of everyday life.[80]

Here is an example. Gail Pryor was my neighbor in the Boston area. A marketing writer in the health care field, she brilliantly turned her house into a compelling narrative when she put it on the market. Here are some excerpts from her description, which is quite novelistic in style. She called her property "The Shire" and the "pitch" starts with a description of her prior home:

> Our babies became boys. Boys with skateboards and lacrosse sticks and friends. . . . Sometimes I had to press myself against a wall in our small house to avoid being knocked over. . . . But what we really needed was a farm . . . [and we found one] just a few blocks away.
>
> The house was built in 1850 in a bit of pasture. . . . Four families moved in over the next 150 years. . . . A child who lived here planted every one of his family's Christmas trees, ringing the house with spruce trees, now towering sentries.
>
> By the time our family came along, the farmhouse was exhausted by 156 years of hard living. "We bought the Boo Radley house," my husband told friends. . . . It frightened potential buyers with peeling paint on original clapboards, an aging roof, and an iffy spot on its foundation. . . . [Yet] the house became ground zero for team dinners, pig roasts for graduations and engagements, games of charades on Christmas afternoon, and end-of-summer clam bakes.

. . . When I kept chickens at The Shire, the first welcome egg told me spring was coming. The hens took their annual break from laying as daylight dwindled in November, and started back up again in early February, with surprised squawks.

After first eggs come snowdrops, then crocuses, which herald daffodils, and then we're off to the races. The garden at The Shire tumbles in one bloom after another through spring and summer. . . . The dwarf pines have years to go until they reach full height. I realize now that I've planted them for another family, for the next gardener. And I feel the same relief I felt when each of my sons fell in love: she will look after him now. . . .

The wisteria vine twines around the rails of the kids' tree fort. Someday, it will tangle itself into a roof, a purple tent high in the spruce for the next set of children who live at the shire.[81]

Is it any wonder the house sold quickly, above asking price? The description abounds with many details that serve as an objective correlative for a feeling of warm attraction—fueling happy expectations for the new family who will forge their own memories. The technique is not simply a "catalogue of items in a scene" but an entire backdrop that describes the world through the character's point of view.[82] (In this case, one might say that the house is the protagonist.) Eloquent description can indeed recreate the past, as the objective correlative becomes subjective in the viewer's mind. That's one of main goals of marketing.

TEN

Make Your Words March

Clichés, Writer's Block, and Plot Patterns

AVOID CLICHÉS LIKE THE PLAGUE

I cannot tell you how many clichés I hear in my consulting practice. "We think like our customers; our technology is robust and scalable; our people are our best asset" and so on. When you are tempted to use a platitude in your messaging, run the other way. Annihilate stereotypes and turn the hackneyed on end.[1] Instead of saying "we embrace our customers," explain that you spend weeks with each of them to try to understand if your products are helping them in the intended way. Rather than bragging about your services with adjectives like "superb" or "unparalleled," describe what you have *done* for those who benefit.

Here is a partial list of clichés to avoid. Don't touch them with a ten-foot keyboard. (Irony intended.)

Little fish in a big pond (or big fish in a little pond)

Cannibalization (as in one business eating another)

Synergy (or worse, 2 + 2 = 5)

Cinderella stories (an unknown quickly rising to the top)

Crash-test dummies

Stranded on a desert island with _____

Fountain of youth

Firing squads (circular or otherwise)

Reinventing the wheel

Life rafts

Parting the Red Sea

Sprinkling pixie dust around _____

Leveraging (often used in the broadest sense, as in "We're leveraging the new design." Huh?)

Buried treasure

Robin Hood maneuver

Thinking outside the box

Strategic communications

Story arc

Ear to the ground

Last but not least

The City of Light (Paris)

The Windy City (Chicago)

The City with the Broad Shoulders (also Chicago)

The Eternal City (Rome)

It would be hard to top this parody of clichés from *Writing News for Broadcast*:

> Once upon a time, in a network newsroom, the writers drew a map of a . . . continent washed on the east by the Restless Ocean, in which, clearly marked beside Desperate Straits, lay the Depths of Despair. . . . The largest country was Major Power, whose political capital, Mounting Tension, lay west of the Undulating Plains. . . . The principal metropolis on the West Coast was Crystal Clear, washed by the Great Expanse of Water. . . . [L]arge X-marks indicated a score of Watery Graves. At the bottom of the map stretched the Sea of Upturned Faces.[2]

On the other hand, an abundance of clichés, when artfully arranged, can be effective. "Two [of them] make us laugh, but a hundred move us because we sense dimly that [they] are talking among themselves, celebrating a reunion."[3] That's a quote from master semiologist (and novelist) Umberto Eco, speaking about the movie *Casablanca* which turns shopworn language into deep irony. But that script, written by the Epstein brothers, won an Academy Award in 1942 and is generally regarded as a masterpiece. The rest of us need to be more careful with hackneyed expressions.

CALISTHENICS TO CURE WRITER'S BLOCK

I would offer some advice about working through writer's block, but I've never experienced it. Ha! Anyone who has ever tried to put words together will find himself or herself writhing in frustration and wondering why he or she ever attempted the task in the first place. It's so much easier to mow the lawn, sweep the front porch, or watch TV. And, I suppose, the malady is no different than pitcher's block, slalom skier's block, or accountant's block. There are days where you just can't manage to do it.

So how do you get started?

Earlier in this book we met Raymond Chandler, best known for noir fiction. He could pack more into a sentence than most of us can squeeze into a paragraph. Here are a few examples of his compressed prose:

- "I don't mind if you don't like my manners. They're pretty bad. I grieve over them during the long winter evenings."[4]

- "Nobody came into the office. Nobody called me on the phone. It kept raining."[5]

- "All she did was take her hand out of her bag, with a gun in it. All she did was point it at me and smile. All I did was nothing."[6]

Chandler was quite disciplined about his writing. He composed on small pieces of paper, about the size of a paperback book, with a capacity of just 12–15 lines. He'd feed them into his typewriter in what we now call landscape mode. This habit forced him to tighten his prose. Plus it made rewriting easier. Lesson: when in doubt, write short.

Here are a few other tips that have often helped me when I'm stuck:

- Try turning your messages into a Tweet, with the outmoded 140-character limit. (The new 280-character maximum encourages verbosity, by comparison!)

- Imagine that you are satisfying a need. What does your business *do*? Focusing on that will push you in a fruitful direction.

- Carry a small notebook with you. Ideas come at random moments, often when you are thinking about something else.

- Write to see what you are thinking. If you are bewildered, then write about bewilderment.

- Open a dictionary and choose three words haphazardly. (Or better yet, find one of the readily available programs that does this online.) Repeat as necessary.

- As mentioned before, ask "what if?" as in, "What if we went out of business? How would our customers react?" Or "what if our best customer were here? What would she/he say?"

HINTS ABOUT PLOT BLUEPRINTS

If you get stuck trying to find the structure of a story, follow basic patterns called "narratemes." Here is a useful list of "Seven Easy Steps to a Better Story," courtesy of Brian McDonald's book *Invisible Ink*:

Once upon a time . . .

And every day . . .

Until one day . . .

And because of this . . .

And because of this . . .

Until finally . . .

And ever since that day . . .[7]

McDonald applies this format to a popular Hollywood movie:

Once upon a time there was a godfather who ran a family business . . .

And every day he did favors and received them in return . . .

Until one day he refused a request and a rival tried to murder him . . .

And because of this his sons took over the business . . .

And because of this one of them was killed and the other driven into exile . . .

And because of this the godfather made peace . . .

And because of this the exiled son was able to return to take over . . .

Until finally the son eliminated the rival bosses . . .

And ever since that day he has been the new godfather.[8]

How might this apply to business? Let's imagine that you are making a case for a new veterinary clinic. The pitch might run as follows, in general terms:

Once upon a time, at least 15,000 years ago, wolves roamed the countryside.

And every day people lived in fear.

Until one day a tame member of a wolf pack started hanging around a village of humans.

And because of this a little girl played with him and begged her parents to keep him as a pet.

And because of this the tame wolf developed a symbiotic relationship with his new family—trading protection for food.

Until finally the tame wolves bred with one another and gave rise to the animal we now know as a dog.

And ever since that day dogs have been our best friends.

Tagline: So don't trust your dog to just anyone. Visit the _____ Clinic.

Here are some other possible plot formats—adapted from various sources—that might get you started. First, Joseph Campbell:

> The mythological hero, setting forth from his common-day hut or castle . . . proceeds . . . to the threshold of adventure. There he encounters a shadowy presence that guards the passage. The hero may defeat or conciliate this power . . . or be slain by the opponent . . . The hero journeys through a world of unfamiliar yet strangely intimate forces . . . [H]e undergoes a supreme ordeal and gains his reward . . . The final work is that of the return . . . [and he] re-emerges from the kingdom of dread. The boon that he brings restores the world.[9]

Campbell's system may be too grandiose for a business story, but it could be a helpful paradigm nonetheless. Consider this: in mythology, the hero often feels he or she is "lacking" an essential element in life:

> The old ideas that have nourished his community for generations no longer speak to him. So he leaves home and endures death-defying adventures. He fights monsters, climbs mountains, traverses dark forests and, in the process, dies to his old self, and gains a new insight or skill, which he brings back to his people. [For instance] Prometheus stole fire from the gods for humanity, and had to endure centuries of agonising punishment; Aeneas was forced to leave his old life behind, see his homeland in flames, and descend to the underworld before he could found the new city of Rome.[10]

Here are a few more ideas, culled from *The Thirty-Six Dramatic Situations*, by Georges Polti: supplication, deliverance, vengeance, pursuit, disaster (ingratitude or outrage suffered), revolt, daring enterprise, enigma, madness, temptations, self-sacrifice for an ideal, family, or passion, or erroneous judgment.[11] Then we have Vladimir Propp, who wrote the landmark

Morphology of the Folktale. Here are some of the narrative elements he identified:

- A family member leaves home.
- The hero receives a stern warning: "you dare not look into this closet; bring breakfast out into the field; or take your brother with you to the woods."
- He violates the warning. Enter the villain, who may be a dragon, a devil, a witch, and so on.
- The villain engages in reconnaissance.
- The villain attempts to deceive his victim, possibly through disguise (a dragon turns into a golden goat or a handsome youth; a witch pretends to be a "sweet old lady"; a thief pretends to be a beggarwoman). Or the villain deceives in a clever way (for example, a dragon rearranges wood shavings that show a young girl the way to her brothers.)
- The victim is fooled.
- The villain causes harm or injury to a member of a family through abduction, magic, seizing the daylight, imprisonment, and so on.
- The hero is tested, interrogated, or attacked, preparing the way for a magical agent or helper/donor (for instance, a witch or a forest knight).
- The hero acquires the use of a magical agent.
- He is led to the whereabouts of the desired object. He may fly through the air, travel over water, or follow bloody tracks.
- The hero and the villain join in direct combat.
- The hero is branded, wounded, or marked with a burning star on his forehead by a princess.
- The villain is defeated.
- The hero is rescued: he may be carried away through the air or transformed into an animal. Perhaps he jumps from tree to tree!
- Unrecognized, he arrives home or in another country.
- He faces a difficult task, for example, ordeal by food, drink, or fire; a riddle; or a test of strength, skill, or courage.
- The hero is transformed, through magic, and builds a beautiful palace or puts on new clothes.

- The villain is punished.
- The hero is married and ascends the throne.[12]

You may think these plots are extreme or far-fetched, but Mary Jo Hatch discovered that epic tales abound in the C-suite. In the book *The Three Faces of Leadership: Manager, Artist, Priest*, she and her co-authors studied 30 interviews with CEOs published in *Harvard Business Review*. The overall themes concerned "beauty, passion and vision"[13] and a full 78 percent of the stories were pure epics, with heroes, villains, great challenges and sacrifices, all with an inspirational edge.[14] Another 13 percent were hybrids involving epic components, bringing the total of partial and complete epics to 91 percent.[15] This confounds expectations. Most observers would assume that CEOs' tales would be more neutral, but Hatch's research shows that they feature bold actors, oversized statements, and big events. For instance, let's experience the tale of the humble origins of Softbank, a multinational finance and high-tech conglomerate. Founder Masayoshi Son is an ethnic Korean who had moved to Japan:

> When I started the company, I used straight bank loans. And that was really difficult. I went to the Dai-ichi Kangyo Bank when the company was only three or four months old. At the time, I had revenues of about $10,000 and I asked for a loan of $750,000. I told them, I have no collateral, I have no business experience, and I am not going to ask my family or my friends to co-sign the loan. I will sign myself, and I'll take all the responsibility. But unless you give me the prime rate, I'm not going to take a loan from you. . . . The people at the . . . bank just started laughing. [Son then offered a key reference who heartily endorsed him.] Then it was up to the branch manager to fill in the formal scorecard of the bank using his judgment. . . . When he used the ordinary scoring, the total was -15 against making the loan. But the last column was "potential growth." He gave us 15 points [for that] . . . So the total came out zero. . . . The branch manager said, "I'm going to give him the loan." Today at Softbank, we have a special day where we honor the few individuals who made contributions to help start [the company]. One [of them] is that bank branch manager.[16]

Here is another epic story from Hatch's book—told by Nicolas Hayek, the CEO of Swatch's parent company in Switzerland:

> How did we launch Swatch in Germany? Did we saturate the airwaves with paid advertisements? No. Anyone can do that. We built a

giant Swatch. It was 500 feet high, weighed 13 tons and actually worked. We suspended [it] outside the tallest skyscraper in Frankfurt, the headquarters of Commerzbank. It was really something to see![17] . . . We also hung a giant Swatch in Tokyo, in the Ginza. . . . By volume, Swiss companies account for more than 50 percent of all the watches sold in Japan. [We] account for 75 percent of that 50 percent. Do you think we broadcast these figures? Or that we act arrogantly in Japan? Of course not. The Japanese are sympathetic to us. We're nice people from a small country. We have nice mountains and clear water. They like us and our products, and we like them.[18]

Both these stories depict audacious managers who are not afraid to make emphatic statements, about themselves and their products. They tell their stories with relish and pride. We can find this sort of drama inside companies as well. Most organizations think their internal narratives are unique, but they nonetheless fall into seven bold, basic patterns:

- Rule breaking
- Is the big boss human?
- Can the little person rise to the top?
- Will I get fired?
- Will the organization help me when I have to move?
- How will the boss react to my mistakes?
- How will the organization deal with obstacles?[19]

Please note that this analysis of plot formats is not meant to be universally applicable. Instead, the lists are mere idea prompts, from scholars who have studied the patterns in detail. As circumstance would have it, however, I recently stumbled across a story that involves many of these elements.

An artist I know received an enticing e-mail, apparently from a prominent corporate lawyer Ms. X, in Washington, DC. She said that she had long admired his work and wanted to buy one of his paintings for $2,000. She asked him to keep the transaction secret because she intended to surprise her husband with the artwork as an anniversary gift. Moreover, she claimed that the family was moving to another country and that "Our shipper will come and pick up the painting." The artist Googled the lawyer and discovered that she was indeed well known and respected. Soon a check arrived, in the amount of $5,000, not $2,000. My friend is an honest man so he took the check to his bank and tried to deposit it, with the full intention of refunding the additional $3,000 ASAP. Fortunately, the bank personnel noticed right away that the printed account numbers on the check were fictitious. At that point, the artist called the 800 number that the "buyer" had left. A man answered who told him that the woman who called herself Ms. X was not there. "Is she a lawyer?" my friend asked. "No, she's a computer expert," the man blurted out. Expert indeed. This is an elaborate scam whereby the rogues send a bogus check in the hope that the recipient will deposit it, then they demand a refund before it clears. They had no intention of buying the painting, of course. They merely wanted to create a fake "debt" so they could extract payment by threat of force or worse. My friend eventually contacted the actual lawyer whose identity was "borrowed" for this scheme, and she in turn told him to call the FBI.

How do the plot categories apply? Polti's enigma takes the form of a strange request with an aura of credibility, with a bold play to the artist's ego. What painter does not want to believe that he or she has unknown admirers, even long-term ones, anxious to pay four-figure amounts for his or her work? And isn't it endearing that the attorney wanted to surprise her husband with a gift? We have subterfuge, disguise, and pretense, coupled with temptation. The hero is tested, but helpers emerge: the alert bankers who immediately perceived the bogus nature of the check; the clumsy accomplice who blurted out that the woman's real occupation was "computer expert" even though she was masquerading as an attorney; last, the real attorney who immediately recognized that she too was a victim of a scam. They assist him the hero in solving the riddle, and he is "rescued."

Returning to our earlier delineation of the villain-victim-hero paradigm, we can assign the categories as follows: the villain is the deceiving woman, the victims are my friend and the real attorney, and the hero is the bank. Let's further suppose that your company specializes in exposing swindles of this sort. You would be able to exploit this anecdote to show that your business could be an überhero by thwarting dishonesty either through a technological filter, a staff education program or both, so that would-be victims would not have to rely on the kindness of bankers who may or may not be schooled in these matters.

Now do you see why this seemingly literary and abstract approach can have direct practical applications? Try to choose a few of the categories above at random and create a story that expresses the essence of the drama in your company. No wonder that English majors sometimes have an edge in business!

Whatever you do, keep pressing forward. As Picasso said, "Inspiration exists . . . but it has to find you working."[20] Norman Mailer, who wrote a book about Picasso, understood this all too well:

> I think from the time I was seventeen, I had no larger desire in life than to be a writer, and I wrote a great deal. Through my Sophomore, Junior, and Senior years at Harvard, and the summers between, I must have written thirty or forty short stories, a couple of plays, a novel, then a short novel, and then a long novel . . .[21] I'm now eighty, but some people still regard me as a wild man. Even at my peak, that was only five to ten percent of my nature. The rest was work. I like work.[22]

We often regard Shakespeare as the towering genius of literary creativity, yet we forget how much *time* he must have spent at his desk. All told, he wrote 37 plays, some 150 sonnets, and long narrative poems—nearly 900,000 words—while acting and running a theater company.[23] He accomplished all this by the time he was 49, when he reportedly retired! The seemingly indefatigable playwright was dead three years later, possibly from exhaustion. Genius, certainly, but without the sweat his gray matter would have mattered not.

ELEVEN

Body Language, Vocal Techniques, and Stage Fright
Your Body Speaks, Your Voice Gestures

Like it or not, deep communication often occurs without words. Nonverbal cues can be more truthful and expressive than spoken language. Most voters, for instance, could choose their favorite political candidate with the sound turned off on the TV. Body language has vast impact in job interviews too. Imagine that your colleagues tell you that Ms. X is not only eminently qualified, but likeable. They ask you to have lunch with her before a decision is made. You will probably make up your mind in the first 30 seconds. Does she "look professional"? Is her handshake firm? Does she slurp when she drinks her tea? These criteria may be unfair, but they're powerful nonetheless. As a species we are conditioned to interpret visual cues, perhaps because our ancestors had to determine whether a nearby beast was regarding them with curiosity, or with hunger. Since cavemen and cavewomen couldn't interrogate animals (a difficulty still faced in veterinary medicine), they relied on their eyes to make the determination. An animal seeking a meal *stalks*. A bored creature merely *walks*.

Modern-day executives in my consulting practice often tell me they have been taught body language "rules" such as "lean forward to signal interest and command"; "sit up straight with the spine perfectly vertical"; "don't gesture too much, or too widely," and so on. I tell them point blank: my only rule is that there are no rules. Simply speak your native body language. That's a fancy way of saying: act as you ordinarily do. Actually that's not entirely accurate. You need to be the most effective, boldest self you can be—but within the confines of your personality as it normally expresses itself physically.

Many years ago, during graduate school, I worked in restaurants. I wasn't sure how to carry a tray of drinks without spilling them while wending through a crowded dining room. "Do you want to know the secret?" a more experienced waiter asked. I nodded vigorously. "Just walk," he said. The trick is to concentrate on the room, not on the tray. If you watch the drinks too closely, you'll be self-conscious and you are almost guaranteed to cause a mishap because your movements will be stiff and mechanical. This is a good metaphor for body language in general.

There is, however, one rule that is applicable in almost all cultures: Eye contact is not only important but *essential*. When you maintain it, you create a connection. If not, a major disconnect results.[1] Eye contact has broad impact: it facilitates learning for students and enhances communication with infants, who instinctively pay more attention to those who gaze into their eyes.[2] If you establish and hold eye contact with a business associate, you will gain an aura of power. In a tense situation, he or she who looks away first cedes ground. There is such a thing, though, as "moral (i.e. limited) looking time," which is zero seconds on a crowded elevator, or a very short time on the street in most big cities, otherwise your glance may be perceived as a challenge. In fact, studies show that most people can tolerate just 3.2 seconds of staring from a stranger.[3] In a normal conversation, we tend to maintain eye contact 30–60 percent of the time. When you are speaking to a group, be sure to sweep your eyes back and forth—while occasionally landing on individuals. "Touching down" will create the impression that you are speaking to each person in the audience. Most speakers tend to look in one direction only, either to the right, or the left. If they do swivel their heads, they tend to move in a narrow arc. I always counsel clients to sweep through a full 180-degree span to encompass everyone, even those seated in the front corners of a room. Missing any sector of the audience will make the people there feel disenfranchised. Be as inclusive as possible.

Yes, the eyes have it, and not just in person. When I am on one of those dreaded conference calls, I try to aim my gaze toward the phone in the middle of the room. I feel that my energy and attention will follow. I can't prove it, but I'm willing to bet that the people on the other side of the voice pod will be more receptive if I pay attention to the direction of my eyesight. Moreover, I believe that I am more focused on them if I am looking at the phone. I recently listened to a webinar that was quite informative. When I stared at the screen, my attention was on the content. When I looked away, even though I was trying to listen, my mind was elsewhere. Please test this yourself and determine if I am correct.

I need to take a moment to address some gender differences in body language—a subject of some sensitivity. Many female clients have told me that other advisors, generally male, admonished them this way: "Whatever you do, don't use your hands when you speak." What is the basis for this "wisdom"? Those "gurus" claim, "Big gestures will make you look aggressive or unprofessional!" Huh? These so-called consultants tell women to leave their arms at their sides, or, worse, to clasp their hands in front. If you don't believe this, ask the women in your office. Probably three-quarters of women executives will say they received gender-biased instruction to remain statue-like—instruction that men rarely receive. This is sexist and demeaning. Likewise, many female clients say they were instructed (usually early in their careers, by male managers) to grip the sides of the podium firmly so they will appear more "authoritative." Gravitas, however, emanates from who you are and what you say rather than your ability to become a monolith with a column of walnut. Too much poise = too little passion. Podiums are nothing more than barriers. So walk away and reveal yourself to the audience. We can't read your body language if we can't see your body. (This applies to men and women alike, of course.)

Studies have actually shown that women are naturally more fluent in body language than men. They are said to be more accurate and sensitive in identifying facial expressions, for instance. This advantage manifests itself across many cultures and has been shown to begin as early as age three. One study shows that women are more accurate than men 80 percent of the time in overall nonverbal sensitivity. Moreover, they have more gray matter in the sections of the limbic system involved in emotional processing.[4] My own experience confirms their superiority in the realm of body language. I have found that women are more adept not only at receiving nonverbal messages but at transmitting them as well. Both of these skills provide an essential edge in business. Therefore, women should not rein in but "rein out." When it comes to gesturing, they win the arms race, uh, hands down. And consultants who don't celebrate this should never be invited back to your company again.

For all of us, regardless of gender, gestures should emanate from the inside out, not the outside in. In other words, they should flow naturally from the core of your personality. If your body language is "quiet"—meaning that you don't tend to gesticulate—then by all means don't force your hands to move when you speak. Otherwise you'll look like you're chopping the air for no apparent reason, in the manner of a hyperkinetic slapstick comedian. Yet the converse is true too. If you tend to gesture passionately and you restrain yourself, you will look like you're caught in an invisible straightjacket. Audiences can quickly perceive if your physical demeanor is authentic, or not. It's very hard to fool people when it comes to nonverbal communication. Any "performance" creates a barrier. So don't act; just be.

Now you may be wondering how you can determine what your natural physical demeanor may be. As odd as it may sound, you need to be analytical about being spontaneous. The next time you are speaking to someone in a relaxed business setting—say a conversation with a colleague at work—pretend that the scene is a video and freeze the interaction mid-sentence. Now notice where your hands are and how you're sitting. If you are in the midst of a wide gesture, chances are you tend to gesticulate expansively. If you are leaning to one side, then you probably don't have perfect posture. If your hands are folded, then that's your style. And that shows what your "native body language" may be.

Whether you're at a podium, standing in a conference room, or sitting at a table, pay attention to the way you start. Think of your initial pose as your "home base position." If you seem uptight and withholding, perhaps with your forearms or palms velcroed to the table in a way that permits no movement, or with your knuckles gripping the side of the lectern, the audience may sense that you are tense. That will set up a negative feedback loop because you will in turn realize that they think you're nervous, which will make them sense your discomfort further and so on. Instead of this vicious cycle of negative impressions, you can set up a virtuous cycle if you're relaxed from the start. Then the audience will feel your comfort, share it, and reflect it back.

Whenever I speak, and this is the only "precept" I follow, I envision the way I want to appear at the outset and then consciously assume that pose, but only for a few seconds. If I don't start with a tranquil physical attitude, I risk looking (and more important *feeling*) diffident. Generally, the position I choose is relaxed: hands reaching out (and not stuck in my pockets!). I also try to walk forward, toward the audience, because it energizes me. After that, I let my body and hands go where they will.

By the way, don't assume that nonverbal cues matter only in person. If you're relaxed on the phone, it will be "visible" in your voice. We don't need to see the speaker to figure out if he or she is engaged or disengaged. That's why mute buttons fool no one on conference calls. We somehow just *know* when someone has tuned out to check his e-mail, don't we?

I firmly believe, as I mentioned earlier, that there are virtually no hard and fast dogma with regard to body language, though there are some general recommendations to consider. These are not rules, just suggestions.

- Count points off on your fingers for emphasis, if appropriate.

- Consider opening your arms wide, with your palms toward the audience on occasion. This conveys openness and inclusion.

- Walk forward, even into the audience, to remove barriers. Don't be afraid to pace around the room. Sometimes the direction you walk can speak volumes, however. A professor I know realized that she always retreated in the face of a tough question. After recognizing this bad habit, she learned to literally stand her ground.

- When you are listening, mirror the body language of the speaker to establish rapport. This often happens unconsciously when communication is purring along. (Successful salespeople engage in this sort of chameleonic behavior in a conscious or manipulative way, so beware.) If you are imitating the other person, then you're silently demonstrating that that you like him or her. If you nod, by the way, you might encourage the other person to nod, which further enhances a bond.

I'll digress for a moment with two amusing stories about head movements. A few years ago I traveled to Albania for a political consulting assignment. I discovered that people there shake their heads when listening. I had read about this in guide books so I knew what to expect, but still found it disconcerting. Were my clients displeased? Not at all. Their head shakes meant "I agree," or at least, "I am listening closely." The second story concerns the late behavioral psychologist B. F. Skinner, who believed in operant conditioning (that is, that we can be taught to behave a certain way with positive or negative reinforcement). One of my professors in college sat next to Skinner at a lecture. The famed behaviorist said, "I'll show you that my theories work. Every time the speaker raises his right hand, I'll nod vigorously." Sure enough, the lecturer was soon raising his right hand repeatedly, apparently responding to the cues. At the end, however, he came over and told my professor, "Skinner is easy to please. All you have to do is raise your right hand."

Here are a few more observations, this time concerning behaviors to avoid. Again, these are merely suggestions, utterly dependent on context and personal style.

- Avoid folding your arms across your torso, as if caressing yourself. That may make you look uncertain, lonely, or self-centered. Folding your arms may also convey disinterest. (Some people assume that position all the time, particularly if they are cold, in which case it will appear natural). By the way, if you look out and see a skein of folded arms in the audience, do not assume that everyone is shivering. Perhaps they are shutting down. In that case, confront the situation directly. Ask, "Am I not being clear? Did I lose you?" Or perhaps just pick up the pace.

- Do not touch your face with your hands. This may be a defensive pose, especially if you reach across to the opposite cheek. Plus it's distracting.

- Don't clasp your hands, as this might convey closure.

- Don't fail to complete a handshake. As a general rule, extend your hand until you lock thumbs with the other person. If you don't reach far enough, then the palms won't meld, and you'll seem tentative.

- Don't pull down the back of your jacket and sit on it (à la *Broadcast News*). It will remove slack in the material and square your shoulders. How can you move freely if your clothing is taut across your back? (This caveat applies equally to men and women.)

- Avoid sitting or standing up straight. This generally seems studied. In the armed forces, a stiff back may be normal but that pose will look awkward in civilian life. In my experience, though, former ballet dancers are the exception. They have an enviable ability to enter a room with upright posture, then sit down without leaning too far from the vertical. And they make it look effortless! I fear that the non-dancers among us would be unable to do this with anywhere near their aplomb. (I am the father of a young woman who spent many years as a pre-professional ballerina, so I can generally spot a dancer at 50 paces.) If you want to see how artificial a deliberate pose can look, assume a ramrod-straight posture and ask those who know you how you appear. I can guarantee that they will say that you seem ill at ease and unnatural.

- Avoid repetitive gestures such as licking your lips, biting your nails, chewing on your glasses, scratching your head, twirling your hair, bouncing your foot, jangling coins in your pocket, or playing with a glass, ring, or bracelet. These habits convey nervousness. If I am holding a pen in my hand, I tend to click and unclick it, which will be quite annoying. Knowing this, I always leave pens on the table.

- Staying behind your desk when speaking to colleagues will create a barrier. Instead, walk around and sit next to them to create more intimacy.

Before we leave the subject of body language, I need to debunk a myth you may have heard that nonverbals (i.e., tone of voice and body language) account for 93 percent of the meaning in a presentation and that content is responsible for just 7 percent. This is a misinterpretation and expansion of the research of Albert Mehrabian, a retired psychology professor from UCLA. Witness his cautionary message:

> Please note that this and other equations regarding relative import-ance of verbal and nonverbal messages were derived from experi-ments dealing with communications of feelings and attitudes (i.e., like-dislike). Unless a communicator is talking about their feelings or attitudes, these equations are not applicable.[5]

Although the exact percentage of meaning generated by nonverbal cues may be uncertain, the physical component is surely important. We need only look at common idiomatic expressions in our language to see how many somatic references and attitudes abound. Here's a partial list:

- Shouldering a burden
- Facing up to facts
- Keeping your chin up
- Gritting your teeth
- Keeping a stiff upper lip
- Catching one's eye
- Shrugging it off
- Elbowing your way to top
- Bare-knuckled tactics

One last tip that I learned at a recent industry conference: When you're networking with someone you just met at an event, look down and observe which way his or her toes are pointing. If they are aimed toward you, then the person may be interested in the conversation. If they are pointed away, then the listener may be ready to leave. (I have no scientific basis for these conclusions, but they appear to make sense.) Famed media philosopher Marshall McLuhan once said that the medium is the message. I paraphrase that as follows with regard to body language: the *movement* may be the message. And now we move on to the human voice.

A VOICE IN THE MATTER

When I started my first job as a TV reporter, my skills as a narrator left a lot to be desired. So much so that the news director sent me to a voice coach, who was kind, but no-nonsense. She greeted me with this observation: "Remember, Greg, you have no charm." After my initial shock wore off, I asked what she meant. "I'm not saying you're not a nice guy," she explained. "It's just that you need to make the audience come to you. You're reaching out too much." She was trying to tell me that the best speakers are not necessarily the most humble. They may not be arrogant, but they are certainly not modest either. The tacit message should be: "Listen to me, or you'll miss something." Try to think of your voice as a font with different variations that will change the emphasis. For instance, sometimes your point may be roman; **sometimes bold;** *AND FOR EXTRA WEIGHT, BOLD, UNDERLINED, ITALIC, AND ALL CAPS*. You don't have to increase the volume to drive your message. Simply modifying the pitch and speed will suffice. If you speak slowly and deliberately, you'll be signaling that your words are essential at that moment. Decide what to underscore vocally, just as you decide what to highlight in the story itself. For instance, if you say, "In the next year, 39% of the audience will be promoted," then slow down when you come to the key statistic. Say it this way: "In the next year [roman font, followed by a pause] *39%* [bold, italic, and underlined] of you will be promoted."

Don't turn a statement into a question, with rising intonation. Make a bold, declarative assertion, like this: "This story will be **captivating** and **emotional**." If your voice rises sharply at the end of the sentence, you will sound as if as you are seeking reassurance: "This ad will be . . . captivating and emotional?"

For both men and women, in-to-na-tion—the way the pitch in your voice rises and falls—is all important. In fact, a study by Professor Kathleen Dolan shows that voters prefer the candidate of either gender with the more "bassy" voice: "Low voices are just more pleasing," she says. "Think Barry White versus Pee-wee Herman."[6] By the way, people often wonder why they sound different when recorded. The reason is that we experience our own voices in two ways: as sound waves striking our eardrums (the way others hear us) but also as vibrations rumbling through the tissue of the head and neck. It's as if we are listening to a guitar, from inside the instrument. When heard from the outside, on tape, the resonance seems to decrease.

The human voice, controlled by the laryngeal nerve, is a truly intricate mechanism. It "has some of the most complex and dense wiring in the body, roughly fifty times as dense as the nerves to the hand or the tongue," according to Dr. Steven Zeitels, a surgeon specializing in vocal repairs at Massachusetts General Hospital in Boston.[7] The ligaments and muscles around the voice box can stretch like an elastic band, with the ability to rev up from 75 to 1,500 vibrations a second "almost instantaneously."[8] In everyday speech, men's vocal cords vibrate about 100 times a second—producing a more "bassy" sound, while women's oscillate about 200 times a second, with more soprano results.[9] My voice coach convinced me, by the way, that I was relying too much on bass sounds. "The treble part of your range is quite pleasant, Greg," she told me. I realized that going up and down the scale for variety or emphasis makes a great deal of sense, for men and women alike. When I was falling into a low pitch and staying there, I tended to keep my chin close to my chest, which impeded airflow.

That would be detrimental because we can think of the human voice as a pipeful of air powering the vocal cords. If you're not breathing properly, you're not speaking properly. You can quickly hear the effect of copious airflow if you place your palm in front of your mouth and say the first ten letters of the alphabet out loud. You feel your breath on your skin, right? If you try to speak while inhaling, however, you'll see that no sound will emerge. The diaphragm is the engine behind this wonderful apparatus. Learn how to use it. Place your palm on your belly and inhale. You should feel your stomach pushing outward as your diaphragm heads toward the floor. This movement will increase the volume of your chest cavity, and air will be sucked in because nature tends to fill a vacuum. (The process works in the opposite direction when you exhale.) It may seem most natural to take a deep breath by puffing out your chest, but the effect is the opposite of what you might except. Your voice will sound hollow. If you inhale with your diaphragm, however, spoken words will have force and timber. That's how actors ensure that the people in the back of the theater can hear them. They are propelling their words, not shouting. If they did yell, then the people in the front rows would have to cover their ears. One extra observation: breathe at the places where you would put commas or periods in your presentation. (If you pause in the middle of a sentence you will sound tentative.)

In addition to adding timber to your voice, deep breathing has other health benefits such as lowering your heart rate and your blood pressure. If you have trouble mastering the mechanics, think of a pitcher of water. You fill it from the bottom up, but empty it from the top down. Your breath works the same way: inhale from the belly up, and exhale from the neck down.

Try to be confident. You know your subject. You've researched it. So proclaim your thoughts with attitude. On the other hand, don't smack expressive words too much. The language has been around longer than you have, and it does a lot of the work for you.

Just remember: you have no charm.

PROPS PROPEL YOUR MESSAGE

Let's go all the way back to 1783. The Revolutionary War had just ended. American soldiers had been fighting for eight years. The new U.S. government was broke. The men had not been paid for some time and they feared that the promise of lifelong pensions, equal to half their salaries, would be abandoned. Mutiny was in the air at the army camp in Newburg, New York. There was a call for a meeting, postponed for four days by a commander in chief by the name of George Washington, no doubt to defuse the tension.

When the meeting day came, Washington stunned the officers when he arrived. They had not expected him. He spoke briefly but passionately, imploring the men "not to open the floodgates of civil discord and deluge our rising empire in blood."[10] They seemed unimpressed by these eloquent words, however, which did nothing to soothe their hunger or fatigue. Washington then fumbled as he opened a letter from Congress. At first, he squinted as he struggled to read the tiny writing. He took out his reading glasses, which the men had never seen him use. Then came the coup de grâce.

"Gentlemen," Washington said, "you will permit me to put on my spectacles, for I have not only grown gray but almost blind in the service of my country."[11] The men cried. Washington finished the letter. Then he left in silence. Conspiracy terminated. The hero of this story, as you now realize, was the prop. Did Washington really need his glasses or was he just acting? I would guess that this was pure political theater.

A prop can carry enormous dramatic weight, far beyond the ounces it would measure on the scale. I have found that most executives are reluctant to use props; or if they do, they handle them awkwardly. Many forget to look at them when they discuss them. Instead they hold them aloft as if they have no significance. *Showcase* your product, as if it were your newborn. Revel in it. Stare at it. Move it around in the air. Churchill had his own version of props: heavy-rimmed black glasses and a cigar.[12] (The glasses would still work today, but the cigar would be taboo, even if unlit.) Alfred Hitchcock also understood the power of props. In *Spellbound*, for instance, we see a menacing close-up of a giant hand with a gun. In *Suspicion*, Gary Grant carries a glass of milk on a tray upstairs to his wife. There is a luminous light *inside the glass* to focus our attention on it. The drink, in a sense, becomes the "villain" of the scene because we share his wife's fear that he is trying to poison her. (I won't spoil the ending, but suffice it to say that Cary Grant would never have played a criminal. A rogue perhaps, but not a criminal.) The point is that a prop can become a character in your story, so "cast" it wisely and introduce it at the right time in your "screenplay." Don't hide it, highlight it.

ARE YOUR KNEES SHAKING? CONQUERING STAGE FRIGHT

Public speaking is downright scary. Jerry Seinfeld once joked that the person delivering a eulogy envies the corpse.[13] Your brain probably works extremely well until you stand up to make a speech. If it's any comfort, though, many famous people have suffered from stage fright, including Adele, Andrea Bocelli, Laurence Olivier, Rihanna, and Barbra Streisand. It is arguably one of the most common anxieties, afflicting just about every live and sentient being. But it can be conquered. Here are some tips:

- Do not try to repress your inner critic. You know, the one who says, "You're going to embarrass yourself. Remember when you flubbed the poetry reading in 6th grade? etc." Instead of squelching that voice, talk back to it and debate it into a stalemate, if not submission.[14]

- Embrace the anxiety by channeling nervous energy into performance intensity. Force the butterflies in your stomach into formation. Stage fright, like guilt or envy, is a useless emotion that ricochets around inside your being. Rather than holding it in, let it out, and translate it into a vector directed toward the audience.

- Just before you start to speak, call to mind a situation when you were at your best and when you performed well. Or picture a pleasant scene, such as a walk on the beach during an island vacation. Sometimes it helps to think of a child in your family who wouldn't care if you failed. There is strong evidence that thoughts, what psychologists call cognitions, can alter your feelings. If you change the way you think, you can in turn modify attitudes, beliefs, feelings, and even your brain chemistry.[15]

- Recognize that the audience cannot read your mind. They will not be able to see your shaking hands or hear your pounding heart. Your inner turmoil will be invisible.

- Prepare early and often. There is a direct relationship between practice and your confidence at the podium. Take a lesson from James Earl Jones, who went to extremes when he prepared for the role of the brute Lenny in *Of Mice and Men*. Jones went so far as to take psychological tests at a medical facility—in costume and in character. His "performance" was so skillful that the grad student who gave him the tests told his professor that they should admit him because he was exhibiting violent tendencies.[16]

- Practice in front of a mirror, in the car, or with family members and colleagues. Videotape yourself and play it back. This may be painful, but necessary. You need to see your faults. Remember: If you prepare, you can say the first thing that comes to mind and you will sound intelligent. If you "wing it," your first comment might be disastrous.

- Do not memorize your presentation. If you try to do so and forget your "lines" you will enter a world of pain. Instead, make an outline and follow that instead. It's quite acceptable to refer to notes. You may consider just memorizing the opening line, however, so you'll know *exactly* how to start. That can be reassuring.

- Make the space your own. Visit the site of your presentation *ahead of time*, preferably the night before. Walk the floor and determine how you will interact with the setting.

- Concentrate on your expertise: After all, you know what you're talking about. Isn't that why you're speaking in front of this audience in the first place?

- We repeat: Breathe deeply, from the diaphragm.

- Tense up all your muscles, then release them. Yawn. Roll your head around. (Don't do this in front of the audience! Retreat to a private space instead.)

- If you fumble, just move on. Even the most fluid actors jam and stammer occasionally.

A word about microphones: Use wireless mikes (lavaliers) for maximum mobility, but learn how to turn them off—especially when attending to personal needs (or engaging in what you think is a private conversation). Some wireless mikes have a range of 100 yards. Need we say more? Also, position the "lav" in the center of your chest, near your sternum. If you're going to be on a dais, audio people tend to place the mike on the side closest to the moderator, which is fine as long as you are facing in that direction. But if you turn the other way, the audio will dim and may become inaudible. For that matter, even if the mike is in the center of your chest, turn your body when you look in a different direction to ensure that your voice will still be captured. A hand-held mike presents other challenges. Hold it about a foot from your chin and aim it toward your mouth at all times. There is nothing worse than a speaker who keeps the mike so far from his lips that the sound dies. On the other hand, don't move it too close, otherwise your voice will be loud and harsh. Practice this until it becomes second nature because you won't be able to tell the difference when you're on stage. The audience may be too polite to shout out, "Can't hear you." By the way, there is an artful way to grasp a mike. When I started in television I was so nervous that I squeezed it so hard that my knuckles were white. A great cameraman by the name of Rich Rumppe taught me to cradle the mike gently and leave some daylight between my fingers. You'll look much more relaxed if you do that.

One last pointer: Bear in mind that the audience wants you to triumph, not fizzle. Remember that as you look out at their faces. Think of them as friends.

TWELVE

Social Media Relations

Printing Presses, Water Coolers, and Crises

When I first heard of social media, I thought the term was redundant. "Aren't all media social?" I wondered. But then I realized that is not the case at all. "Traditional" media move in one direction as they push content from TV stations, radio stations, or printing presses toward the consumer. For the first time readers (or viewers or listeners) can now speak *to one another* through social media—creating in effect a water cooler discussion writ large. At first businesses saw these venues as just another advertising channel but then the smart ones came to understand that their presence needs to be subtle to avoid violating unwritten rules of decorum. Venues like Facebook and Twitter are great places to listen first, then start a conversation where the dialogue is already occurring. Moreover, you can unearth new ideas and trends, forge connections with audiences in novel ways, bring traffic and attention to your company and strengthen your brand.[1] At the moment, 8 out of 10 people in America have a social media account[2] and the number of users on what I will call the "Big Four" is staggering: some 500 million for LinkedIn, 330 million for Twitter, 1 billion on Instagram (owned by Facebook) and Facebook itself, which boasts over 2 billion users. You may be wondering if posting is worth the trouble, and what the ROI may be. Yet according to Sree Sreenivasan, a widely regarded social media expert, that's like asking what the ROI may be for your cell phone.[3] Does it really matter? Don't avoid a useful tool just because the metrics may not be clear.

No matter what venue you choose, there are rules to follow: First, ask for nothing. Second, try to create posts that could be described with any combination of these adjectives: useful, helpful, informative, relevant, practical, actionable, timely, generous, credible, brief, entertaining, fun and occasionally funny.[4] Sreenivasan explains it this way:

> Whenever anyone asks me, "How can I get more followers on Twitter, more followers on Facebook, more connections?" I say, "Take your last 50 Tweets or Facebook postings. Cut and paste them into a Word document. And then, take those words [above]. Put little tick marks next to each posting for these attributes."[5]

One sure fire way to get traction is to be a pointer, that is, to refer people to articles, blogs or statistics that are valuable, rather than merely publicizing your own activities.[6] If you have established yourself as a thought leader, or are trying to become one, then share your expertise, not your accomplishments.[7]

Here are some specific tips about the various venues:

- LinkedIn is the "quintessential professional network," most suitable for career development rather than job hunting. If you are writing an article for this venue, add a catchy headline and a picture and promote it through other media.

- Instagram, at 1 billion users, is now "increasingly part of the business world"[8] and its platform of photos, captions, and videos is especially effective. The service also has a feature called stories that allows you to post sequences with multiple photos that last for just 24 hours. You can also create a narrative with the captions, or curate content from users.[9] (When in doubt about visuals, by the way, use the "flat-lay" style with an overhead shot of skillfully arranged items on your desk, a relevant article or book, for instance. Shoot horizontally because the image is less likely to be truncated when uploaded.[10])

- Twitter recently doubled its character maximum from 140 to 280—which I decry, as I mentioned, because the prior brevity enforced greater clarity and discipline. When you tweet, add a photo or a video, or even numerous photos at once, which will vastly increase the appeal. And if you retweet something, add a "quote tweet" with your own thoughts. You can also send a "tweet storm"—a barrage of messages to emphasize your point (like a certain prominent person we know!)

- On Facebook, the grandma of all social media, you can also employ consecutive posts to build a story, or you can create a relevant photo album. Facebook live may be useful if you are trying to publicize an event as it is occurring, but it is hard to attract an audience. If the viewers miss the beginning, you may need to repeat the introduction periodically to bring them up to speed.

Whatever you do, try not to place too much emphasis on the number of followers or friends you have on the various media. Sreenivasan calls this the "million follower fallacy" in that you "might have a million of them, but that doesn't mean they care about what you're doing."[11] Bear in mind, however, that social media tools are free. Many businesses experience measurable progress with as little as 15 minutes a day of effort. It's far from a full-time job. But "think more about authenticity than about how to position [your] brand."[12]

Before we leave the subject of social media, let's consider the possibility that they create the same sort of "impromptu and uncontrolled" interactions between customers and businesses that we see in improvisational theater, as explained in a fascinating new article called "Brand Performances in Social Media."[13] This process permits co-creation of the brand, with positive or negative results emanating (1) from conversation or provocative dialogue (witness Dove's Real Beauty campaign that encouraged women to celebrate their natural appearance)[14] or (2) from the "fan who praises the brand, [the] evangelist who preaches [it], [the] critic who challenges [it, or the] hacker who slanders [it]."[15] These interactions come to resemble a pinball machine: "The brand owner continues to manage the ball (the narrative) with the agile use of flippers but the ball often does not go where the owner intends."[16] Moreover, roles blur since business and customers can both play director, actor, and spectator in this arena.[17] In fact, the old lexicon no longer applies:

> The current marketing and branding terminology still reflects the one-to-many thinking, with its use of the military language: target group, campaign, positioning, strategy, tactic, or planning. . . . [T]hese military marketing terms are no longer suitable in the era of democratized and interactive media, where the consumer not only responds to branding communication but also helps co-create it.[18]

No longer is marketing a one-to-many phenomenon; now it's many-to-many. We spoke earlier about intertextuality, with media and stories intersecting with one another. Now that term also has new meaning in that anecdotes, websites, Facebook, Twitter, and conversation converge, diverge, and reconverge in a "polylogue" that can get away from us unless we take pains to be visible and participate. This is why it's a misconception to treat communication on social media as a strategy or even as a tactic. It is neither. It's a place to listen first and participate second.

CRISES DON'T JUST HAPPEN TO OTHERS

No book on storytelling would be complete without addressing crises, which flare on traditional and social media alike. There's an old Texas saying that during a crisis "you'll be like a coyote in a hailstorm. Just hunker down and be pelted." There are ways to dodge some of the hailstones, however. The first step is anticipation. Here is a list[19] of egregious problems that may visit your company:

- acquisition
- age discrimination
- bankruptcy
- boycotts
- bribery
- chemical spills or leaks
- contamination
- cybersecurity issues
- domestic violence
- drug trafficking
- earthquakes
- embezzlement
- explosions
- fatalities
- fires
- floods
- hurricanes
- insider trading
- kickbacks
- kidnapping
- lawsuits
- layoffs
- mergers

- murders
- negative legislation
- plant closings
- product failures
- protests
- racial issues
- robberies
- rumors
- sexual discrimination
- sexual harassment or assault
- strikes
- substance abuse
- suicides
- takeovers
- tax problems
- terrorism
- tornadoes
- toxic waste
- transportation accidents
- whistleblowers (justified or not)
- workplace violence

Should one of these calamities land at your office door, there are simple but effective rules to follow. First and foremost, express sympathy for any injured parties. Doing so is not an admission of guilt; it's an expression of your humanity. Beyond this: You MUST respond, probably in one of three ways:

- "We know what happened and here's all the information.
- We don't know everything at this time. Here's what we do know. We'll find out more and keep you informed.
- We have no idea, but we'll find out and tell you."[20]

Public and media alike can forgive many transgressions, except arrogance or indifference. If your initial response is lacking, then you will spawn a secondary crisis that will double the damage to your reputation. In any event the media will want to know:

- What happened and why
- Whether there were any deaths or injuries
- Who or what is responsible
- What is being done about it
- When it will be over
- The extent of the damage and danger
- Whether it happened before
- Whether there were any warning signs[21]

I have no animosity against lawyers, but they tend to advise clients to remain silent during crises, which is counterproductive. In a courtroom, you may be innocent until proven guilty, but in the court of public opinion you are guilty until proven innocent. Governmental agencies, on the other hand, tend to follow an equally deleterious course. Here's a parody of their typical statements: Week 1: "It never happened"; Week 2: "It might have happened, but we didn't do it"; Week 3: "We weren't responsible, but we'll never do it again."

It is important to *anticipate* crises. Set up a chain of command and make sure that contact information for key personnel is shared. Designate a spokesperson, preferably in senior management, just in case. Unfortunately, most businesses don't establish a crisis plan until an emergency strikes, which is too late.

Here are a few more suggestions:

- Be emphatic: "We really want the public to know _____; Our number-one priority is _____; It is important to note that_____."
- Don't bring up past good deeds: nobody cares about the little league team you sponsor when people are injured.
- Avoid a protracted discussion about the incident; instead focus on future remedies or investigations.
- Remember that companies which enjoy good communication with the press beforehand tend to weather crises more effectively.

Vicious rumors deserve special attention. Here are examples of patently false stories that have plagued responsible companies:

- Corona Beer contains urine
- Procter & Gamble's old logo was satanist
- Coca-Cola contains bug-based dye

Again, the above stories are completely false. Yet unfortunately "the bigger the company—the more iconic the brand—the more persistently it is dogged by rumor and conspiracy theories."[22] An MIT study showed that popular rumors that had been fact-checked and determined to be false not only spread "significantly farther, faster, deeper and more broadly than the truth" but reached 1,500 people six times faster.[23] Rumors tend to fall into these categories:

- Intentional
- Premature fact (i.e., a leak of the truth)
- Malicious
- Outrageous (so much so that people assume it has to be factual)
- Nearly true
- Birthday (arising repeatedly)[24]

Possible recommendations for dealing with rumors:

- Publish accurate information as soon as possible to contradict the story
- Deny the rumor vigorously
- Find an expert to refute it
- Buy ads to convey positive messages[25]

Let's turn to two classic crisis case studies that remain instructive. The first concerns the Johnson & Johnson Tylenol scare in 1982—an example that all should follow. We'll tell the story in the historical present.

Seven people die from cyanide poisoning from tampered Tylenol bottles. James Burke, the CEO at the time, is out in front and available. 180,000 stories run nationally in newspapers; the company fields 2,000 calls from the media. Burke says, "We were all scared to death."

J&J has one overriding goal: warning the public. It recalls the product (some 31 million bottles) and asks Americans for their trust—appealing to a sense of fair play. In six weeks, Tylenol is reborn, in tamper-resistant bottles. Not only does the product recover, but it *surpasses* its previous market share.

A leading TV personality invites Burke onto his show and gives him permission to use the podium as a "48-minute commercial" because he sees J&J as a *victim*! Burke says, "I think the answer comes down to the value system. . . . What's right works. It really does. The cynics will tell you it doesn't, but they're wrong. . . . All of the previous managements who built this corporation handed us, on a silver platter, the most powerful tool you could possibly have," that is *"real, palpable, bankable trust. . . .* Without a moral center, you can swim in chaos."

By the way, the case has never been solved and the murderer or murderers are still at large. Cost to J&J: $100 million (in 1982 dollars).[26]

And now we turn to the sad case of the *Exxon Valdez* tanker, from 1989. This is an example to *avoid.*

Exxon's ship crashes into a reef off the coast of Alaska and dumps 11 million gallons of crude oil into Prince William Sound—enough to fill 17 Olympic-sized swimming pools. Some 2 million birds, seals, sea lions, otters, and other animals die, not to mention countless fish.

Four days after the spill, Exxon CEO Lawrence Rawl explains that he did not travel to Alaska because he feels "technologically obsolete." (He has been at the company for 40 years at that point.) He later issues a statement informing the public of the chemicals that would be used in the cleanup, but makes no apology to fishermen and shows no reaction. Ten days after spill, the company takes out full-page ads expressing concern and promising to clean up the site, but assuming no responsibility. Three weeks after the spill, Rawl finally goes to Alaska.[27]

"If the media had captured, on video and film, the CEO on the site at Prince William Sound holding an oil-covered bird in his hand and looking as if he were crying, the entire story would be told differently today."[28] Instead, to this day the phrase *"Exxon Valdez"* is synonymous with environmental disaster.

THIRTEEN

More Stories to Emulate

Prevail with a Tale

This chapter offers more intriguing examples of stories well told and challenges well met—further illustrations of the villains-victims-heroes model.

ATTORNEY AT LAW AND AT NARRATIVE

Daniel Dwyer, a lawyer at Murphy & King, a boutique Boston firm specializing in business litigation, bankruptcy, corporate law, and white-collar defense, began his career as a federal agent with the Drug Enforcement Administration. He sees similarities between those two realms:

> Many business cases amount to a game of cops and robbers, somebody did something wrong, somebody cheated you or somebody is trying to get away with something, and that has to be stopped. . . . It's not as decisive as an arrest or a raid or a high speed chase, certainly not that colorful, but in a way it's similar. You're trying to make someone stop what he's doing or prevent him from getting away with it.[1]

Dan regards his work as an attempt to tell the client's story:

> I like to think of this exercise in portrayal or trial as a movie or a storyboard, and our job is to portray the facts, what you have lived through, to a jury or a judge who wasn't there . . . and to make them almost see your experience as if it were a movie playing in their own mind. They have to reimagine where you were, what you went through, what somebody did to you, and how it hurts financially, usually—but otherwise too. Beneath the financial skin of a case

there is humanity and emotion, and that is not to be exploited so much as explained and felt. We have to communicate all of that as you have lived it and a lot of that involves peeling away the things that either aren't true or are irrelevant or are advanced by an opponent for purely tactical purposes.[2] . . . The goal is not to fake perfection or to tell a false story. The goal is to find out what is true in your client's story, to get into that part of the case, so to speak, to make that the center of the case, and to push the case out from the inside from the place where your client is right.[3]

In litigation, Dwyer believes you "have to be someone's champ" and take the clients' affairs and livelihoods seriously.[4] He also says that he never met a true story he couldn't tell."[5] Sometimes that calls for a tough posture, however:

When we roll our cannons up to the line, so to speak, that's when the other side gets nervous and then they want to parlay and talk peace. And it's very effective, but it's not just effective for show, because you may have to fire the cannons. [Quoting Shakespeare:] "Beware of entrance into a quarrel, but being in it bear that the opposed may beware of thee."[6]

The villain: Confusion stemming from the potential ill winds of business

The victim: Clients undergoing bankruptcy or failure

The hero: The core of the client's narrative

AN ORGANIC TALE

Jesse Laflamme is the CEO of Pete and Gerry's Organic Eggs, a third-generation family operation that produces free-range eggs that are certified organic and humane. It all started with his childhood companion Nellie:

One day my parents decided that they would bring a hen home, and that would be my pet. I was about four or five years old. I had just learned how to ride a bike, which had a basket on it. So naturally I put Nellie in the basket everywhere I went. She was my constant companion.

The best part was I'd take her to the sandbox, and I'd be playing with trucks, and she'd be scratching around, doing what chickens do the whole time. She was always under my arm, you know, like a football.[7]

As an animal lover, Jesse sees his egg business as a moral imperative. In his view, the "villains" are (1) uncertainty over the composition of our food, with "more and more consumers asking, 'Was this produced with pesticides, genetically modified feed or antibiotics?'" and (2) the massive industrial farms that often don't take animal welfare into account.[8] The victims are the mistreated animals. In battery cage operations, for instance, there may be hundreds of thousands of hens in one barn with

> nine hens living in a space equal to the volume of a microwave oven. And these battery cage buildings are often five or six hundred feet long. It's a giant machine, with rows of these cages, 13 decks high. They actually have to have catwalks in between them. All artificial light, artificial ventilation. And the hens are living on wire their entire lives. The smell of ammonia is often overwhelming, because of the manure. . . . And it's taking agriculture and egg production to sort of this utmost efficiency at the complete expense of animal welfare and natural behavior.[9]

Even so-called cage-free farms are often grossly overcrowded. The open space available to the hens can be as small as a 10' x 10' square of macadam! By contrast, Pete and Gerry's form of "heroism" is reassuring consumers that

> livestock should be able to go outside, and be in the sunshine, and further, that they should be able to find some grass and vegetation, and roam around and act like the animals that they are. And that's the vision and the picture that consumers have in their minds of how food should be produced.
>
> So that's sort of our compass, is listening to those consumers, and what are they expecting of us. Along with producing food, we're telling a story we want them to believe in and pay more for, so we better be doing it right. And a huge part of that is free range, and letting the hens go outside, and do what chickens do outside.
>
> In fact, the day after they're hatched, they're fed certified organic grain that is free of herbicides, pesticides, and any of the prohibited chemicals or preservatives that are not part of the prescribed USDA organic program. And that certification trail comes from all the farmers, suppliers, goes all the way back to the seeds. The seeds

we're planting in the field actually have to be certified organic. Plus the flock is never given antibiotics or medications at any point.[10]

Good business is good for business. Pete and Gerry's is now the number two producer in the country—working with more than 125 small farms in 15 states—yielding three million eggs a day. Moreover, all of their suppliers are family operations. "We depend on them and they depend on us," Jesse says. He derives great satisfaction from supporting so many small, independent operations.[11] His "heroism" takes many forms.

EMPOWERING WOUNDED VETERANS, ONE FAIRWAY AT A TIME

The problem and the victims: Since 9/11 countless veterans have returned from Iraq and Afghanistan with dire physical and mental injuries, including loss of limbs, facial disfigurement, brain trauma, and post-traumatic stress disorder (PTSD). Coming home is only the beginning of the journey. Veterans often struggle with low self-esteem, depression, anxiety, and substance abuse. The "hero" of this tale, as you'll see, is actually the game of golf.

Enter Jerry Shanahan, who runs the New England chapter of an organization called the Salute Military Golf Association (SMGA), whose motto is "Empowering Wounded Veterans One Fairway at a Time."[12] Jerry eloquently explains the mission:

We believe that golf has a healing power. . . . There's nothing really uplifting about [the veterans] new existence—their new bodies, their new minds or whatever. So golf gets them out of that, gets them to focus on something else, a sport with other veterans.

When they're in the military, they are constantly told what to do, when to wake up, how to dress, where to go. And they're doing it with their buddies and everybody's got each other's backs.

So when they come back, that's all gone. Relationships are totally broken up. The central command is gone. Golf brings these guys back together so that the camaraderie is being rebuilt. . . . It does have some military aspects to it because when you're playing golf, there are certain rules that you have to follow that make you an effective golfer, as you would if you were a rifleman, so to speak. Plus a golf course is very strategic, just like combat.

They're just out there with three or four other guys and they're doing something together in some sort of competition. They're helping the other guy as much as they're helping themselves.[13]

Does this work? The numbers speak for themselves. One hundred and twenty-five wounded veterans have received golf instruction in "warrior clinics" and have participated in more than 1,250 golf experiences. Jerry Shanahan volunteers full-time, seven days a week for the organization:

I'm motivated by the enjoyment they get out of the game and the smiles on their faces and the laughter and the kidding and all that sort of stuff, it's a hoot. And they come back in and they'll have a beer or a soft drink or whatever, and what they're sharing together, I just sit back and take it all in. It's cool. It really is. I mean, that's where I get my reward and my motivation for doing what I do and the time that I spend doing it.[14]

A TINY SOLUTION WITH HUGE IMPACT

About 10 years ago I helped a CEO of a large hi-tech firm prepare a speech for a conference focused on the promise of engineering. I did extensive research to discover which inventions had the greatest impact on history, under the heading of "Disastrous Times Spawn Innovation." It turns out that one of the most pivotal inventions of all time was the eyed sewing needle. And what "villains" did it slay? Imagine a freezing winter, tens of thousands of years ago. If prehistoric hunters were fortunate enough to slay a furry animal, they would have to remove the skin, dry it, then fashion a crude garment that would hang loosely off the shoulders like a cape. Not exactly a recipe for warmth or comfort. Once the needle arrived, however, sewing came into being, and tailoring with it, which meant that "clothes" could be fitted to the body with fewer openings. This in turn made layering possible and made it easier to work, hunt, and fish outdoors for longer periods of time. As a consequence, migration would have been easier.

The exact date of origin for the eyed needle is unclear. It may have been 61,000 years ago in South Africa,[15] or 50,000 years ago in Siberia,[16] though some say it came into use about 25,000 years ago not only "to stich hides together for warmth but also for sewing and decorating textiles for social and erotic display."[17] Early needles were probably slivers of bone, polished smooth with sand, and the eyes were made with a crude awl or drill.

You may be thinking that this has little to do with business, but the invention satisfied a real, unmet, if non-obvious need at the time. Without tailoring, people would have shivered in their shelters and experienced shorter and hungrier lives until some entrepreneuring spirit figured out a way to stitch furs together with animal tendons or sinew. That "may have been what allowed [*Homo sapiens*] to prosper and flourish over the Neanderthals."[18] The villain was the cold, the victims were our ancestors, and the hero of the story is the smart woman or man who fashioned the first sewing tool, not to mention the needle itself. This makes me wonder what other simple inventions are waiting to be hatched to solve problems that we either don't recognize or that we view as intractable.

A TALE OF BEER RETAIL

Suzanne Schalow and Kate Baker have an instinctive understanding of the food and beverage service business because they ran a popular pub in Cambridge, Massachusetts, for a dozen years—"giving customers burgers, tater tots and beer."[19] They started a crash course in craft beer on their own in the early 2000s and soon discovered that there were a lot of brews with "cool packaging, cool labels, cool people and great stories." At the same time they came to the conclusion that "people really suck at beer retail in the United States":[20]

> Dirty, dusty old stores and a lack of knowledge about products being sold. You ask a question, you get nothing in return, or you get a grunt, a groan, or a, "Well, I don't know. We'll have to look that up." Or a general really disconcerting feeling that "These people are not interested in what they're selling and what they're doing."[21]

Seven and a half years ago they created an antidote: the Craft Beer Cellar boutique store, in their hometown of Belmont, Massachusetts. They bootstrapped it—financing it themselves. The store features a large selection, efficient design, and a huge dose of passion:

> So it was like a true love and adoration for the product, and a deep-seated care for the community.[22] . . . We wanted to give customers something to believe in. And they're going to say, "This was money well spent. And it wasn't all because of the liquid, it was because of the experience provided."[23]

They now have 32 franchise stores in 15 states, from coast to coast, with a creed in the form of a trinity: "quality beer on the shelves, the way we treat people, and our know-how."[24] As Kate explains, "customer service is a handshake, hospitality is a hug."[25] It's all about "a community of people [who] come in here and shop and support us. It's also a community of brewers, distributors, suppliers and importers. We speak with people literally all over the world to bring certain products here."[26] In unison, Kate and Suzanne say, "They're all our family."[27] They want to extend those relationships as far as possible. Although 27 percent of beer buyers in Boston drink craft brews, nationwide only about 7 percent do so.[28] That spells further growth for their concept.

Their villains: poor beer retailing, with no finesse; ignorance about craft brews

The victims: consumers who never had a store where they could be educated

The heroes: two women with deep knowledge and passion for their products and their communities alike

WHISPERED ENLIGHTENMENT

Marcie Schorr Hirsch never met a corporate problem she couldn't solve or at least reduce in severity. Carrying a PhD in organizational behavior and management, she helps companies and executives perceive hidden issues that get in the way of productivity:

> I think some people call me the organizational whisperer. I think I'm a thought partner. I do two things. . . . One is management consulting, which is really where I'm looking at the organization and its needs. And the other is one-on-one coaching, typically with senior executives. . . . And anybody who's inside immediately has a skewed view. It's like looking at your own baby and saying, "Is that baby cute?" You know, tell me somebody who doesn't think their own baby is cute. It doesn't happen. And yet, in a world of babies, if you were to line them up and take an impartial judge, and say, "Pick the cutest baby," it wouldn't necessarily be our own.[29]

Marcie finds many villains in this process such as the overwhelming need for large public companies to concentrate on quarterly earnings, or the myopia of senior management:

It's the structural villains that often drive the outcomes that you maybe didn't see coming, when people are blindsided. And the reason we don't see them is the same reason that you don't notice that there's a smell in your own house. It's because you live in it. And so it's not until you go away for a month, and you come back, open the door, and you go, "Ooh, my house has a smell." Not necessarily a bad smell, but there's actually sort of a fragrance to this space. And when you're in it, it doesn't smell like anything at all.[30]

Marcie says most executives think their decisions are rational, but they don't realize (or admit) that emotions play a large role:

Bad decisions are often triggered by irrational reactions. Maybe we were burned in our last job by a terrible boss. Or maybe we got laid off because the industry took a downturn. Or maybe the new head of the board reminds us of our mother, and we didn't like her. I've seen people react adversely to résumés because they have a negative association with the name. You see a résumé from Frederica _____, and you knew a Frederica in seventh grade, and she just gave you a miserable time. She was a mean girl, kept you out of the in-group, tormented you forever. And it all kind of comes up from the gut. . . . And you get into confirmation bias, where you're looking for everything about Frederica that's negative. Whereas Jane gets a total pass, and she may have been an axe murderer in 1997! "Oh, well that's in the past," you say to yourself. You give that person a lot of leeway. . . . Everybody has a different lens, just something that's a little idiosyncratic.[31]

Surprisingly, for someone who trains leaders, Marcie does not believe in motivation:

I believe that nobody motivates another person. . . . There's a reason you get out of bed in the morning. There's a reason that you choose to eat Wheaties rather than Cheerios. You have preferences. You have expectations. Leaders need to capture and embrace the existing motivations of a diverse workforce. They can't inject motivation. We know this from the research on salaries. The American ethos is, if you have to give somebody something crummy, you pay them more. If you want to keep somebody on the job who wants to leave, throw money at it. Well, the reality is, that doesn't work. It just doesn't work. If what somebody really wants is more time with their kids, giving them more money is not going to be the answer.[32]

That's why she favors "servant leadership," meaning that you don't lead people, you serve and guide them.

Marcie's villains: problems that can't be seen, residing either in executives' psyches or in the structure of the overall organization

The victims: the leaders and the employees

The heroes: revealing obscured issues through an outside perspective, along with the concept of servant leadership

FOURTEEN

The End of the Story

My Own Saga

You may have heard the myth that Albert Einstein failed math. This may emanate from a misunderstanding of his statement "Do not worry about your difficulties in mathematics. I can assure you mine are still greater."[1] No doubt he was referring to his complicated calculations concerning the structure of the entire universe, not to simple arithmetic like adding eight and seven to get 15. In fact, not only did young Einstein *excel* at math in school, but he quickly surpassed a medical student named Talmud who was giving him weekly geometry lessons—starting when the boy was 10. "After a short time, a few months, he had worked through the whole book," Talmud said. "Soon the flight of his mathematical genius was so high that I could no longer follow."[2] Moreover, Albert mastered differential and integral calculus before he was 15.[3] I believe that one major factor in the development of his fertile imagination was his interaction with his Uncle Jakob, an engineer who managed to make algebra *interesting*. "It's a merry science," Jakob explained. "When the animal that we are hunting cannot be caught, we call it X temporarily and continue to hunt until it is bagged."[4] Jakob turned a dry subject into an adventure that no doubt captivated his creative nephew. If only we had all learned algebra this way! Instead we were tormented with silly problems like this: "Jane is 10 years older than Sally, and the sum of their ages is 30. How old is each sister?" As you recall, you can solve it two ways. If X = Sally's age, then $X + (X + 10) = 30$. If, on the other hand, X = Jane's age, then $X + (X - 10) = 30$. Either way, who cares? This is merely boring data, not a story. The point is that anything can be interesting, if explained with verve and idiosyncrasy. (My high school algebra teacher Mr. Gerber used to insist on the first iteration, with X and $X + 10$, because he thought the plus sign was more optimistic. "People would say, 'Gerber, do you really think this way?'" he would say. "Yes, I do?")

When I tell a story, I imagine a vector emanating from my mouth toward the audience. I hope that my words and meaning arrive undisturbed and intact in the minds of the listeners. You recall that I mentioned earlier that my first boss in television news sent me to a voice coach. She was fond of reminding me to "feel the words in your mouth when you speak." I think about that all the time. To me, the language is a friend who performs a noble service: carrying our messages from place to place. I try to be kind to English in the hope that it in turn will be kind to me. I treat it with respect and deference. Now some people might ask, "Stone, do you really think this way?" I can answer with three words: "Yes, I do."

Like money, language is a means of exchange and a store of value. We tend to think that humans have a monopoly on it, though AI may be changing that. Yet the appeal of the human voice persists:

> Fairy tales, like myths, capitalize on the kaleidoscopic with its multifaceted meanings: sparkling beauty, austere form, and visual power. Once told around the fireside or at the hearth, with adults and children sharing the storytelling space, they captured the play of light and shadow in their environment, creating special effects that yoked luminous beauty with the dark side. Imagine a time before electronic entertainments, with long nights around campsites and other sources of heat and light, and it is not much of a challenge to realize that human beings, always quick to adapt, began exchanging information, trading wisdom, and reporting gossip.[5]

As with all stories, though, we need to return to the most colorful characters of all: the villains. We delight in them because they *intrigue* us. In our personal lives they often dominate our thinking. We can recall specifics about negative events much more clearly and in greater detail than happy ones.[6] I can attest to this. When I call to mind a given vacation, when my kids were younger, I tend to envision a tender scene with my two children cavorting in the pool. I might have difficulty remembering the resort, or the year, because the edges of the images are shrouded in benign imprecision. But ask me about the time a nun embarrassed me in front of the entire 6th grade catechism class, and I can recount the story in astounding detail. Problems often dominate our thinking, sometimes to the point of obsession. But as business storytellers we can hold consumers' attention by addressing their concerns and fears, as long as we offer hope or resolution.

Sometimes the possibility of extreme (and real) danger carries a bizarre appeal. In Japan, for instance, the pufferfish fugu is considered a delicacy. Even when prepared by specially licensed chefs, it can still be deadly:

> [I]ts skin, ovaries, liver, and intestines contain tetrodotoxin, one of the most poisonous chemicals in the world, hundreds of times more lethal than strychnine or cyanide. A shred small enough to fit under one's fingernail could kill an entire family. . . . That's the appeal of the dish: eating the possibility of death. . . . The most highly respected fugu chefs are the ones who manage to leave in the barest touch of the poison, just enough for the diner's lips to tingle from his brush with mortality but not enough to actually kill him.[7]

Fugu aficionados actually seek out this thrill. Granted, most situations in business are not so dire, but we should still reach for the drama in the daily or the metaphor in the mundane when we tell our own stories.

As we approach the end of this book—and I hope, dear reader, that it has been a worthwhile ride for you—I'd like to share some of my own experiences in this crazy part of the universe that we call everyday commerce. After a decade or so as a journalist, at Time Inc., in New York and on television in Minneapolis, Boston, and on PBS, I started my own venture. At first I was just doing video production for hire, until one day a business school professor called me up and said, "I got your name from _____. I'm on TV a lot and I need some pointers. Can you help me?" I had no idea what I would do to improve his delivery, but nonetheless, that day, Greg Stone Media Consultant was born. At first consulting was a sideline, then it became my mainstay. I help executives craft and deliver compelling messages that they can transform into stories, and I teach business leaders how to speak with greater authority, either to the media or other key audiences.

Along the way, I have cultivated a "personality" that in large part comes naturally. I was a middle-class kid with working-class roots. My maternal grandparents emigrated from Italy to Pennsylvania, where my grandpa toiled underground in the coalmines. As teenagers, my older uncles were miners too, but legend has it that my grandmother did not want that life for her boys so the family migrated again, heading east this time, toward New Jersey where I grew up. My paternal roots are also in Italy, though my dad's family originally came from Albania. (It's a little-known fact that some 800,000 Albanians still reside in Italy.) Now why does all this matter to you? Eastern European and Italian genes have given me a flair for the histrionic, which I can summon when necessary and quell when decorum demands. Here are a few incidents from my career that may be amusing and, I hope, instructive.

August 1980. I had just graduated from Columbia Journalism School and passed the writing test for the Associated Press. They told me I could be sent anywhere, but I was gunning for a job with AP's New York Bureau for personal reasons. I knew that working as an intern at the Democratic National Convention at Madison Square Garden would be a good entry point. There were 60 reporters and editors from AP splayed out in concentric arcs of desks, right behind the podium. It was a great vantage point. Although we never saw the speakers' faces, we looked out at the immense crowd at the Garden. My high-level job involved carrying manual typewriters (the preferred writing tool in those days) from place to place, and going down to street level to pick up advance copies of speeches from the press booth. At that time documents were Xeroxed and handed out to reporters ahead of time, then as now a matter of professional courtesy, so they could prepare their stories and be ready to release them once the politicians started their addresses. Imagine the scene: 30 or so reporters converging on the press booth, in a tangle of extended arms, grabbing the copy and running back to their desks. I did the same thing once or twice, racing upstairs to hand the copy to the writers. Then it dawned on me: "The copies had to be printed somewhere." During an idle moment I sauntered down to the press booth and asked, with as much mock innocence as I could muster, "Do you know where the speeches come from?"

The answer was, "Yeah, from the print shop."

"Where is that?" I asked.

"Somewhere upstairs, I think."

Game on. I hustled up to the Garden's upper floors, with long, empty corridors with shiny linoleum, and eventually found the mythical print shop at the end of one of the hallways. I introduced myself in the most official manner possible as "Greg Stone, from the Associated Press," and turned on whatever charm I could muster. "Any chance I can get a copy of the next speech before it goes downstairs?" Yup.

For a time I was a hero. I was delivering speech after speech to the bureau on the convention floor probably half an hour before they were distributed to the hordes. Why did this matter? The AP writers were able to prepare their stories way in advance so they could get the jump on UPI, at a time when wire services were engaged in a blood war every day. Winning by minutes was considered a victory.

Then came the anxiously awaited "dream shall never die" speech, delivered by Ted Kennedy. I went upstairs to the print shop, grabbed a copy, sprinted down several flights and delivered it to the editor. I was winded but ecstatic. It seemed that everyone who counted at the bureau was admiring my chutzpah and resourcefulness. A born reporter. Aggressive and shrewd, right? Not quite.

When I went back to the print shop to get Jimmy Carter's speech, the capstone of the convention, my buddies there said they couldn't give it to me. "Why not?" I asked in a panic—watching my newfound reputation collapsing. "Do you see those two guys over there in the corner, Greg?" I peered over and noticed two non-descript gentlemen in suits staring at me with cold, efficient eyes. I nodded. "Well they're Secret Service," my print shop pal said. "And they told me to tell you that if you value your life, you'll get out of the print shop RIGHT NOW."

Now, my parents didn't raise any fools. I said "OK," raised my hands, and retreated, empty-handed. I figured that if I was going to die on assignment there should be more at stake than a Xerox of a speech.

I learned several valuable lessons from this escapade:

1. Look beyond the obvious. Ask yourself where things come from. (The copies didn't just *materialize*, they had to be printed somewhere.)
2. Be cool. The Secret Service had probably been in the print shop at all times. When I sprinted out with the Kennedy speech under my arm I am sure I attracted too much attention. I could imagine them saying, "Don't let that guy in here again." If I had walked out calmly, they might not have noticed me.

Postscript: I didn't get a job offer from AP's New York bureau. Why? I later found out from one of my professors, who worked there, that they thought I was "too aggressive" because I asked so many people to hire me. The last lesson is: don't be a pest.

Now, if we apply the villain-victim-hero paradigm to this tale, the "characters" play out as follows: The "villain" is the obvious, the victims were the writers who had to wait for the copy, and the "hero" was the shortcut. On another level, the villain was my youthful impatience and bumptiousness, the victim was ultimately the AP for not receiving the key Carter speech ahead of time, and the hero was my willingness to learn from my mistakes. (Never did I imagine that I would be writing about all this in a book so many years later.)

Here's another tale, also from 1980. After striking out at the AP, I landed a job as an apprentice writer at Time Inc. The New York bureau from *Time* magazine gave me a freelance assignment to report on violence in baseball. I remember including the old joke, "I went to the fights the other night and a baseball game broke out." Anyway, I was able to visit the locker room at Yankee Stadium, which was quite a thrill for a kid who grew up as a Yankees fan. Yogi Berra was gracious and accommodating, Ron Guidry was unfriendly, and Reggie Jackson was in the middle of a monologue—cursing out his rival Joe Morgan. "****ing Joe Morgan, how can anyone say he's a great baseball player, he *&%*88" etc."

I waited for an opening and tried to butt in. "Mr. Jackson, my name is Greg Stone and I'm here on assignment from *Time* magazine and—"

"I'm having a baseball conversation, and YOU'RE interrupting me," he snarled.

I waited a few minutes then went back at him. "C'mon, Reg, give me a break. I just want to ask you a few questions."

"What are you gonna do? Put me on the cover?" he asked.

"No, Reggie, we're gonna make you man of the year," I joked.

At that point he relaxed a bit and answered my questions.

Afterwards an older reporter came up to me and said, "You handled him just right. He's really not a bad guy. He's just arrogant on the surface."

"Thanks," I said. "What is your name, sir?"

"Dave Anderson," he said.

"Mr. Anderson," I answered. "It's an honor to meet you. I read you all the time." (He was a famous sportswriter at the *New York Times*.)

"Call me Dave" was the reply.

"What a class act," I said to myself.

Once again, let's apply the paradigm. The "villain" was Reggie Jackson's apparent arrogance, the victim was yours truly, and the "hero" was my persistence and success in convincing him to speak with me. On another level, the villain was my own inexperience, the victim could have been the magazine in losing some good quotes, and the hero was Dave Anderson's kindness and encouragement.

Fast forward to 2006. I asked a branding consultant I know to evaluate my own messaging. The good news was that clients had positive reactions to my work. They used words like accomplished, curious, and passionate to describe me. Slide 13 in the presentation fell like a cleaver, however: "A communicator who does not communicate. . . . No outreach from Greg—ever. . . . Wish I would hear from him." I was dumbfounded. Wasn't it enough just to do the work? Why did I need to send out updates when my clients seemed satisfied? I was like the proverbial shoemaker with holes in his soles. And I quickly responded. As a result of these insights (that only an independent consultant could have unearthed, since most clients will not tell you point blank what they think), I started sending out newsletters at regular intervals. At first quarterly, then perhaps every two months, with a twofold purpose: (1) to inform my clients about recent events in media and technology and the places they intersect and (2) to a much lesser extent, to keep my business top of mind. (I keep promotional references to a minimum.)

The villain here: a news vacuum

The victim: the writer of this book, who was missing opportunities

The hero: the branding consultant who unearthed the problem

People won't know what you're doing unless you tell them!

Here is a general observation: It is a common myth that creativity in business is inductive (the result of factual analysis). In fact, it is often deductive (the product of a theory or a concept that will fit the circumstances—or so we hope). Artists, scientists, and inventors often function this way too. The idea comes first, then the execution. There is no doubt, for instance, that Steve Jobs's mind worked deductively, and perhaps that's why he was so skeptical about market research. "Customers don't know what they want until we've shown them," he said. "Our task is to read things that are not yet on the page."[8]

The villain is overthinking. Reading too much, doing too much market research, or conducting too many focus groups often yields paralysis through analysis. If Steve Jobs had asked people whether they would like to have a hand-held device that would play music, send and receive messages, allow them to watch movies, and, by the way, also make phone calls, they might have told him that he was way off base. Sometimes we have to proceed as if success is the only option. Diffidence can be the enemy. Like Picasso, we just have to jump in and start painting. As he once said, "I don't seek, I find."[9]

I hope I have helped you find your stories. And may they be replete with villains, victims, and heroes. Thanks for taking this trip with me. I greatly appreciate your time.

Notes

PREFACE

1. William H. Whyte, "Is Anybody Listening?" *Fortune*, September 1950.

2. Garry Wills, *Lincoln at Gettysburg: The Words That Remade America* (New York: Simon and Schuster, 1992), 28.

3. Rudyard Kipling, "I Keep Six Honest . . ." from *The Elephant's Child*, accessed August 3, 2018, https://www.poetryloverspage.com/poets/kipling/i_keep_six_honest.html.

4. Tana French, accessed August 3, 2018, http://www.tanafrench.com/about.html.

CHAPTER 1

1. James C. Humes, *Speak Like Churchill, Stand Like Lincoln: 21 Powerful Secrets of History's Greatest Speakers* (New York: Three Rivers Press, 2002), 20.

2. Belle Linda Halpern and Kathy Lubar, *Leadership Presence: Dramatic Techniques to Reach Out, Motivate and Inspire* (New York: Gotham Books, 2003), 8.

3. Greg Stone, "What Is Executive Presence Anyway?" *Huffington Post*, May 18, 2015, accessed August 3, 2018, https://www.huffingtonpost.com/greg-j-stone/what-is-executive-presenc_b_7307648.html.

4. Robert Steven Kaplan, *What to Ask the Person in the Mirror: Critical Questions for Becoming a More Effective Leader and Reaching Your Potential* (Boston: Harvard Business Review Press, 2011), 162–163.

5. Peter Guber, "The Four Truths of the Storyteller," *Harvard Business Review*, December 2007, accessed August 3, 2018, https://hbr.org/2007/12/the-four-truths-of-the-storyteller.

6. Ibid.

7. Mary Jo Hatch, Monika Kostera, and Andrzej K. Koźmiński, *The Three Faces of Leadership: Manager, Artist, Priest* (Malden, MA: Blackwell, 2005), 42.

8. Howard E. Gardner, *Leading Minds: An Anatomy of Leadership* (New York: Basic Books, 2011), Kindle edition, "The Antecedents of Following" section.

9. Ibid., "Stories Struggling with One Another" and "The Story as Central" sections.

CHAPTER 2

1. Greg Stone, "For Better Presentations, Start with a Villain," *Harvard Business Review*, November 12, 2015, accessed August 3, 2018, https://hbr.org/2015/11/for-better-presentations-start-with-a-villain?autocomplete=true.

2. François Truffaut and Helen G. Scott, *Hitchcock* (New York: Simon & Schuster, 1983), 316.

3. Guber, "The Four Truths." See also, Muhammed Yunus, "Nobel Lecture," December 10, 2006, accessed August 3, 2018, https://www.nobelprize.org/nobel_prizes/peace/laureates/2006/yunus-lecture-en.html.

4. Stone, "For Better Presentations."

5. Glen Stansberry, "10 Examples of Shockingly Excellent Customer Service," American Express OPEN Forum, May 4, 2010, accessed August 3, 2018, https://www.americanexpress.com/us/small-business/openforum/articles/10-examples-of-shockingly-excellent-customer-service-1/. See also https://www.reddit.com/r/reddit.com/comments/agsb4/trader_joes_did_something_awesome/.

6. Eduardo Andrade and Joel Cohen, "On the Consumption of Negative Feelings," *Journal of Consumer Research* 34 (2007): 284.

7. Ibid.

8. Ibid., 283.

9. Edmund Burke, from "On the Sublime and Beautiful," The Harvard Classics, 1909–14, as quoted in Adam Gopnik, "The Right Man: Who Owns Edmund Burke?" *New Yorker*, July 29, 2013, accessed August 3, 2018, https://www.newyorker.com/magazine/2013/07/29/the-right-man.

10. Stuart Fischoff, "Why Are Some People More Attracted to Scary Movies than Others Are?" Science + Religion Today, October 28, 2011, accessed August 3, 2018, http://www.scienceandreligiontoday.com/2011

/10/28/why-are-some-people-more-attracted-to-scary-movies-than-others-are/.

11. Truffaut and Scott, *Hitchcock*, 201.

12. Dr. Steven Schlozman, Assistant Professor of Psychiatry, Harvard Medical School. Interview by the author, March 18, 2018.

13. Ibid.

14. M. R. James, *Collected Ghost Stories* (Oxford: Oxford University Press, 2011), 406.

15. Ibid., 407.

16. Ibid., 406.

17. Maria Tatar, *The Hard Facts of Grimms' Fairy Tales*, 2nd ed. (Princeton, NJ: Princeton University Press, 2003), 181.

18. Craig Lambert, "The Horror and the Beauty: Maria Tatar Explores the Dazzle and the 'Dark Side' in Fairy Tales—and Why We Read Them," *Harvard Magazine*, November–December 2007, accessed August 3, 2018, https://www.harvardmagazine.com/2007/11/the-horror-and-the-beaut.html.

19. Maria Tatar, *Enchanted Hunters: The Power of Stories in Childhood* (New York: Norton, 2009), Kindle edition, ch. 2.

20. Tatar, *Hard Facts*, 20–21.

21. Lambert, "Horror."

22. Tatar, *Enchanted Hunters*, Introduction.

23. Schlozman, Interview.

24. Maria Tatar, ed., *The Classic Fairy Tales*, Second Norton Critical Edition (New York: Norton, 2016), Kindle edition, introduction.

25. Professor Mary Jo Hatch, Professor, Emerita, McIntyre School of Commerce, University of Virginia, and visual artist, Interview by the author, February 7, 2018.

26. Hatch, Kostera, and Koźmiński, *The Three Faces*, 111.

27. Joseph Campbell, *The Hero with a Thousand Faces*, 3rd ed. (Novato, CA: New World Library, 2008), 330.

28. Robert A. Segal, *Myth: A Very Short Introduction*, 2nd ed. (Oxford: Oxford University Press, 2015), Kindle edition, introduction, "Definition of Myth."

29. Ibid., ch. 6, quoting Jacob Arlow.

30. Karen Armstrong, *A Short History of Myth* (Edinburgh: Canongate, 2005), Kindle edition, ch. 1.

31. Walter Benjamin, "From the Storyteller: Reflections on the Work of Nikolai Leskov," in Tatar, *Classic Fairy Tales*, Kindle edition.

32. Campbell, *The Hero*, 57.

33. Ibid.

34. Armstrong, *Short History*, ch. 2.

35. Schlozman, Interview.

36. Ovid, *Metamorphoses*, trans. David Raeburn (London: Penguin Books, 2004), 635.

37. Alison Griswold, "Everything You Think You Know about Thomas Edison Might Be Wrong," Business Insider, November 6, 2013, accessed August 3, 2018, http://www.businessinsider.com/thomas-edison-light-bulb-publicity-stunt-2013-11.

38. Mark A. Lemley, "The Myth of the Sole Inventor," *Michigan Law Review* 110 (2012): 722.

39. Ibid., 710–711.

40. Ibid., 721.

41. Ibid., 719.

42. Ibid., 725.

43. Ibid., 726.

44. Greg Stone, "No One Avoid Tabloids," *Huffington Post*, July 21, 2016, accessed August 3, 2018, https://www.huffingtonpost.com/greg-j-stone/toupee-or-not-to-pay_b_7925586.html.

45. I saw a similar quiz in Steven Pinker, *How the Mind Works* (New York: W. W. Norton, 1997), 542. Pinker, in turn, credited this book for the idea: R. Lederer and M. Gilleland, *Literary Trivia: Fun and Games for Book Lovers* (New York: Vintage, 1994).

CHAPTER 3

1. Michele Gorman, "Yogi Berra's Most Memorable Sayings," *Newsweek*, September 23, 2015, accessed August 3, 2018, http://www.newsweek.com/most-memorable-yogi-isms-375661.

2. Humes, *Speak Like Churchill*, 7.

3. Ibid., 9.

4. Ibid., 2.

5. Walter Isaacson, *Leonardo da Vinci* (New York: Simon & Schuster, 2017), Kindle edition, conclusion.

6. Patricia Benesh, "Mark Twain's Discourse: A Timeless Writing Course," *Huffington Post*, October 25, 2010, accessed August 3, 2018, https://www.huffingtonpost.com/patricia-benesh/mark-twains-discourse-a-t_b_772701.html.

7. Ethan C. Rouen, Assistant Professor at Harvard Business School. Interview by author. January 31, 2018.

8. Ibid.

9. Ibid.

10. Ibid.

11. Ibid.

12. Gabriel García Márquez, *One Hundred Years of Solitude* (New York: HarperCollins, 2006), 1.

13. Gabriel García Márquez, "The Art of Fiction No. 69," Interview, *Paris Review*, Winter 1981.

14. Stephen Jay Gould, *The Panda's Thumb: More Reflections in Natural History* (New York: W. W. Norton, 1982), 21.

15. Ibid., 21–22.

16. Joan Detz, *How to Write & Give a Speech* (New York: St. Martin's Press, 2002), 31–32.

17. Clayton M. Christensen, Taddy Hall, Karen Dillon, and David S. Duncan, *Competing Against Luck: The Story of Innovation and Customer Choice* (Sydney: HarperCollins, 2016), Kindle edition, ch. 8.

18. Arlene Croce, "Balanchine Said: What Was the Source of the Choreographer's Celebrated Utterances?" *New Yorker*, January 26, 2009, accessed August 3, 2018, https://www.newyorker.com/magazine/2009/01/26/balanchine-said.

19. Franklin Delano Roosevelt, First Inaugural Address, March 4, 1933, accessed August 3, 2018, http://www.americanrhetoric.com/speeches/fdrfirstinaugural.html.

20. Terry Gross, Graduation Speech, Bryn Mawr College, May 17, 2014, accessed August 3, 2018, https://www.youtube.com/watch?v=U42981EtGdQ.

21. Mary Jo Hatch, Professor, Emerita, McIntyre School of Commerce, University of Virginia, and visual artist. Interview by the author, February 7, 2018.

22. Andrey Tarkovsky, *Sculpting in Time: Reflections on the Cinema*, trans. Kitty Hunter-Blair (Austin: University of Texas Press, 1991), 10.

23. Christensen et al., *Luck*, Kindle edition, introduction.

24. Ibid., ch. 1.

25. Ibid., ch. 2.

26. Ibid., ch. 1.

27. Ibid., ch. 5.

28. Schlozman, Interview.

29. Christensen et al., *Luck*, ch. 8.

30. Carmen Nobel, "Clay Christensen's Milkshake Marketing," Harvard Business School Working Knowledge, February 14, 2011, accessed August 3, 2018, https://hbswk.hbs.edu/item/clay-christensens-milkshake-marketing.

31. Christensen et al., *Luck*, introduction.

32. Winston Churchill, "First Speech as Prime Minister to House of Commons," International Churchill Society, May 13, 1940, accessed August 3, 2018, https://winstonchurchill.org/resources/speeches/1940-the-finest-hour/blood-toil-tears-and-sweat-2/.

33. Suzanne B. Shu and Kurt A. Carlson, "When Three Charms but Four Alarms: Identifying the Optimal Number of Claims in Persuasion Settings," *Journal of Marketing* 78 (2014): 127–139.

34. Gina Barreca, "Does 'Handsome, Ruthless, and Stupid' Sound Like Your Type?: Do Women Respond More to a Man's Forgetfulness Than His Attention?" *Psychology Today*, July 27, 2014, accessed August 3, 2018, https://www.psychologytoday.com/us/blog/snow-white-doesnt-live-here-anymore/201407/does-handsome-ruthless-and-stupid-sound-your-type.

CHAPTER 4

1. Philip Kotler and Kevin Lane Keller, *Marketing Management* (Upper Saddle River, NJ: Prentice Hall, 2012), 7.

2. Adam Waytz, John Cacioppo, and Nicholas Epley, "Who Sees Human? The Stability and Importance of Individual Differences in Anthropomorphism," *Perspectives on Psychological Science* 5 (2010): 220.

3. Nicholas Epley, Adam Waytz, and John T. Cacioppo, "On Seeing Human: A Three-Factor Theory of Anthropomorphism," *Psychological Review* 114 (2007): 865.

4. "Xenophanes," *Stanford Encyclopedia of Philosophy*, January 24, 2018, accessed August 3, 2018, https://plato.stanford.edu/entries/xenophanes/.

5. Chris Malone and Susan T. Fiske, *The Human Brand: How We Relate to People, Products, and Companies* (San Francisco: Jossey-Bass, 2013), 37.

6. Ibid.

7. Youngme Moon, "Intimate Exchanges: Using Computers to Elicit Self-Disclosure from Consumers," *Journal of Consumer Research* 26 (2000): 325.

8. Scott Akalis and John T. Cacioppo, "When We Need a Human: Motivational Determinants of Anthropomorphism," *Social Cognition* 26 (2008): 144.

9. Malone and Fiske, *Human Brand*, 37.

10. Eply, Waytz, and Cacioppo, "On Seeing Human," 880.

11. Waytz, Cacioppo, and Epley, "Who Sees Human," 227.

12. Ibid., 226.

13. Ibid., 227.

14. Matthew Hutson, "Love Objects: Why People Fall for Things," *Atlantic*, December 2017, 20.

15. Kotler and Lane Keller, *Marketing*, 292.

16. Matt Haig, *Brand Success: How the World's Top 100 Brands Thrive and Survive* (London: Kogan Page, 2011), 172–173.

17. Kotler and Lane Keller, *Marketing*, 291.

18. Tony Schwartz, *The Responsive Chord* (Garden City, NY: Anchor Books, 1974), 25.

19. Ibid., 93.

20. Margalit Fox, "Tony Schwartz, Father of the 'Daisy Ad' for the Johnson Campaign, Dies at 84," *New York Times*, June 17, 2008, accessed August 3, 2018, https://www.nytimes.com/2008/06/17/business/media/16cnd -schwartz.html.

21. Sam Roberts, "On the Streets, Discovering the Voice of the City," *New York Times*, November 8, 2011, accessed August 3, 2018, https://cityroom .blogs.nytimes.com/2011/11/08/on-the-streets-discovering-the -voice-of-the-city/.

CHAPTER 5

1. Jennifer Aaker, Professor of Marketing, Stanford Graduate School of Business, Harnessing the Power of Stories Video, March 13, 2013, accessed August 3, 2018, https://www.youtube.com/watch?v=9X0weDMh9C4.

2. Supporting information for Greg J. Stephens, Lauren J. Silbert, and Uri Hasson, "Speaker-Listener Neural Coupling Underlies Successful Communication," *Proceedings of the National Academy of Sciences of the United States of America* (32), accessed August 3, 2018, http://www.pnas. org/content/pnas/suppl/2010/07/14/1008662107.DCSupplemental /pnas.201008662SI.pdf?targetid=nameddest%3DSTXT.

3. Greg J. Stephens, Lauren J. Silbert, and Uri Hasson, "Speaker-Listener Neural Coupling Underlies Successful Communication,"

Proceedings of the National Academy of Sciences of the United States of America (32), https://doi.org/10.1073/pnas.1008662107.

4. Ibid.

5. Katherine Hobson, "Clicking: How Our Brains Are in Synch," *Princeton Alumni Weekly*, April 11, 2018, accessed August 3, 2018, https://paw.princeton.edu/article/clicking-how-our-brains-are-sync.

6. Stephens, Silbert, and Hasson, "Speaker-Listener."

7. Jennifer Ouellette, "Meet Me Halfway: Cocktail Party Physics," *Scientific American*, January 31, 2012, accessed August 3, 2018, https://blogs.scientificamerican.com/cocktail-party-physics/meet-me-halfway/.

8. Jerome Bruner, *Making Stories: Law, Literature, Life* (Cambridge, MA: Harvard University Press, 2002), 86.

9. Hobson, "Clicking."

10. Paul J. Zak, "Why Inspiring Stories Make Us React: The Neuroscience of Narrative," *Cerebrum* 2 (2015), accessed August 3, 2018, http://www.dana.org/Cerebrum/2015/Why_Inspiring_Stories_Make_Us_React__The_Neuroscience_of_Narrative/.

11. Paul Zak, Paul, "Why Your Brain Loves Good Storytelling," *Harvard Business Review*, October 28, 2014, accessed August 3, 2018, https://hbr.org/2014/10/why-your-brain-loves-good-storytelling.

12. Ibid.

13. Schlozman, Interview.

14. Steven C. Schlozman, "Why Teens Do Dumb Things—and How You Can Stop Them," *U.S. News*, January 19, 2018, accessed August 3, 2018, https://health.usnews.com/wellness/for-parents/articles/2018-01-19/why-teens-do-dumb-things-and-how-you-can-stop-them.

15. Cristina Bacchilega, "The Fairy-Tale Web," in Tatar, *The Classic Fairy Tales*, Kindle edition.

16. Arthur Asa Berger, *Media Analysis Techniques*, rev. ed. (Newbury Park, CA: Sage Publications, 1991), 21.

17. Noah Isenberg, *We'll Always Have* Casablanca: *The Life, Legend and Afterlife of Hollywood's Most Beloved Movie* (New York: Norton, 2017), Kindle edition, ch. 6.

18. Ibid.

19. Jorge Luis Borges, "The Library of Babel," in *Collected Fictions*, trans. Andrew Hurley (New York: Penguin Books, 1998), 116.

20. Bruner, *Making Stories*, 85.

21. Ibid., 93,

22. Maria Tatar, *Off with Their Heads!: Fairy Tales and the Culture of Childhood* (Princeton, NJ: Princeton University Press, 1992), 230.

23. Jon Gertner, *The Idea Factory: Bell Labs and the Great Age of American Invention* (New York: Penguin Press, 2012), 127.

24. Ibid., 128, 130–131.

25. Robert Darnton, "Peasants Tell Tales: The Meaning of Mother Goose," in Tatar, *Classic Fairy Tales.*

26. Bacchilega, in Tatar, *Classic Fairy Tales.*

27. Ibid.

28. Bruner, *Making Stories*, 51.

29. Ibid., 48.

30. Ella Saltmarshe, "Using Story to Change Systems," *Stanford Social Innovation Review*, February 20, 2018, accessed August 3, 2018, https://ssir.org/articles/entry/using_story_to_change_systems.

31. Ibid.

32. "Microsoft Story Labs," accessed March 29, 2018, accessed August 3, 2018, https://news.microsoft.com.

33. Aaron Foley, "Why Detroit's City Storyteller Wants to Ban the Word 'Gritty,'" CNN, October 5, 2017, accessed August 3, 2018, https://www.cnn.com/travel/article/detroit-storyteller-aaron-foley/index.html.

34. Edward Helmore, "Detroit Redefined: City Hires America's First Official 'Chief Storyteller,'" *The Guardian*, September 5, 2017, accessed August 3, 2018, https://www.theguardian.com/cities/2017/sep/05/detroit-redefined-america-first-official-chief-storyteller.

35. Jack Simpson, "What the Hell Is a Chief Storyteller Anyway?" Econsultancy, June 29, 2015, accessed August 3, 2018, https://econsultancy.com/blog/66630-what-the-hell-is-a-chief-storyteller-anyway.

CHAPTER 6

1. William E. Wallace, *Michelangelo: The Artist, the Man, and His Times* (Cambridge: Cambridge University Press, 2010), 5, 338.

2. Ibid., 68–69, 340.

3. Haig, *Brand Success*, 113–114.

4. Ibid., 60.

5. Margalit Fox, "Helen Gurley Brown, Who Gave 'Single Girl' a Life in Full, Dies at 90," *New York Times*, August 13, 2012, accessed August 3, 2018, https://www.nytimes.com/2012/08/14/business/media/helen-gurley-brown-who-gave-cosmopolitan-its-purr-is-dead-at-90.html.

6. Anna Escher and Lora Kolodny, "Causes of the Global Water Crisis and 12 Companies Trying to Solve It," TechCrunch, March 23, 2017,

accessed August 3, 2018, https://techcrunch.com/2017/03/22/causes-of-the
-global-water-crisis-and-12-companies-trying-to-solve-it/.

7. Waterislife.com.

8. Ibid.

9. Malone and Fiske, *Human Brand*, 95.

10. Ibid.

11. Alaina McConnell, "Zappos' Outrageous Record for the Longest
Customer Service Call Ever," Business Insider, December 20, 2012,
accessed August 3, 2018, http://www.businessinsider.com/zappos-longest
-customer-service-call-2012-12.

12. Emmie Martin, "Why Multi-millionaire Zappos CEO Tony Hsieh
Chooses to Live in a Trailer Park," CNBC, May 8, 2017, accessed August
3, 2018, accessed August 3, 2018, https://www.cnbc.com/2017/05/08/why
-multi-millionaire-zappos-ceo-tony-hsieh-lives-in-a-trailer-park.html.

13. Kotler and Lane Keller, *Marketing*, 379.

14. Ibid.

15. George Daley, Speech delivered at Massachusetts General Hospital
in Boston, MA, January 30, 2018.

16. Ian Todreas, e-mail to the author, December 11, 2017.

17. Ibid.

18. Deborah Burke, e-mail to the author, December 9, 2017.

19. Jimmy Breslin, "It's an Honor," *New York Herald Tribune*, November
26, 1963, accessed August 3, 2018, http://teachers.sduhsd.net/mgaughen
/docs/Breslin.Honor.pdf.

20. Roy Peter Clark, "Remembering Jimmy Breslin and the 'Gravedigger' School of News Writing," Poynter, March 20, 2017, accessed August
3, 2018, https://www.poynter.org/news/remembering-jimmy-breslin-and
-gravedigger-school-news-writing.

CHAPTER 7

1. "Weekly Terrestrial Radio Listenership," Pew Research Center,
June 16, 2017, accessed August 3, 2018, http://www.journalism.org/chart
/weekly-terrestrial-radio-listenership/.

2. Brendan Regan, "Podcasts Took Off This Year: What Will the New
Year Bring?" *Newsweek*, December 26, 2017, accessed August 3, 2018,
http://www.newsweek.com/podcasts-took-year-what-will-new-year-bring
-758304.

3. Ibid.

4. Diane Ackerman, *A Natural History of the Senses* (New York: Vintage Books, 1991), 190.

5. Peter Brunette, *Michael Haneke* (Champaign: University of Illinois Press, 2010).

6. Robert Bresson, *Notes on the Cinematographer*, trans. Jonathan Griffin (Los Angeles: Green Integer Books, 1997), 61.

7. Edward Bliss Jr. and John M. Patterson, *Writing News for Broadcast*, 2nd ed. (New York: Columbia University Press, 1978), 20.

8. Michiko Kakutani, "The Bronx, The Bench and the Life In Between, review of *My Beloved World: A Memoir*, by Sonia Sotomayor," *New York Times*, January 21, 2013, accessed August 3, 2018, https://www.nytimes.com/2013/01/22/books/my-beloved-world-a-memoir-by-sonia-sotomayor.html.

9. Schlozman, Interview.

10. Tony Castro, Interview.

11. John Brandon, "25 Quotes from Bill Gates on How to Succeed," Inc.com, February 15, 2016, accessed August 3, 2018, https://www.inc.com/john-brandon/25-of-the-best-bill-gates-quotes-on-success.html.

12. George Brown Jr., "Windshields and Rear View Mirrors," *IndustryWeek*, April 17, 2013, accessed August 3, 2018, http://www.industryweek.com/change-management/windshields-and-rear-view-mirrors.

13. George H. W. Bush, Address Accepting the Presidential Nomination at the Republican National Convention in New Orleans, August 18, 1988, accessed August 3, 2018, http://www.presidency.ucsb.edu/ws/index.php?pid=25955.

14. "Facts and Statistics, Physical Activity," President's Council on Sports, Fitness & Nutrition, accessed August 3, 2018, https://www.hhs.gov/fitness/resource-center/facts-and-statistics/index.html.

15. Morgan Smart, "Finding Love at Work: Patterns in Glassdoor Data," July 29, 2015, accessed August 3, 2018, https://www.glassdoor.com/research/love-in-the-workplace/.

16. Minda Zetlin, "11 Best Lines Steve Jobs Used in an Interview: The Apple Co-Founder's Insights Will Make You Question Everything," Inc., November 30, 2015, accessed August 3, 2018, https://www.inc.com/minda-zetlin/11-steve-jobs-quotes-about-work-and-life-that-will-make-you-question-everything.html.

17. Kathleen Elkins, "9 of Warren Buffett's Funniest and Most Frugal Quirks," CNBC, February 3, 2017, accessed August 3, 2018, https://www.cnbc.com/2017/02/03/9-of-warren-buffetts-funniest-and-most-frugal-quirks.html.

18. Beth Armogida, "The United States of Yelling," *Huffington Post*, May 25, 2011, accessed August 3, 2018, https://www.huffingtonpost.com /beth-armogida/the-united-states-of-yell_b_258804.html.

19. Blaise Pascal, *Provincial Letters*, Letter XVI, December 4, 1656.

20. Wills, *Lincoln at Gettysburg*, 34.

21. Ibid., 213.

22. Ibid., 158.

23. Humes, *Speak Like Churchill*, 27.

24. Rachel Fershleiser, and Larry Smith, eds., *Not Quite What I Was Planning: Six-Word Memoirs by Writers Famous and Obscure* (Pymble, Australia: HarperCollins, 2008), Kindle edition, introduction.

25. Ibid., beginning of body of book.

26. Ibid., introduction.

27. Ibid.

28. Greg Stone, *Artful Business: 50 Lessons from Creative Geniuses* (Amazon CreateSpace, 2016), 91; see also, Dan Piepenbring, "George Plimpton on Muhammad Ali, the Poet," *Paris Review*, June 6, 2016, accessed August 3, 2018, https://www.theparisreview.org/blog/2016/06/06 /george-plimpton-on-muhammad-ali-the-poet/.

29. Laurence Perrine, *Sound and Sense: An Introduction to Poetry* (New York: Harcourt, 1963), 186–187.

30. Winston Churchill, "We Shall Fight on the Beaches," June 4, 1940, accessed August 3, 2018, https://www.winstonchurchill.org/resources /speeches/1940-the-finest-hour/we-shall-fight-on-the-beaches/.

31. Bill Goldstein, *The World Broke in Two: Virginia Woolf, T. S. Eliot, D. H. Lawrence, E. M. Forster, and the Year That Changed Literature* (New York: Henry Holt, 2017), Kindle edition, ch. 10.

32. Ibid.

33. *Romeo and Juliet*, Act II, Scene 2.

CHAPTER 8

1. Edward Bliss Jr. and James L. Hoyt, *Writing News for Broadcast*, 3rd ed. (New York: Columbia University Press, 1994), 34.

2. Stephen King, *On Writing: A Memoir of the Craft* (New York: Pocket Books, 2000), 222.

3. Truffaut and Scott, *Hitchcock*, 103.

4. Greg Stone, "What Ever Happened to the New Journalism?" (Master's thesis, Columbia University Journalism School, 1980), 7.

5. Ibid.

6. David Sterritt, *The Films of Jean-Luc Godard: Seeing the Invisible* (Cambridge: Cambridge University Press, 1999), 20.

7. John Gardner, *The Art of Fiction: Notes on Craft for Young Writers* (New York: Vintage Books, 1991), Kindle edition, ch. 6.

8. Stone, "New Journalism," 9–10.

9. Yoko Ogawa, "Afternoon at the Bakery," in *Revenge: Eleven Dark Tales*, trans. Stephen Snyder (New York: Picador, 2013), 1.

10. King, *On Writing*, 97.

11. Paul Valéry, *Degas, Manet, Morisot*, trans. David Paul (New York: Pantheon, 1960).

12. "The Lightning Bug vs. the Lightning," American Management Association, accessed August 3, 2018, https://www.amanet.org/training/articles/the-lightning-bug-vs-the-lightning.aspx.

13. Rudy De Reyna, *How to Draw What You See* (New York: Watson-Guptill Publications, 1996), 10.

14. Berger, *Media Analysis*, 88.

15. Ibid., 91

16. Guy de Maupassant, *Pierre et Jean* (Paris: Pocket, 2006), 16 (translated by author).

17. "Top 20 B2B Marketing Charts of 2017," accessed August 3, 2018, https://www.marketingcharts.com/top-20-b2b-marketing-charts-2017.

18. Ibid.

19. William Foster-Harris, *The Basic Patterns of Plot* (Norman: University of Oklahoma Press, 1959), 23.

20. Naomi Eppel, *The Observation Deck: A Tool Kit for Writers* (San Francisco: Chronicle Books, 1998), 90.

21. Gardner, *Art of Fiction*, ch. 2.

22. Ibid., ch. 5.

23. Ibid., ch. 2.

24. Ibid., ch. 5.

25. Ibid., ch. 7.

26. Norman Mailer, *The Spooky Art: Some Thoughts on Writing* (New York: Random House, 2003), Kindle edition, Style section.

27. Ibid., Real Life Versus Plot Life section.

28. Ibid., Living in the World section.

29. E. M. Forster, *Aspects of the Novel* (Orlando: Harcourt, 1955), 78.

30. Ibid., 78–79.

31. Ibid., 169.

32. Stone, *Artful Business*, 7.
33. Ibid., 13.
34. Isenberg, Casablanca, ch. 1, quoting Robert McKee.
35. Tatar, *Enchanted Hunters*, introduction.
36. Isenberg, Casablanca, ch. 6.
37. Ibid., ch. 6.
38. Truffaut and Scott, *Hitchcock*, 287.
39. Foster-Harris, *Basic Patterns*, 107–108.
40. Aristotle, *Poetics*, trans. S. H. Butcher (Mineola, NY: Dover, 1997), Kindle edition, VI, XI.
41. Foster-Harris, *Basic Patterns*, 63.
42. Schlozman, Interview.
43. Tatar, *Off with Their Heads!*, 237.
44. Foster-Harris, *Basic Patterns*, 6, italics in original.
45. "Ford's Assembly Line Starts Rolling," History.com, December 1, 1913, accessed August 3, 2018, https://www.history.com/this-day-in -history/fords-assembly-line-starts-rolling.
46. William Duggan, *Strategic Intuition: The Creative Spark in Human Achievement* (New York: Columbia Business School, 2007), 93–95.
47. Ibid., 95.
48. Ibid.
49. Ibid.
50. Ibid., 95–99.
51. Bruner, *Making Stories*, 13–16.
52. Tatar, *Hard Facts*, 101.
53. Max Lüthi, "Abstract Style," in Tatar, *Classic Fairy Tales*, Kindle ed.
54. Sergei Eisenstein, *Film Form: Essays in Film Theory*, trans. Jay Leyda (San Diego: Harcourt Brace, 1977), 39.
55. Ibid., 12 and 14.
56. Sergei Eisenstein, *The Film Sense*, trans. Jay Leyda (San Diego: Harcourt Brace Jovanovich, 1974), 30.
57. Ovid, *Metamorphoses*, 394–396.
58. Ibid., 210–217.
59. Ibid., 32–33.
60. Mathew Dixon, Karen Freeman, and Nicholas Toman, "Stop Trying to Delight Your Customers," *Harvard Business Review*, July–August 2010, accessed August 3, 2018, https://hbr.org/2010/07/stop-trying-to-delight -your-customers.

61. Ibid.
62. Ibid.
63. Ibid.
64. Truffaut and Scott, *Hitchcock*, 277.
65. Ibid., 138.
66. Ibid., 138–139.

CHAPTER 9

1. Molière, *The Would-be Gentleman*, in *The Misanthrope and Other Plays*, trans. Donald M. Frame (New York: Signet Classics, 2005), 235–236.
2. Wills, *Lincoln at Gettysburg*, 27.
3. Ibid.
4. Ibid., 162.
5. Ibid., 163.
6. Ibid., 164.
7. Inaugural Address of President John F. Kennedy, Washington, DC, January 20, 1961, accessed August 3, 2018, https://www.jfklibrary.org/Research/Research-Aids/Ready-Reference/JFK-Quotations/Inaugural-Address.aspx.
8. William Safire, "On Language; Who Trusts Whom?" *New York Times Magazine*, October 4, 1992, accessed August 3, 2018, https://www.nytimes.com/1992/10/04/magazine/on-language-who-trusts-whom.html.
9. Humes, *Speak Like Churchill*, 159.
10. Churchill, "We Shall Fight on the Beaches."
11. Humes, *Speak Like Churchill*, 127.
12. Wills, *Lincoln at Gettysburg*, 263.
13. For the rhetorical techniques explained here, I am indebted to two excellent sources: Mark Forsyth, *The Elements of Eloquence: Secrets of the Perfect Turn of Phrase* (New York: Berkley Books, 2013), Kindle edition; and Richard Nordquist's articles on thoughtco.com. In all cases I did my best to rephrase the concepts in my own words.
14. Forsyth, *Elements of Eloquence*, Kindle edition, ch. 9.
15. Barack Obama, "Barack Obama's New Hampshire Primary Speech," *New York Times*, January 8, 2008, italics added, accessed August 3, 2018, https://www.nytimes.com/2008/01/08/us/politics/08text-obama.html.
16. Nordquist, thoughtco.com.

17. Forsyth, *Elements of Eloquence*, ch. 17.

18. Nordquist, thoughtco.com.

19. Inaugural Address of President John F. Kennedy.

20. Frank Boers, Seth Lindstromberg, and June Eyckmans, "Are Alliterative Word Combinations Comparatively Easy to Remember for Adult Learners?" *RELC Journal* 43 (2012), accessed August 3, 2018, http://journals.sagepub.com/doi/metrics/10.1177/0033688212439997.

21. Forsyth, *Elements of Eloquence*, Kindle position 154.

22. "Famous Synesthetes: Franz Liszt," accessed August 3, 2018, http://sdl.granthazard.com/exhibits/show/famous-synesthetes/famous-synesthetes-closer-look/franz-liszt.

23. Stone, *Artful Business*, 67.

24. William Shakespeare, *History of Henry IV, Part II*, Act III, Scene 1, accessed August 3, 2018, https://www.opensourceshakespeare.org/views/plays/play_view.php?WorkID=henry4p2&Act=3&Scene=1&Scope=scene.

25. "The Starwars.com 10 Best Yoda Quotes," accessed August 3, 2018, https://www.starwars.com/news/the-starwars-com-10-best-yoda-quotes.

26. Wills, *Lincoln at Gettysburg*, 161.

27. Raymond Chandler, *Farewell My Lovely*, in *Stories and Early Novels* (New York: Library of America, 1995), 943.

28. Dave Barry, "Dave's World," *International Herald Tribune*, April 8, 2001.

29. Mark Forsyth, "Rhetorical Reasons That Slogans Stick," *New York Times*, November 13, 2014, accessed August 3, 2018, https://www.nytimes.com/2014/11/14/business/international/rhetorical-reasons-that-slogans-stick.html.

30. Forsyth, *Elements of Eloquence*, ch. 27.

31. Nordquist, thoughtco.com.

32. "Snowclone," accessed August 3, 2018, http://knowyourmeme.com/memes/snowclone.

33. Paul McFedries, "Snowclone Is the New Cliché," IEEE Spectrum, February 1, 2008, accessed August 3, 2018, https://spectrum.ieee.org/at-work/education/snowclone-is-the-new-clich.

34. "The Snowclones Database," accessed August 3, 2018, https://snowclones.org/index/.

35. McFedries, "Snowclone." See also https://snowclones.org/about/.

36. Marianne Moore, *New Collected Poems* (New York: Farrar, Straus and Giroux, 2017), Kindle edition, 27.

37. Stone, *Artful Business*, 69.

38. Berger, *Media Analysis*, 4.

39. Ibid., 12.

40. Ibid., 22–23.

41. Ibid., 24.

42. Rory McDonald, "Becoming a Cognitive Referent: Market Creation and Cultural Strategy," Harvard Business School Working Paper, No. 16-095, February 2016, accessed August 3, 2018, http://nrs.harvard.edu /urn-3:HUL.InstRepos:25680334, quoting Santos and Eisenhardt, 3.

43. Ibid., 3.

44. Stone, *Artful Business*, 73.

45. Aristotle, *Poetics*, XXII.

46. Stone, *Artful Business*, 73.

47. Tihamér Von Ghyczy, "The Fruitful Flaws of Strategy Metaphors," *Harvard Business Review*, November 11, 2013, accessed August 3, 2018, https://hbr.org/2003/09/the-fruitful-flaws-of-strategy-metaphors, 2.

48. Ibid., 2.

49. Stone, *Artful Business*, 73.

50. Von Ghyczy, "Fruitful Flaws," 5.

51. F. Scott Fitzgerald, *The Crack-up* (New York: New Directions, 1993), 69.

52. Adam Kirsch, "Extracting the Woodchuck: Robert Frost's 'Doubleness' Revealed in his Letters—and Poems," *Harvard Magazine*, January–February 2014, accessed August 3, 2018, https://www.harvardmagazine. com/2014/01/extracting-the-woodchuck.

53. "Umberto Eco's Rules for Writers," Of Course Italian, accessed August 3, 2018, http://ofcourseitalian.com/italian-culture-2/umberto-ecos -rules-for-writers/.

54. Stone, *Artful Business*, 73.

55. Ibid.

56. Hatch, "Jazz," 77.

57. Ibid., 76.

58. Ibid., 79.

59. Ibid., 80–81.

60. Ibid., 81.

61. Hatch, Interview.

62. George Lakoff, *Don't Think of an Elephant!: Know Your Values and Frame the Debate* (White River Junction, VT: Chelsea Green Publishing, 2004), xv.

63. Ibid.

64. Ibid., 73.

65. Bonnie Azab Powell, "Framing the Issues: UC Berkeley Professor George Lakoff Tells How Conservatives Use Language to Dominate Politics," UCBerkeleyNews, October 27, 2003, accessed August 3, 2018, https://www.berkeley.edu/news/media/releases/2003/10/27_lakoff.shtml.

66. Magda Szabó, *The Door*, trans. Len Rix (New York: New York Review of Books, 2007), Kindle edition, Sutu chapter.

67. Umberto Eco, *A Theory of Semiotics* (Bloomington: Indiana University Press, 1979), 7, italics in original.

68. Margaret Macdonald, "The Language of Fiction," in *Philosophy of Art and Aesthetics: From Plato to Wittgenstein*, ed. Frank A. Tillman and Steven M. Cahn (New York: Harper & Row, 1969), 620.

69. Stone, "New Journalism," 21.

70. Ibid., 29–30.

71. "Hamlet," in T. S. Eliot, *Selected Prose of T. S. Eliot* (San Diego: Harvest, 1975), 48; Eliot may have disavowed this concept in an oblique reference in a speech in front of 14,000 people at the University of Minnesota when he mentioned that "a few notorious phrases of his own . . . have had a truly embarrassing success in the world." See also Richard Poirier, *Trying It Out in America: Literary and Other Performances* (New York: Farrar, Straus and Giroux, 1999), 93.

72. Stone, *Artful Business*, 25.

73. Eliot, "Hamlet," 47–49.

74. T. S. Eliot, *The Sacred Wood: Essays on Poetry and Criticism* (New York: Alfred A. Knopf, 1921), 114.

75. Washington Allston, "Introductory Discourse" of Lectures on Art, 1840.

76. George Santayana, *Interpretations of Poetry and Religion* (Cambridge, MA: MIT Press, 1989), 164–165.

77. Edgar Allan Poe, Excerpt from a Review of Hawthorne's *Twice-Told Tales* in *Graham's Magazine*, May 1842, accessed August 3, 2018, http://www.people.virginia.edu/~sfr/enam315/texts2/eaphawthorne.html.

78. Michel de Montaigne, "On Diversion," accessed August 3, 2018, http://www.gutenberg.org/cache/epub/3594/pg3594-images.html.

79. Judith Williamson, *Decoding Advertisements: Ideology and Meaning in Advertising* (London: Marion Boyars, 1978), 38, italics in original.

80. Stone, *Artful Business*, 103.

81. Gale Pryor, Description of home for sales purposes.

82. Cathren Koehlert-Page, "A Look Inside the Butler's Cupboard: How the External World Reveals Internal State of Mind in Legal Narratives," *NYU Annual Survey of American Law* 69 (2013): 12, 13, 14, 29, accessed August 3, 2018, https://lawpublications.barry.edu/cgi/viewcontent.cgi?arti cle=1049&context=facultyscholarship.

CHAPTER 10

1. Stone, *Artful Business*, 19.
2. Bliss and Hoyt, *Writing News*, 43.
3. Isenberg, Casablanca, ch. 5.
4. Chandler, *The Big Sleep*, in *Stories and Early Novels*, 601.
5. Ibid., 717.
6. Chandler, *Farewell My Lovely*, in *Stories and Early Novels*, 976.
7. Brian McDonald, *Invisible Ink* (Omaha, NE: Concierge Marketing, 2003–2005), 16.
8. Sean Hood, "A New Class at USC," *Genre Hacks*, January 27, 2015, accessed August 3, 2018, http://genrehacks.blogspot.com/2015/01/.
9. Campbell, *The Hero*, 211.
10. Armstrong, *Short History*, ii.
11. Georges Polti, *The Thirty-Six Dramatic Situations* (Boston: Writer, 1999).
12. V. Propp, *Morphology of the Folktale*, 2nd ed. (Austin: University of Texas Press, 2009).
13. Hatch, Kostera, and Koźmiński, *Three Faces*, xi.
14. Ibid., 23–24.
15. Ibid., 23.
16. Ibid., 39.
17. Ibid., 58.
18. Ibid., 58–59.
19. Joanne Martin, Martha S. Feldman, Mary Jo Hatch, and Sim B. Sitkin, "The Uniqueness Paradox in Organizational Stories," *Administrative Science Quarterly* 28 (1983): 438–453.
20. Ed Vere, "Picasso: His Art Was an Expression of What It Means to be Alive," *The Guardian*, May 17, 2016, accessed August 3, 2018, https://www.theguardian.com/childrens-books-site/2016/may/17/picasso-ed-vere.
21. Mailer, *Spook Art*, Writing Courses chapter.
22. Ibid., Stamina chapter.

23. "Shakespeare FAQ," Folger Shakespeare Library, accessed August 3, 2018, https://www.folger.edu/shakespeare-faq. See also "Shakespeare FAQ," Absolute Shakespeare, accessed August 3, 2018, https://absolute shakespeare.com/trivia/faq/faq.htm.

CHAPTER 11

1. This section relies heavily on an unproduced corporate training video script I wrote about body language in 1992—based on the work of the late Julius Fast, author of the book *Body Language* and on many conversations with him.

2. Katherine Schreiber and Heather Hausenblas, "What Eye Contact Can Do to You: For Better or Worse, the Gaze of Others has a Powerful Effect on Our Behavior," *Psychology Today*, September 20, 2016, accessed August 3, 2018, https://www.psychologytoday.com/us/blog/the-truth-about-exer cise-addiction/201609/what-eye-contact-can-do-you.

3. Ibid.

4. Greg Stone, "Go Ahead, Act Like a Guy: Body Language for Women," *Huffington Post*, October 6, 2014, accessed August 3, 2018, https://www.huffingtonpost.com/greg-j-stone/go-ahead-act-like-a-guy -b_b_5922902.html. See also Monika Gulabovska and Peter Leeson, "Why Are Women Better Decoders of Nonverbal Language?" *Gender Issues* 31 (2014): 202–218; Ronald E. Riggio, "Women's Intuition: Myth or Reality?: Do Women Have Some Special Ability?" *Psychology Today*, July 14, 2011, https://www.psychologytoday.com/us/blog/cutting-edge -leadership/201107/women-s-intuition-myth-or-reality; Jeff Thompson, "Are Man and Woman Equals in Nonverbal Communication?" *Psychology Today*, February 12, 2012, accessed August 3, 2018, https://www.psychologytoday.com/us/blog/beyond-words/201202/are-man-and-woman-equals-in-nonverbal-communication.

5. Albert Mehrabian, "'Silent Messages'—A Wealth of Information about Nonverbal Communication (Body Language)," accessed August 3, 2018, http://kaaj.com/psych/smorder.html.

6. Rich Kirchen, "Career Advancement for Women: Barry White vs. Pee-wee Herman?" *Milwaukee Business Journal*, July 8, 2013, accessed August 3, 2018, https://www.bizjournals.com/milwaukee/blog/2013/07 /career-advancement-barry-white-vs.html.

7. John Colapinto, "Giving Voice: A Surgeon Pioneers Methods to Help Singers Sing," *New Yorker*, March 4, 2013, accessed August 3, 2018, https://www.newyorker.com/magazine/2013/03/04/giving-voice.

8. Ibid.

9. Ibid.

10. "George Washington Prevents the Revolt of His Officers," History Place, March 15, 1783, accessed August 3, 2018, http://www.historyplace.com/speeches/washington.htm.

11. Ibid.

12. Humes, *Speak Like Churchill*, 18.

13. Eric Barker, "How to Overcome Fear of Public Speaking and Give a Great Presentation," *Time*, May 7, 2014, accessed August 3, 2018, http://time.com/89814/how-to-overcome-fear-of-public-speaking-and-give-a-great-presentation/.

14. David D. Burns, *Feeling Good: The New Mood Therapy* (New York: Quill, 1980), 62.

15. Ibid., xviii, xxii, and 12.

16. Greg Stone, "Don't Let Stage Fright Make You Uptight." American Management Association Playbook, July 28, 2014, accessed August 3, 2018, http://playbook.amanet.org/dont-let-stage-fright-make-uptight/.

CHAPTER 12

1. Sree Sreenivasan, Social Media Expert, Interview by author, June 20, 2010.

2. Sree Sreenivasan, "How to Use Social Media in Your Career," *New York Times*, April 2018, accessed August 3, 2018, https://www.nytimes.com/guides/business/social-media-for-career-and-business.

3. Sreenivasan, Interview.

4. Ibid.

5. Ibid.

6. Ibid.

7. Courtesy of Christy McMann, Assistant Director of Digital Engagement at Harvard Business School.

8. Sreenivasan, Interview.

9. Alfred Lua, "20 Creative Ways to Use Social Media for Storytelling," Buffer, January 30, 2018, accessed August 3, 2018, https://blog.bufferapp.com/social-media-storytelling.

10. Courtesy of Christy McMann.

11. Sreenivasan, Interview.

12. John Deighton, "Brands and the Dark Side of Social Media," *Harvard Business Review*, May 18, 2010, accessed August 3, 2018, https://hbr.org/2010/05/brands-and-the-dark-side-of-so.html.

13. Sangeeta Singh and Stephan Sonnenburg, "Brand Performances in Social Media," *Journal of Interactive Marketing* 26 (2012): 189–197.

14. Ibid., 190.

15. Ibid., 192.

16. Ibid., 193.

17. Ibid., 191.

18. Ibid., 195.

19. Kathleen Fearn-Banks, *Crisis Communications: A Casebook Approach* (Mahwah, NJ: Lawrence Erlbaum, 1996), 19.

20. Ibid., 66.

21. Ibid., 65.

22. Joe Mont, "10 Bizarre Company Rumors," TheStreet, October 24, 2011, accessed August 3, 2018, https://www.thestreet.com/story/112855 89/1/10-bizarre-company-rumors.html.

23. Cass R. Sunstein, "Commentary: False Rumors Spread Fast. So Do Some True Ones," *Chicago Tribune*, March 19, 2018, accessed August 3, 2018, http://www.chicagotribune.com/news/opinion/commentary /ct-perspec-rumors-false-true-social-media-katy-perry-taylor-smith-twitter -facebook-0319-story.html.

24. Fearn-Bank, *Crisis Communications*, 37–38.

25. Ibid., 39–40.

26. The Johnson & Johnson story is based on Fearn-Banks, *Crisis Communications*, 102–111; and Greg Stone, "An Interview Survival Guide: Forging Relationships with Reporters," A private manual, 2018, 16.

27. Fearn-Banks, *Crisis Communications*, 143–150.

28. Ibid., 149–150.

CHAPTER 13

1. Dan Dwyer, Interviews with author, May 16, 2016, and December 12, 2016.

2. Dwyer, Interview, December 12, 2016.

3. Dwyer, Interview, May 16, 2016.

4. Ibid.

5. Dwyer, Interview, December 12, 2016.

6. Ibid.

7. Jesse Laflamme, Interview with author, April 4, 2018.

8. Ibid.

9. Ibid.

10. Ibid.

11. Ibid.

12. The Salute Military Golf Association, smgaboston.org.

13. Jerry Shanahan, Volunteer Operators Director, The Salute Military Golf Association, Interview with author, April 3, 2018.

14. Ibid.

15. L. Backwell, F. d'Errico, and L. Wadley, "Middle Stone Age Bone Tools from the Howiesons Poort Layers, Sibudu Cave, South Africa," *Journal of Archaeological Science* 35 (2008): 1566–1580, doi:10.1016/j.jas.2007.11.006.

16. "World's Oldest Needle Found in Siberian Cave That Stiches Together Human History," *Siberian Times*, August 23, 2016, accessed August 3, 2018, http://siberiantimes.com/science/casestudy/news/n0711 -worlds-oldest-needle-found-in-siberian-cave-that-stitches-together-human-history/.

17. "A Brief History of the Sewing Needle," Apparel Science, accessed August 3, 2018, http://apparelscience.com/index.php/apparel-science /technical/85-apparel-science/technical/148-a-brief-history-of-the-sewing -needle.

18. Robert Horvat, "Bone Sewing Needles (a brief history of . . .)," Rearview Mirror, October 22, 2013, accessed August 3, 2018, https://rear -view-mirror.com/2013/10/22/bone-sewing-needles-a-brief-history-of/.

19. Suzanne Schalow, Craft Beer Cellar, Interview with the author, April 28, 2018.

20. Schalow, Interview.

21. Kate Baker, Craft Beer Cellar, Interview with the author, April 28, 2018.

22. Schalow, Interview.

23. Baker, Interview.

24. Schalow, Interview.

25. Baker, Interview.

26. Ibid.

27. Baker and Schalow together, Interview.

28. Schalow, Interview.

29. Marcie Schorr Hirsch, Management Consultant and Coach, Interview with the author, April 26, 2018.

30. Ibid.

31. Ibid.

32. Ibid.

CHAPTER 14

1. Alice Calaprice, ed., *Dear Professor Einstein: Albert Einstein's Letters to and from Children* (Amherst, MA: Prometheus, 2002), 140.

2. Walter Isaacson, *Einstein: His Life and Universe* (New York: Simon & Schuster, 2007), 20. (The entire story spans pp. 16–20.)

3. Ibid., 16.

4. Ibid., 17.

5. Tartar, *Classic Fairy Tales*, introduction.

6. Andrea Thompson, "Bad Memories Stick Better than Good," Live Science, September 5, 2007, accessed August 3, 2018, https://www.livescience.com/1827-bad-memories-stick-good.html; Jennifer Warner, "Bad Memories Easier to Remember: Negative Memories May Be More Vivid than Happy Ones," WebMD, August 29, 2007, accessed August 3, 2018, https://www.webmd.com/brain/news/20070829/bad-memories-easier-to-remember.

7. Ackerman, *Natural History*, 169.

8. Walter Isaacson, "The Real Leadership Lessons of Steve Jobs," *Harvard Business Review*, April 2012, accessed August 3, 2018, https://hbr.org/2012/04/the-real-leadership-lessons-of-steve-jobs.

9. Tarkovsky, *Sculpting in Time*, 97.

Bibliography

Ackerman, Diane. *A Natural History of the Senses*. New York: Vintage Books, 1991.

Aggarwal, Pankaj, and Ann L. McGill. "Is That Car Smiling at Me? Schema Congruity as a Basis for Evaluating Anthropomorphized Products." *Journal of Consumer Research* 34 (2007): 468–479.

Akalis, Scott, and John T. Cacioppo. "When We Need a Human: Motivational Determinants of Anthropomorphism." *Social Cognition* 26 (2008): 143–155.

Aldama, Frederick Luis. "The Science of Storytelling: Perspectives from Cognitive Science, Neuroscience, and the Humanities." *Projections* 9 (2015): 80–95.

Allston, Washington. Introductory Discourse of Lectures on Art. Accessed July 19, 2018. https://ipfs.io/ipfs/QmXoypizjW3WknFiJnKLwHC nL72vedxjQkDDP1mXWo6uco/wiki/Objective_correlative.html.

Andrade, Eduardo B., and Joel B. Cohen. "On the Consumption of Negative Feelings." *Journal of Consumer Research* 34 (2007): 283–300.

Angier, Natalie. "You Share Everything with Your Bestie. Even Brain Waves." *New York Times*, April 16, 2018. Accessed July 19, 2018. https://www.nytimes.com/2018/04/16/science/friendship-brain -health.html.

Aristotle. *The Philosophy of Aristotle*. Translated by A. E. Wardman and J. L. Creed. New York: New American Library, 1963.

Aristotle. *Poetics*. Translated by S. H. Butcher. Mineola, NY: Dover, 1997. Kindle edition.

Armstrong, Karen. *A Short History of Myth*. Edinburgh: Canongate, 2005. Kindle edition.

Baker, Kate. Craft Beer Cellar. Interview with the author. April 28, 2018.

Barreca, Gina. "Does 'Handsome, Ruthless, and Stupid' Sound Like Your Type?: Do Women Respond More to a Man's Forgetfulness Than his Attention?" *Psychology Today*, July 27, 2014. Accessed August 3, 2018. https://www.psychologytoday.com/us/blog/snow-white -doesnt-live-here-anymore/201407/does-handsome-ruthless-and -stupid-sound-your-type.

Barro, Josh. "That Company You Love Won't Love You Back." *New York Times*, December 13, 2015.

Benesh, Patricia. "Mark Twain's Discourse: A Timeless Writing Course." *Huffington Post*, October 25, 2010. Accessed August 3, 2018. https://www.huffingtonpost.com/patricia-benesh/mark-twains-dis course-a-t_b_772701.html.

Berger, Arthur Asa. *Media Analysis Techniques*. Revised ed. Newbury Park, CA: Sage Publications, 1991.

Bliss, Edward, Jr., and James L. Hoyt. *Writing News for Broadcast*. 3rd ed. New York: Columbia University Press, 1994.

Bliss, Edward, Jr., and John M. Patterson. *Writing News for Broadcast*. 2nd ed. New York: Columbia University Press, 1978.

Boers, Frank, Seth Lindstromberg, and June Eyckmans. "Are Alliterative Word Combinations Comparatively Easy to Remember for Adult Learners?" *RELC Journal* 43 (2012). Accessed August 3, 2018. http://journals.sagepub.com/doi/metrics/10.1177/003368821243 9997.

Borges, Jorge Luis. *Collected Fictions*. Translated by Andrew Hurley. New York: Penguin Books, 1998.

Bragg, Melvyn. *The Adventure of English: The Biography of a Language*. New York: Arcade, 2004.

Breslin, Jimmy. "It's an Honor." *New York Herald Tribune*, November 26, 1963. Accessed August 3, 2018. http://teachers.sduhsd.net/ mgaughen/docs/Breslin.Honor.pdf.

Bresson, Robert. *Notes on the Cinematographer*. Translated by Jonathan Griffin. Los Angeles: Green Integer Books, 1997.

"A Brief History of the Sewing Needle." Apparel Science. Accessed August 3, 2018. http://apparelscience.com/index.php/apparel-science /technical/85-apparel-science/technical/148-a-brief-history-of -the-sewing-needle.

Bruner, Jerome. *Making Stories: Law, Literature, Life*. Cambridge, MA: Harvard University Press, 2002.

Brunette, Peter. *Michael Haneke*. Champaign: University of Illinois Press, 2010.

Burns, David D. *Feeling Good: The New Mood Therapy*. New York: Quill, 1980.

Campbell, Joseph. *The Hero with a Thousand Faces*. 3rd ed. Novato, CA: New World Library, 2008.

Castro, Tony. Attorney at Law. Interview with the author. September 20, 2017.

Chandler, Raymond. *Stories and Early Novels*. New York: Library of America, 1995.

Christensen, Clayton M., Taddy Hall, Karen Dillon, and David S. Duncan. *Competing Against Luck: The Story of Innovation and Customer Choice*. Sydney: HarperCollins, 2016. Kindle edition.

Ciotti, Gregory. "10 Stories of Unforgettable Customer Service." *Entrepreneur*, July 2, 2014. Accessed August 3, 2018. https://www.entrepreneur.com/article/234956.

Clark, Roy Peter. "Remembering Jimmy Breslin and the 'Gravedigger' School of News Writing." Poynter. March 20, 2017. Accessed August 3, 2018. https://www.poynter.org/news/remembering-jimmy-breslin-and-gravedigger-school-news-writing.

Colapinto, John. "Giving Voice: A Surgeon Pioneers Methods to Help Singers Sing." *New Yorker*, March 4, 2013. Accessed August 3, 2018. https://www.newyorker.com/magazine/2013/03/04/giving-voice.

Croce, Arlene. "Balanchine Said: What Was the Source of the Choreographer's Celebrated Utterances?" *New Yorker*, January 26, 2009. Accessed August 3, 2018. https://www.newyorker.com/magazine/2009/01/26/balanchine-said.

Daley, George. Speech delivered at Massachusetts General Hospital in Boston, MA, January 30, 2018.

Deighton, John. "Brands and the Dark Side of Social Media." *Harvard Business Review*, May 18, 2010. Accessed August 3, 2018. https://hbr.org/2010/05/brands-and-the-dark-side-of-so.html.

Deighton, John, and Leora Kornfeld. "Interactivity's Unanticipated Consequences for Marketers and Marketing." *Journal of Interactive Marketing* 23 (2009): 4–10.

Demers, Jayson. "6 Stories of Super Successes Who Overcame Failure." *Entrepreneur*, December 8, 2014. Accessed August 3, 2018. https://www.entrepreneur.com/article/240492.

De Reyna, Rudy. *How to Draw What You See*. New York: Watson-Guptill Publications, 1996.

Detz, Joan. *How to Write & Give a Speech*. New York: St. Martin's Press, 2002.

Dickinson, Emily. *Final Harvest: Emily Dickinson's Poems*. Boston: Little Brown, 1961.

Dixon, Matthew, Karen Freeman, and Nicholas Toman. "Stop Trying to Delight Your Customers." *Harvard Business Review*, July–August 2010. Accessed August 3, 2018. https://hbr.org/2010/07/stop-trying -to-delight-your-customers.

Duggan, William. *Strategic Intuition: The Creative Spark in Human Achievement*. New York: Columbia Business School, 2007.

Dwyer, Dan. Partner, Murphy & King, Boston. Interviews by author. May 16, 2016, and December 12, 2016.

Eco, Umberto. *A Theory of Semiotics*. Bloomington: Indiana University Press, 1979.

Eisenstein, Sergei. *Film Form: Essays in Film Theory*. Translated by Jay Leyda. San Diego: Harcourt Brace, 1977.

Eisenstein, Sergei. *The Film Sense*. Translated by Jay Leyda. San Diego: Harcourt Brace Jovanovich, 1974.

Eliot, T. S. *The Sacred Wood: Essays on Poetry and Criticism*. New York: Alfred A. Knopf, 1921.

Eliot, T. S. *Selected Prose of T. S. Eliot*. New York: Harvest, 1975.

Elkins, Kathleen. "9 of Warren Buffett's Funniest and Most Frugal Quirks." CNBC, February 3, 2017. Accessed August 3, 2018. https://www.cnbc.com/2017/02/03/9-of-warren-buffetts-funniest- and-most-frugal-quirks.html.

Epel, Naomi. *The Observation Deck: A Tool Kit for Writers*. San Francisco: Chronicle Books, 1998.

Epley, Nicholas, Adam Waytz, and John T. Cacioppo. "On Seeing Human: A Three-Factor Theory of Anthropomorphism." *Psychological Review* 114 (2007): 864–886.

Escher, Anna, and Lora Kolodny. "Causes of the Global Water Crisis and 12 Companies Trying to Solve It." TechCrunch, March 23, 2017. Accessed August 3, 2018. https://techcrunch.com/2017/03/22 /causes-of-the-global-water-crisis-and-12-companies-trying-to -solve-it/.

"Facts and Statistics, Physical Activity." President's Council on Sports, Fitness & Nutrition. Accessed August 3, 2018. https://www.hhs. gov/fitness/resource-center/facts-and-statistics/index.html.

Fast, Julius. *Body Language*. New York: Pocket Books, 1971.

Fast, Julius, and Greg Stone. "Body Language Video Script" (unproduced). 1992.

Fearn-Banks, Kathleen. *Crisis Communications: A Casebook Approach.* Mahwah, NJ: Lawrence Erlbaum, 1996.

Fershleiser, Rachel, and Larry Smith, eds. *Not Quite What I Was Planning: Six-Word Memoirs by Writers Famous and Obscure.* Pymble, Australia: HarperCollins, 2007. Kindle edition.

Field, Syd. *The Foundations of Screenwriting: A Step-by-Step Guide from Concept to Finished Script.* New York: Dell, 1982.

Field, Syd. *The Screenwriter's Workbook.* New York: Dell, 1984.

Fischoff, Stuart. "Why Are Some People More Attracted to Scary Movies than Others Are?" *Science + Religion Today,* October 28, 2011. Accessed August 3, 2018. http://www.scienceandreligiontoday. com/2011/10/28/why-are-some-people-more-attracted-to-scary -movies-than-others-are/.

Fitzgerald, F. Scott. *The Crack-up.* New York: New Directions, 1993.

Fitzgerald, F. Scott. *The Love of the Last Tycoon.* New York: Scribner, 1993.

Flaherty, Francis. *The Elements of Story: Field Notes on Nonfiction Writing.* New York: Harper, 2009.

Foley, Aaron. "Why Detroit's City Storyteller Wants to Ban the Word 'Gritty.'" CNN, October 5, 2017. Accessed August 3, 2018. https:// www.cnn.com/travel/article/detroit-storyteller-aaron-foley/index .html.

"Ford's Assembly Line Starts Rolling." History.com. Accessed August 3, 2018. https://www.history.com/this-day-in-history/fords-assembly-line -starts-rolling.

Forster, E. M. *Aspects of the Novel.* Orlando: Harcourt, 1955.

Forsyth, Mark. *The Elements of Eloquence: Secrets of the Perfect Turn of Phrase.* New York: Berkley Books, 2013. Kindle edition.

Forsyth, Mark. "Rhetorical Reasons That Slogans Stick." *New York Times,* November 13, 2014. Accessed August 3, 2018. https://www .nytimes.com/2014/11/14/business/international/rhetorical-reasons -that-slogans-stick.html.

Foster-Harris, William. *The Basic Patterns of Plot.* Norman: University of Oklahoma Press, 1959.

Fox, Margalit. "Helen Gurley Brown, Who Gave 'Single Girl' a Life in Full, Dies at 90." *New York Times,* August 13, 2012. Accessed August 3, 2018. https://www.nytimes.com/2012/08/14/business /media/helen-gurley-brown-who-gave-cosmopolitan-its-purr-is -dead-at-90.html.

Fox, Margalit. "Tony Schwartz, Father of the 'Daisy Ad' for the Johnson Campaign, Dies at 84." *New York Times*, June 17, 2008. Accessed August 3, 2018. https://www.nytimes.com/2008/06/17/business /media/16cnd-schwartz.html.

French, Tana. "Author Note." Tanafrench.com. Accessed August 3, 2018. http://www.tanafrench.com/about.html.

Gallo, Carmine. "Data Alone Won't Get You a Standing Ovation." *Harvard Business Review*, April 30, 2014. Accessed August 3, 2018. https://hbr.org/2014/04/data-alone-wont-get-you-a-standing -ovation.

Gardner, Howard E. *Leading Minds: An Anatomy of Leadership.* New York: Basic Books, 2011. Kindle edition.

Gardner, John. *The Art of Fiction: Notes on Craft for Young Writers.* New York: Vintage Books, 1991. Kindle edition.

Gavetti, Giovanni, and Jan W. Rivkin. "How Strategists Really Think: Tapping the Power of Analogy." *Harvard Business Review*, April 2005. Accessed August 3, 2018. https://hbr.org/2005/04/how -strategists-really-think-tapping-the-power-of-analogy.

Gavetti, Giovanni, and Jan W. Rivkin. "The Use and Abuse of Analogies." Harvard Business School Background Note 9-703-429, February 28, 2006.

"George Washington Prevents the Revolt of His Officers." History Place, Great Speeches Collection. Accessed August 3, 2018. http://www .historyplace.com/speeches/washington.htm.

Gertner, Jon. *The Idea Factory: Bell Labs and the Great Age of American Invention.* New York: Penguin Press, 2012.

Goldstein, Bill. *The World Broke in Two: Virginia Woolf, T. S. Eliot, D. H. Lawrence, E. M. Forster, and the Year That Changed Literature.* New York: Henry Holt, 2017. Kindle edition.

Gopnik, Adam. "The Right Man: Who Owns Edmund Burke?" *New Yorker*, July 29, 2013. Accessed August 3, 2018. https://www .newyorker.com/magazine/2013/07/29/the-right-man.

Gorman, Michele. "Yogi Berra's Most Memorable Sayings." *Newsweek*, September 23, 2015. Accessed August 3, 2018. http://www .newsweek.com/most-memorable-yogi-isms-375661.

Gould, Stephen Jay. *The Panda's Thumb: More Reflections in Natural History.* New York: W. W. Norton, 1982.

Griswold, Alison. "Everything You Think You Know about Thomas Edison Might Be Wrong." Business Insider, November 6, 2013.

Accessed August 3, 2018. http://www.businessinsider.com/thomas
-edison-light-bulb-publicity-stunt-2013-11.

Gross, Terry. Graduation Speech. Bryn Mawr College, May 17, 2014.
Accessed August 3, 2018. https://www.youtube.com/watch?v=U429
81EtGdQ.

Grosz, Stephen. *The Examined Life: How We Lose and Find Ourselves.*
New York: W. W. Norton, 2013.

Guber, Peter. "The Four Truths of the Storyteller." *Harvard Business
Review*, December 2007. Accessed July 19, 2018. https://hbr
.org/2007/12/the-four-truths-of-the-storyteller.

Gulabovska, Monika, and Peter Leeson. "Why Are Women Better Decoders of Nonverbal Language?" *Gender Issues* 31 (2014): 202–218.

Haig, Matt. *Brand Success: How the World's Top 100 Brands Thrive and
Survive.* London: KoganPage, 2011.

Halpern, Belle Linda, and Kathy Lubar. *Leadership Presence: Dramatic
Techniques to Reach Out, Motivate and Inspire.* New York:
Gotham Books, 2003.

Hamilton, Edith. *Mythology.* Boston: Little, Brown, 1998.

Hatch, Mary Jo. "Exploring the Empty Spaces of Organizing: How Improvisational Jazz Helps Redescribe Organizational Structure." *Organization Studies* 20 (1999): 75–100.

Hatch, Mary Jo. Professor, Emerita, McIntyre School of Commerce, University of Virginia, and visual artist. Interview by author. February
7, 2018.

Hatch, Mary Jo, Monika Kostera, and Andrzej K. Koźmiński. *The Three
Faces of Leadership: Manager, Artist, Priest.* Malden, MA: Blackwell, 2005.

Hauge, Michael. *Writing Screenplays That Sell.* New York: McGraw-Hill,
1988.

Helmore, Edward. "Detroit Redefined: City Hires America's First Official
'Chief Storyteller.'" *The Guardian*, September 5, 2017. Accessed
August 3, 2018. https://www.theguardian.com/cities/2017/sep/05
/detroit-redefined-america-first-official-chief-storyteller.

Hobson, Katherine. "Clicking: How Our Brains Are in Synch." *Princeton
Alumni Weekly*, April 11, 2018. Accessed August 3, 2018. https://
paw.princeton.edu/article/clicking-how-our-brains-are-sync.

Horvat, Robert. "Bone Sewing Needles (a Brief History of . . .)." Rearview
Mirror, October 22, 2013. Accessed August 3, 2018. https://rear-view-
mirror.com/2013/10/22/bone-sewing-needles-a-brief-history-of/.

Humes, James C. *Speak Like Churchill, Stand Like Lincoln: 21 Powerful Secrets of History's Greatest Speakers*. New York: Three Rivers Press, 2002.

Hutson, Matthew. "Love Objects: Why People Fall for Things." *Atlantic*, December 2017.

Impelluso, Lucia. *Myths: Tales of the Greek and Roman Gods*. New York: Abrams, 2008.

Isaacson, Walter. *Einstein: His Life and Universe*. New York: Simon & Schuster, 2007.

Isaacson, Walter. *Leonardo da Vinci*. New York: Simon & Schuster, 2017. Kindle edition.

Isaacson, Walter. "The Real Leadership Lessons of Steve Jobs." *Harvard Business Review*, April 2012. Accessed August 3, 2018. https://hbr.org/2012/04/the-real-leadership-lessons-of-steve-jobs.

Isenberg, Noah. *We'll Always Have* Casablanca*: The Life, Legend and Afterlife of Hollywood's Most Beloved Movie*. New York: Norton, 2017. Kindle edition.

James, M. R. *Collected Ghost Stories*. Oxford: Oxford University Press, 2011.

Johnson, Khari. "Google Empathy Lab Founder: AI Will Upend Storytelling and Human-Machine Interaction." VentureBeat, March 11, 2018. Accessed August 3, 2018. https://venturebeat.com/2018/03/11/google-empathy-lab-founder-ai-will-upend-storytelling-and-human-machine-interaction/.

Kakutani, Michiko. "'The Bronx, The Bench and the Life In Between,' review of *My Beloved World: A Memoir*, by Sonia Sotomayor." *New York Times*, January 21, 2013. Accessed August 3, 2018. https://www.nytimes.com/2013/01/22/books/my-beloved-world-a-memoir-by-sonia-sotomayor.html.

Kaplan, Robert Steven. *What to Ask the Person in the Mirror: Critical Questions for Becoming a More Effective Leader and Reaching Your Potential*. Boston: Harvard Business Review Press, 2011.

King, Stephen. *On Writing: A Memoir of the Craft*. New York: Pocket Books, 2000.

Kipling, Rudyard. "I Keep Six Honest . . ." Poetry Lover's Page. Accessed August 3, 2018. https://www.poetryloverspage.com/poets/kipling/i_keep_six_honest.html.

Kirchen, Rich. "Career Advancement for Women: Barry White vs. Pee-wee Herman?" *Milwaukee Business Journal*, July 8, 2013. Accessed

August 3, 2018. https://www.bizjournals.com/milwaukee/blog/2013
/07/career-advancement-barry-white-vs.html.

Kirsch, Adam. "Extracting the Woodchuck: Robert Frost's 'Doubleness,'
Revealed in his Letters—and Poems." *Harvard Magazine*,
January–February 2014. Accessed August 3, 2018. https://www
.harvardmagazine.com/2014/01/extracting-the-woodchuck.

Koehlert-Page, Cathren. "A Look Inside the Butler's Cupboard: How the
External World Reveals Internal State of Mind in Legal Narratives." *NYU Annual Survey of American Law* 69 (2013): 441–501.
Accessed August 3, 2018. https://lawpublications.barry.edu/cgi/
viewcontent.cgi?article=1049&context=facultyscholarship.

Kotler, Philip, and Kevin Lane Keller. *Marketing Management.* Upper
Saddle River, NJ: Prentice Hall, 2012.

Laflamme, Jesse. CEO of Pete and Gerry's Organic Eggs. Interview with
the author. April 4, 2018.

Lakoff, George. *Don't Think of an Elephant!: Know Your Values and
Frame the Debate.* White River Junction, VT: Chelsea Green Publishing, 2004.

Lambert, Craig. "The Horror and the Beauty: Maria Tatar Explores the
Dazzle and the 'Dark Side' in Fairy Tales—and Why We Read
Them." *Harvard Magazine*, November–December 2007. Accessed
August 3, 2018. https://www.harvardmagazine.com/2007/11/the
-horror-and-the-beaut.html.

Lemley, Mark A. "The Myth of the Sole Inventor." *Michigan Law Review*
110 (2012): 709–760.

Lévi-Strauss, Claude. "The Structural Study of Myth." *Journal of American Folklore* 68 (1955): 428–444.

Lua, Alfred. "20 Creative Ways to Use Social Media for Storytelling."
Buffer, January 30, 2018. Accessed August 3, 2018. https://blog
.bufferapp.com/social-media-storytelling.

Mailer, Norman. *The Spooky Art: Some Thoughts on Writing.* New York:
Random House, 2003. Kindle edition.

Malone, Chris, and Susan T. Fiske. *The Human Brand: How We Relate to
People, Products, and Companies.* San Francisco: Jossey-Bass,
2013.

Mankoff, Bob. "The Great Clichés: The Complete List So Far." *New
Yorker*, April 7, 2017.

Márquez, Gabriel García. "The Art of Fiction." Interview. *Paris Review.*
Winter 1981.

Márquez, Gabriel García. *One Hundred Years of Solitude*. Translated by Gregory Rabassa. New York: HarperCollins, 2006.

Martin, Emmie. "Why Multi-millionaire Zappos CEO Tony Hsieh Chooses to Live in a Trailer Park." CNBC, May 8, 2017. Accessed August 3, 2018. https://www.cnbc.com/2017/05/08/why-multi-millionaire-zappos-ceo-tony-hsieh-lives-in-a-trailer-park.html.

Martin, Joanne, Martha S. Feldman, Mary Jo Hatch, and Sim B. Sitkin. "The Uniqueness Paradox in Organizational Stories." *Administrative Science Quarterly* 28 (1983): 438–453.

Maupassant, Guy de. *Pierre et Jean*. Paris: Pocket, 2006.

May, Lisa. Real Estate Agent from Sotheby's in Cambridge, MA. Description of property for sale.

McConnell, Alaina. "Zappos' Outrageous Record for the Longest Customer Service Call Ever." Business Insider, December 20, 2012. Accessed August 3, 2018. http://www.businessinsider.com/zappos-longest-customer-service-call-2012-12.

McDonald, Brian. *Invisible Ink*. Omaha, NE: Concierge Marketing, 2003–2005.

McDonald, Rory. "Becoming a Cognitive Referent: Market Creation and Cultural Strategy." Harvard Business School Working Paper, No. 16-095, February 2016. Accessed August 3, 2018. http://nrs.harvard.edu/urn-3:HUL.InstRepos:25680334.

McFedries, Paul. "Snowclone Is the New Cliché." IEEE Spectrum, February 1, 2008. Accessed August 3, 2018. https://spectrum.ieee.org/at-work/education/snowclone-is-the-new-clich.

McLuhan, Marshall. *Understanding Media: The Extensions of Man*. New York: Mentor, 1964.

McMenemy, Lauren. "What Is a Chief Storyteller? Five Business Leaders Share Their Stories." ContentStandard, March 22, 2018. Accessed August 3, 2018. https://www.skyword.com/contentstandard/marketing/what-is-a-chief-storyteller-five-business-leaders-share-their-stories/.

Mehrabian, Albert. "'Silent Messages'—A Wealth of Information about Nonverbal Communication (Body Language)." Accessed August 3, 2018. http://kaaj.com/psych/smorder.html.

Molière. *The Misanthrope & Other Plays*. Translated by Donald M. Frame. New York: Signet Classics, 2005.

Monarth, Harrison. "The Irresistible Power of Storytelling as a Strategic Business Tool." *Harvard Business Review*, March 11, 2014.

Accessed August 3, 2018. https://hbr.org/2014/03/the-irresistible -power-of-storytelling-as-a-strategic-business-tool.

Mont, Joe. "10 Bizarre Company Rumors." TheStreet, October 24, 2011. Accessed August 3, 2018. https://www.thestreet.com/story /11285589/1/10-bizarre-company-rumors.html.

Moon, Youngme. "Intimate Exchanges: Using Computers to Elicit Self-Disclosure from Consumers." *Journal of Consumer Research* 26 (2000): 323–339.

Moore, Marianne. *New Collected Poems.* New York: Farrar, Straus and Giroux, 2017. Kindle edition.

Mootee, Idris. *60-Minute Brand Strategist: The Essential Brand Book for Marketing Professionals.* Hoboken, NJ: Wiley, 2013.

"Newburgh Conspiracy." Accessed August 3, 2018. https://en.wikipedia. org/wiki/Newburgh_Conspiracy.

Nobel, Carmen. "Clay Christensen's Milkshake Marketing." Harvard Business School Working Knowledge, February 14, 2011. Accessed August 3, 2018. https://hbswk.hbs.edu/item/clay-christensens-milk shake-marketing.

Nohria, Nitin, and Rakesh Khurana, eds. *Handbook of Leadership Theory and Practice.* Boston: Harvard Business Press, 2010.

Obama, Barack. "Barack Obama's New Hampshire Primary Speech." *New York Times,* January 8, 2008. Accessed August 3, 2018. https:// www.nytimes.com/2008/01/08/us/politics/08text-obama.html.

O'Brien, Lucy. "The Curious Appeal of Horror Movies: Why Do We Like to Feel Scared?" IGN, September 9, 2013. Accessed August 3, 2018. http://www.ign.com/articles/2013/09/09/the-curious-appeal -of-horror-movies.

Ogawa, Yoko. *Revenge: Eleven Dark Tales.* Translated by Stephen Snyder. New York: Picador. 2013.

O'Hara, Carolyn. "How to Tell a Great Story." *Harvard Business Review,* July 30, 2014. Accessed August 3, 2018. https://hbr.org/2014/07 /how-to-tell-a-great-story.

Olsen, Flemming. *Eliot's Objective Correlative: Tradition or Individual Talent, Contributions to the History of a Topos.* Brighton, UK: Sussex Academic Press, 2012.

On Leadership. Boston: Harvard Business Review Press, 2011.

On Managing People. Boston: Harvard Business Review Press, 2011.

Ong, Walter J. "A Dialectic of Aural and Objective Correlatives." *Essays in Criticism* 8 (1958): 166–181.

Ouellette, Jennifer. "Meet Me Halfway: Cocktail Party Physics." *Scientific American*, January 31, 2012. Accessed August 3, 2018. https:// blogs.scientificamerican.com/cocktail-party-physics/meet -me-halfway/.

Ovid. *Metamorphoses*. Translated by David Raeburn. London: Penguin Books, 2004.

Parks, Tim. "Is It a Good Thing to Stimulate Our Emotions? Montaigne, Brecht and Others Thought Not." *New York Times Book Review*, October 13, 2016, 35.

Perrine, Laurence. *Sound and Sense: An Introduction to Poetry*. New York: Harcourt, 1963.

Pierce, John R. *An Introduction to Information Theory: Symbols, Signals & Noise*. New York: Dover Publications, 1980.

Pinker, Steven. *How the Mind Works*. New York: W. W. Norton, 1997.

Poe, Edgar Allan. Excerpt from a Review of Hawthorne's *Twice-Told Tales* in *Graham's Magazine*, May 1842. Accessed August 3, 2018. http://www.people.virginia.edu/~sfr/enam315/texts2 /eaphawthorne.html.

Poirier, Richard. *Trying It Out in America: Literary and Other Performances*. New York: Farrar, Straus and Giroux, 1999.

Polti, Georges. *The Thirty-Six Dramatic Situations*. Boston: Writer, 1999.

Pound, Ezra. "Vorticism." *Fortnightly Review* 96 (1914): 461–471. Accessed August 3, 2018. http://fortnightlyreview.co.uk/vorticism/.

Powell, Bonnie Azab. "Framing the Issues: UC Berkeley Professor George Lakoff Tells How Conservatives Use Language to Dominate Politics." *UCBerkeleyNews*, October 27, 2003. Accessed August 3, 2018. https://www.berkeley.edu/news/media/releases/2003/10/27 _lakoff.shtml.

Propp, Vladimir. *Morphology of the Folktale*. 2nd ed. Translated by Laurence Scott. Austin: University of Texas Press, 2009. Kindle edition.

Regan, Brendan. "Podcasts Took Off This Year: What Will the New Year Bring?" *Newsweek*, December 26, 2017. Accessed August 3, 2018. http://www.newsweek.com/podcasts-took-year-what-will-new -year-bring-758304.

Riggio, Ronald E. "Women's Intuition: Myth or Reality?: Do Women Have Some Special Ability?" *Psychology Today*, July 14, 2011. Accessed August 3, 2018. https://www.psychologytoday.com/us/blog/cutting -edge-leadership/201107/women-s-intuition-myth-or-reality.

Roberts, Sam. "On the Streets, Discovering the Voice of the City." *New York Times*, November 8, 2011. Accessed August 3, 2018. https://cityroom.blogs.nytimes.com/2011/11/08/on-the-streets-discovering-the-voice-of-the-city/.

Roosevelt, Franklin Delano. First Inaugural Address, March 4, 1933. Accessed August 3, 2018. http://www.americanrhetoric.com/speeches/fdrfirstinaugural.html.

Rouen, Ethan C. Assistant Professor at Harvard Business School. Interview by author. January 31, 2018.

Safire, William. "On Language; Who Trusts Whom?" *New York Times Magazine*, October 4, 1992. Accessed August 3, 2018. https://www.nytimes.com/1992/10/04/magazine/on-language-who-trusts-whom.html.

Saltmarshe, Ella. "Using Story to Change Systems." *Stanford Social Innovation Review*, February 20, 2018. Accessed August 3, 2018. https://ssir.org/articles/entry/using_story_to_change_systems.

The Salute Military Golf Association. Accessed August 3, 2018. http://www.smgaboston.org.

Santayana, George. *Interpretations of Poetry and Religion*. Cambridge, MA: MIT Press, 1989.

Sawyer, Tom, and Arthur David Weingarten. *Plots Unlimited*. Malibu, CA: Ashleywilde, 1994.

Schalow, Suzanne. Craft Beer Cellar. Interview with the author. April 28, 2018.

Schlozman, Steven. Assistant Professor of Psychiatry, Harvard Medical School. Interview by author. March 18, 2018.

Schlozman, Steven. "Why Teens Do Dumb Things—and How You Can Stop Them." *U.S. News*, January 19, 2018. Accessed August 3, 2018. https://health.usnews.com/wellness/for-parents/articles/2018-01-19/why-teens-do-dumb-things-and-how-you-can-stop-them.

Schorr Hirsch, Marcie. Management Consultant and Coach. Interview with the author. April 26, 2018.

Schreiber, Katherine, and Heather Hausenblas. "What Eye Contact Can Do to You: For Better or Worse, the Gaze of Others Has a Powerful Effect on Our Behavior." *Psychology Today*, September 20, 2016. Accessed August 3, 2018. https://www.psychologytoday.com/us/blog/the-truth-about-exercise-addiction/201609/what-eye-contact-can-do-you.

Schwartz, Tony. *The Responsive Chord*. Garden City, NY: Anchor Books, 1974.

Segal, Robert A. *Myth: A Very Short Introduction.* 2nd ed. Oxford: Oxford University Press, 2015. Kindle edition.

Seger, Linda. *Making a Good Script Great: A Guide for Writing and Rewriting.* Hollywood, CA: Samuel French, 1987.

"Sewing Needle." Wikipedia. Accessed August 3, 2018. https://en.wikipedia.org/wiki/Sewing_needle.

Shanahan, Jerry. Volunteer Operations Director, The Salute Military Golf Association, New England. Interview with the author. April 3, 2018.

Shu, Suzanne, and Kurt A. Carlson. "When Three Charms but Four Alarms: Identifying the Optimal Number of Claims in Persuasion Settings." *Journal of Marketing* 78 (2014): 127–139.

Simpson, Jack. "What the Hell Is a Chief Storyteller Anyway?" *Econsultancy,* June 29, 2015. Accessed August 3, 2018. https://econsultancy.com/blog/66630-what-the-hell-is-a-chief-storyteller-anyway.

Singh, Sangeeta, and Stephan Sonnenburg. "Brand Performances in Social Media." *Journal of Interactive Marketing* 26 (2012): 189–197.

Smart, Morgan. "Finding Love at Work: Patterns in Glassdoor Data." July 29, 2015. Accessed August 3, 2018. https://www.glassdoor.com/research/love-in-the-workplace/.

"Snowclone: Part of a Series on Internet Slang." Accessed April 20, 2018. http://knowyourmeme.com/memes/snowclone.

"The Snowclones Database: Snowclones are the new Eggcorns." Accessed August 3, 2018. https://snowclones.org/index/.

Snyder, Blake. *Save the Cat!: The Last Book on Screenwriting That You'll Ever Need.* Studio City, CA: Michael Wiese Productions, 2005.

Sreenivasan, Sree. "How to Use Social Media in Your Career." *New York Times,* April 2, 2018. Accessed August 3, 2018. https://www.nytimes.com/guides/business/social-media-for-career-and-business.

Sreenivasan, Sree. Social Media Expert. Interview by author. June 20, 2010.

Stallman, Robert Wooster, ed. *Critiques and Essays in Criticism 1920–1948: Representing the Achievement of Modern British and American Critics.* New York: Ronald Press, 1949.

Stansberry, Glen. "10 Examples of Shockingly Excellent Customer Service." American Express OPEN Forum, May 4, 2010. Accessed August 3, 2018. https://www.americanexpress.com/us/small-business/openforum/articles/10-examples-of-shockingly-excellent-customer-service-1/.

Stephens, Greg J., Lauren J. Silbert, and Uri Hasson. "Speaker-Listener Neural Coupling Underlies Successful Communication." *Proceedings of the National Academy of Sciences* 32 (2010): 14425–14430, https://doi.org/10.1073/pnas.1008662107.

Sterritt, David. *The Films of Jean-Luc Godard: Seeing the Invisible.* Cambridge: Cambridge University Press, 1999.

Stone, Greg. *Artful Business: 50 Lessons from Creative Geniuses.* Scotts Valley, CA: Amazon CreateSpace, 2016.

Stone, Greg. "Don't Let Stage Fright Make You Uptight." American Management Association Playbook, July 28, 2014. Accessed August 3, 2018. http://playbook.amanet.org/dont-let-stage-fright -make-uptight/.

Stone, Greg. "Don't Provoke, Evoke." *Huffington Post*, July 23, 2015. Accessed August 3, 2018. https://www.huffingtonpost.com/greg-j -stone/dont-provoke-evoke_b_7849554.html.

Stone, Greg. "Drumming with Words." *Huffington Post*, June 11, 2015. Accessed August 3, 2018. https://www.huffingtonpost.com/greg-j -stone/drumming-with-words_b_7552800.html.

Stone, Greg. "'The Focus Group Was Ecstatic': Facts and Feelings in Stories." *Huffington Post*, September 22, 2015. Accessed August 3, 2018. https://www.huffingtonpost.com/greg-j-stone/the-focus-group -was-ecsta_b_8173100.html.

Stone, Greg. "For Better Presentations, Start with a Villain." *Harvard Business Review*, November 12, 2015. Accessed August 3, 2018. https://hbr.org/2015/11/for-better-presentations-start-with-a -villain?utm_source=twitter&utm_medium=social&utm _campaign=harvardbiz.

Stone, Greg. "Go Ahead, Act Like a Guy: Body Language for Women." *Huffington Post*, October 6, 2014. Accessed August 3, 2018. https:// www.huffingtonpost.com/greg-j-stone/go-ahead-act-like-a-guy -b_b_5922902.html.

Stone, Greg. "Hard to Disagree with the Power of Three." *Huffington Post*, April 11, 2016. Accessed August 3, 2018. https://www.huffington post.com/greg-j-stone/hard-to-disagree-with-the_b_9646740.html.

Stone, Greg. "An Interview Survival Guide: Forging Relationships with Reporters." A private manual, 2018.

Stone, Greg. "Name It and It's Yours." *Huffington Post*, September 16, 2015. Accessed August 3, 2018. https://www.huffingtonpost.com /greg-j-stone/name-it-and-its-yours_b_8005572.html.

Stone, Greg. "No One Avoid Tabloids." *Huffington Post*, July 21, 2016. Accessed August 3, 2018. https://www.huffingtonpost.com/greg-j -stone/toupee-or-not-to-pay_b_7925586.html.

Stone, Greg. "The Pictures Are Better on Radio." *Huffington Post*, September 22, 2016. Accessed August 3, 2018. https://www.huffing tonpost.com/greg-j-stone/the-pictures-are-better-o_b_12074406 .html.

Stone, Greg. "Soundbiting with Teeth: How to be More Quotable." American Management Association Playbook, June 30, 2014. Accessed August 3, 2018. http://playbook.amanet.org/soundbiting-with-teeth -how-to-be-more-quotable/.

Stone, Greg. "A Speech Is All about the Word 'About.'" *Huffington Post*, October 5, 2014. Accessed August 3, 2018. https://www.huffing-tonpost.com/greg-j-stone/a-speech-is-all-about-the_b_5932764 .html.

Stone, Greg. "10 Things to Avoid Doing to the Media." American Management Association Playbook, April 24, 2014. Accessed August 3, 2018. http://playbook.amanet.org/10-things-to-avoid-doing-to -the-media/.

Stone, Greg. "To Pitch or Not to Pitch: What Makes a Story." American Management Association Playbook, September 25, 2014. Accessed August 3, 2018. http://playbook.amanet.org/to-pitch-or-not-to-pitch -what-makes-a-story/.

Stone, Greg. "Voices Carry More than Words." American Management Association Playbook, April 10, 2014. Accessed August 3, 2018. http://playbook.amanet.org/voices-carry-words/.

Stone, Greg. "What Ever Happened to the New Journalism?" Master's thesis, Columbia University Journalism School, 1980.

Stone, Greg. "What Is Executive Presence Anyway?" *Huffington Post*, May 18, 2015. Accessed August 3, 2018. https://www.huffington post.com/greg-j-stone/what-is-executive-presenc_b_7307648.html.

Stone, Greg. "What's News and What Ain't." *Huffington Post*, June 25, 2015. Accessed August 3, 2018. https://www.huffingtonpost.com /greg-j-stone/whats-news-and-what-aint_b_7656804.html.

Sunstein, Cass R. "Commentary: False Rumors Spread Fast. So Do Some True Ones." *Chicago Tribune*, March 19, 2018. Accessed August 3, 2018. http://www.chicagotribune.com/news/opinion/commentary /ct-perspec-rumors-false-true-social-media-katy-perry-taylor -smith-twitter-facebook-0319-story.html.

Swaminathan, Nikhil. "Why Does the Brain Need so Much Power?" *Scientific American*, April 29, 2008. Accessed August 3, 2018. https://www.scientificamerican.com/article/why-does-the-brain-need-s/.

Szabó, Magda. *The Door*. Translated by Len Rix. New York: New York Review of Books, 2007. Kindle edition.

Tarkovsky, Andrey. *Sculpting in Time: Reflections on the Cinema*. Translated by Kitty Hunter-Blair. Austin: University of Texas Press, 1991.

Tatar, Maria, ed. *The Classic Fairy Tales*. Second Norton Critical Edition. New York: Norton, 2017. Kindle edition.

Tatar, Maria. *Enchanted Hunters: The Power of Stories in Childhood*. New York: Norton, 2009. Kindle edition.

Tatar, Maria. *The Hard Facts of Grimms' Fairy Tales*. 2nd ed. Princeton, NJ: Princeton University Press, 2003.

Tatar, Maria. *Off with Their Heads!: Fairy Tales and the Culture of Childhood*. Princeton, NJ: Princeton University Press, 1992.

Thompson, Andrea. "Bad Memories Stick Better than Good." Live Science, September 5, 2007. Accessed August 3, 2018. https://www.livescience.com/1827-bad-memories-stick-good.html.

Thompson, Jeff. "Are Man and Woman Equals in Nonverbal Communication?" *Psychology Today*, February 12, 2012. Accessed August 3, 2018. https://www.psychologytoday.com/us/blog/beyond-words/201202/are-man-and-woman-equals-in-nonverbal-communication.

Tillman, Frank A., and Steven M. Cahn, eds. *Philosophy of Art and Aesthetics: From Plato to Wittgenstein*. New York: Harper & Row, 1969.

"Top 20 B2B Marketing Charts of 2017." Source: Aberdeen Group. Accessed August 3, 2018. https://www.marketingcharts.com/top-20-b2b-marketing-charts-2017.

Truffaut, François, and Helen G. Scott. *Hitchcock*. New York: Simon & Schuster, 1983.

Twain, Mark. *How to Tell a Story and Other Essays*. Alexandria: Library of Alexandria, 2012. Kindle edition.

Von Ghyczy, Tihamér. "The Fruitful Flaws of Strategy Metaphors." *Harvard Business Review*, November 11, 2013. Accessed August 3, 2018. https://hbr.org/2003/09/the-fruitful-flaws-of-strategy-metaphors.

Wallace, William E. *Michelangelo: The Artist, the Man, and His Times*. Cambridge: Cambridge University Press, 2010.

Warner, Jennifer. "Bad Memories Easier to Remember: Negative Memories May Be More Vivid than Happy Ones." WebMD, August 29, 2007. Accessed August 3, 2018. https://www.webmd.com/brain/news/20070829/bad-memories-easier-to-remember.

"War's End: The Promises of the American Revolution." June 1783. Accessed August 3, 2018. http://shaysrebellion.stcc.edu/shaysapp/scenehtml.do?shortName=War.

WATERisLIFE. "New Clean Sip Straw Filters." Accessed August 3, 2018. https://waterislife.com/impact/clean-water/#waterislife-new-clean-sip-straw-filters.

Waytz, Adam, John Cacioppo, and Nicholas Epley. "Who Sees Human? The Stability and Importance of Individual Differences in Anthropomorphism." *Perspectives on Psychological Science* 5 (2010): 219–232.

"Weekly Terrestrial Radio Listenership." Pew Research Center, June 16, 2017. Accessed August 3, 2018. http://www.journalism.org/chart/weekly-terrestrial-radio-listenership/.

Wheeler, Alina. *Designing Brand Identity: An Essential Guide for the Whole Branding Team.* Hoboken, NJ: Wiley, 2013.

Williamson, Judith. *Decoding Advertisements: Ideology and Meaning in Advertising.* London: Marion Boyars, 1978.

Wills, Garry. *Lincoln at Gettysburg: The Words That Remade America.* New York: Simon & Schuster, 1992.

Witkoski, Michael. "The Bottle That Isn't There and the Duck That Can't be Heard: The 'Subjective Correlative' in Commercial Messages." *Studies in Media & Information Literacy Education* 3 (August 2003): 1–11.

Yunus, Muhammad. "Nobel Lecture." December 10, 2006. Accessed August 3, 2018. https://www.nobelprize.org/nobel_prizes/peace/laureates/2006/yunus-lecture-en.html.

Zak, Paul J. "Why Inspiring Stories Make Us React: The Neuroscience of Narrative." *Cerebrum* 2 (2015). Accessed August 3, 2018. http://www.dana.org/Cerebrum/2015/Why_Inspiring_Stories_Make_Us_React__The_Neuroscience_of_Narrative/.

Zak, Paul J. "Why Your Brain Loves Good Storytelling." *Harvard Business Review*, October 28, 2014. Accessed August 3, 2018. https://hbr.org/2014/10/why-your-brain-loves-good-storytelling.

Zeleznock, Tom. "7 Entrepreneurs Whose Perseverance Will Inspire You." growthink, February 29, 2008. Accessed August 3, 2018. https://

www.growthink.com/content/7-entrepreneurs-whose-persever
ance-will-inspire-you.en.

Zetlin, Minda. "11 Best Lines Steve Jobs Used in an Interview: The Apple
Co-Founder's Insights Will Make You Question Everything." Inc.,
November 30, 2015. Accessed August 3, 2018. https://www.inc
.com/minda-zetlin/11-steve-jobs-quotes-about-work-and-life-that
-will-make-you-question-everything.html.

Index

About the Author

Greg Stone is a highly sought after media strategist and the author of the acclaimed book *Artful Business: 50 Lessons from Creative Geniuses*, featuring a dazzling collection of masterpieces and stimulating ideas for thinking managers. Greg began his career as a print and broadcast journalist. His professional honors include three Emmy nominations.

He founded Stone Communications in 1989. Since then he has conducted media and presentation skills workshops for a broad range of clients including Ancestry.com, Arbor Networks, The Boston Red Sox, Capitol One, Citizens Bank, Dunkin' Donuts, Fidelity Investments, Harvard Medical School, IBM, Lego, Massachusetts General Hospital, MIT, 3M, Timberland, and four spokespeople facing interviews on *60 Minutes*. As a recognized expert, Greg has frequently guest-lectured at Harvard Business School.

He studied French, Italian, and German as an undergraduate, earning an AB with honors from Harvard University, followed by two master's degrees from Columbia University in journalism and business. Visit gregstone.com for more details.